Body-Mind
Psychotherapy

A Norton Professional Book

Body-Mind
Psychotherapy

Principles, Techniques,
and Practical Applications

Susan Aposhyan

W. W. Norton & Company
New York • London

For information about permission to reproduce
selections from this book, write to
Permissions, W. W. Norton & Company, Inc.,
500 Fifth Avenue, New York, NY 10110

Production Manager: Leeann Graham
Manufacturing by Haddon Craftsmen, Inc.

Library of Congress Cataloging-in-Publication Data

Aposhyan, Susan M.
Body-mind psychotherapy / by Susan Aposhyan.
    p.   ; cm.
"A Norton professional book."
Includes bibliographical references and index.
ISBN 978-0-393-70441-9
1. Mind and body therapies.   2. Mind and body.   I. Title.
[DNLM: 1. Psychotherapy—methods.   2. Mind-Body Relations
(Metaphysics).   3. Psychological Theory.   WM 420 A645b 2004]

RC489.M53A667   2004
616.89'14—dc22   2004041485

W. W. Norton & Company, Inc., 500 Fifth Avenue, New York, N.Y. 10110
www.wwnorton.com

W. W. Norton & Company Ltd., Castle House, 75/76 Wells St., London
W1T 3QT

5 7 9 0 8 6

Dedication

To my father, whose passing
coincided with the birth of this book,
sealing his gift of joyful work.

Contents

Preface

This book is about Body-Mind Psychotherapy (BMP), an approach to psychotherapy integrating somatic (body-based) techniques into the basic framework of psychotherapy. Since the early 1980s, psychotherapists have been increasingly integrating body-mind techniques into psychotherapy. BMP is an attempt to accomplish this integration in a simple, sensible, and seamless manner, so that the techniques are not just tacked on, but fit integrally and intelligently into the theory and practice of psychotherapy. Furthermore, the practice of embodiment, fundamental to BMP, offers a potent and practical way to enhance the clinician's ability to attune, both with themselves and with their clients.

In the 1930s, Wilhelm Reich, once a close student of Freud, began to use the body as a tool in the psychoanalytic treatment of his patients. Since then, Reich's work has been extended by later researchers and it has branched out in many directions. Many other psychological theorists have made significant and independent contributions to the field of somatic psychology, or body psychotherapy. In addition, many psychotherapists are spontaneously working various techniques of body-mind integration into their clinical practices. The body is increasingly included in the practice of psychotherapy today with a wide range of populations.

Despite the expanded attention to the body, many psychotherapists are anxious about the idea of utilizing the body in psychotherapy. They are concerned about boundary violations and the confusing use of touch. This book presents a simple and safe approach that does not rely on touch, but is fundamentally about somatic awareness and body-mind integration. From one perspective it is evident that psychotherapy is firmly ensconced in body-mind dualism. The body is seen as a dangerous source of strong, primal instincts that must be firmly contained to the point of suppression and denial. It is thought that, once provoked, our primitive self, animal instinct, or the id—as the body is variously described—will run rampant. This is one end of the continuum of perspectives on the body. On the other hand, over the decades, the seemingly polarized battle between id and ego has softened its charge. Now, psychotherapists speak about honoring emotions and meeting needs. Psychotherapists of many persuasions are recognizing the importance of the direct experience of psychological issues as accessed through the body. Out of this interest, psychotherapists are seeking out further information and training in somatic or body-based approaches.

This book provides a basic framework for understanding how the body and the mind are fundamentally connected in psychological development and growth. In Part 1 a theoretical background to BMP is provided. Chapter 1 reviews the larger contexts which engendered BMP: psychotherapy, somatic psychology, body-mind integration, and Body-Mind Centering (BMC). In Chapter Two the theoretical and scientific basis for the body-mind connection is defined as the basis of BMP. In Chapter 3 the fundamental principles of BMP are articulated, creating an atmosphere for the technical details that follow. Part 2 reviews first, in Chapter 4, the basic tasks of psychotherapy: healing developmental deficiencies, resolving trauma, and supporting psychological growth. Case examples are provided for each of these to give a more specific flavor to the BMP approach. (In order to protect the identity of the individuals in these vignettes, the specifics are changed and cases are composites.) Chapters 5 and 6 delineate basic BMP techniques. Part 3 introduces the reader to the BMP approach to observing the basic systems of the body and how that information might be used therapeutically. Part 4 provides the final technical details of the BMP approach, involving movement observation, early motor development, and the cellular experience. Chapter 12 looks at the clinical situations involving birth, death, sexuality, bonding, and trauma. Overall, this book is designed to give the reader a full introduction to BMP techniques and principles.

There are a few structural features of this book that are worth noting. Throughout the book technical terms are presented in boldface. The reader will find these terms fully defined in the glossary that appears at the back of the book. Case vignettes are also featured throughout and those parts of the case vignettes that reflect close, moment-by-moment clinical work appear in italics. Readers will also find therapeutic exercises interspersed over the chapters. These exercises appear in bold so as to set them off from the regular text.

This is an exciting time to be writing this book. The research base for body psychotherapy or somatic psychology is somewhat diffuse and still developing (Smith, 1985; Young, 2002), but theoretical support is growing strong. Since 1985, with the publication of *The Interper-*

sonal World of the Infant, Daniel Stern irrevocably impressed upon the psychological world the importance of nonverbal attunement between infant and caregivers to the development of the self and future styles of relationship. In addition, more sophisticated brain-imaging techniques have provided neuroscientists and psychiatrists with a great deal of evidence regarding the importance of nonverbal processing, autonomic regulation, and implicit memory in psychological development and health. All of these developments point to the central role of the body in psychological development. Furthermore, as the fields of developmental psychology and neuroscience grow and intertwine, the multidisciplinary research of developmental neuroscience also points to the importance of nonverbal techniques in psychotherapy. Much of this research will be discussed in Chapter 2.

Body-mind psychotherapy has been greatly enhanced by developments in neuroscience in the 1990s. The basis of BMP lies in anatomy, physiology, and early motor development, and therefore BMP is in a good position to integrate and apply the science of early development and neurological processing directly into its theoretical and technical structures. BMP draws the foundations of its principles from BMC, developed by Bonnie Bainbridge Cohen (1993). BMC involves the study of experiential anatomy, physiology, and early motor development. The BMC approach is well suited to application in psychology in that it is so centrally focused on how the body and the mind work together to produce functional behavior. In addition, BMC takes an extremely direct approach to the human experience, at once simple and profound, that renders it easily translatable into the world of psychology. BMC points to the inseparability of body and mind. This fundamental inseparability makes this work so potent and undeniable.

My own professional life began with dual interests in psychology and the body. As a part of my undergraduate psychological studies, I worked in a group home with adolescents and did research in social psychology, developing community interventions to simultaneously support pregnant teens and educate childless teens regarding parenting. During this time, I was also studying dance, yoga, and meditation. I had some inkling that there was an important interface there, but very little idea of how to bring those disparate worlds together. I did graduate work in developmental psychology, psycholinguistics, and dance movement therapy, as well as continuing to work in many psychological and psychiatric settings with a variety of populations, including developmentally delayed children and adults, inpatient and outpatient addictions, trauma, and chronic psychosis. In addition to working in these clinical and academic settings, I was involved in postmodern dance and performance art, which led me into the study of many different forms of bodywork, massage, and movement reeducation. The most significant of all these studies was BMC. This work gave me the lens through which I could truly integrate my psychological studies and my studies of the body. I have also studied and practiced Buddhist meditation for 30 years, and this discipline provides a very powerful psychophysical map of human development. These dual influences of BMC and Buddhist meditation inform BMP at the deepest level.

I have written this book to demonstrate the ways in which BMP can contribute to the field of psychotherapy. I also have a broader and deeper desire: Our world is suffering in so many ways. As we will explore in this text, much of this suffering is rooted in our fundamental ignorance about ourselves as humans—how we function, and the optimal ways for our bodyminds to work. Throughout this text I use the term *bodymind* to acknowledge the fundamental integrity among these aspects of ourselves. The term *body-mind* acknowledges the functional duality that has been cultivated by our culture. In order to understand both the unity and the duality of the body and the mind, we must reacquaint ourselves with the human evolutionary process. This process has included the unique and profound process of body-mind dualism that has evolved over the past 500 years or so. What needs to evolve within the human psyche and culture that could allow us to reintegrate ourselves with the life of this planet? How can we recognize human nature as part of the larger natural world? How can we directly experience the natural biological processes occurring within our bodies? *Feeling* our bodies in the fullest sense of the word can help us feel our own vitality and the path toward psychological health, but it can also connect us to the rest of life that exists around us. Our bodies are our link to life and the natural world. Understanding our bodily selves as complex human animals can reconnect us to a creative role on this planet.

Acknowledgments

T hanks to so many.

For inspiration and sustenance: this beautiful planet, my unbelievably loving husband, precious daughters, wonderful family and friends.

For the work itself: my stellar teachers, Chogyam Trungpa, Rinpoche, and Bonnie Bainbridge Cohen. And to my clients and students who have given from their hearts.

For collegial stimulation: all the great thinkers I encounter in my work, particularly those in the United States and European Associations of Body Psychotherapy and the growing body of scientists stepping forward for dialogue about the bodymind.

For generous and insightful feedback on the manuscript: Reesa Porter, Babette Rothschild, and Courtenay Young.

For patient and steady editorial and publication support: Deborah Malmud, Andrea Costella, Pat Connolly, Michael McGandy, and the rest of the W.W. Norton staff.

For an exhilarating ride through the 21st century illustration world: Chris Sayres and Ryan Bramwell.

And for consummate personal and professional hand holding: Larry Welsh, Mindy Upton, Reesa Porter, Pat Ogden, Elena Welsh, and Leia Welsh.

Body-Mind
Psychotherapy

PART I

THEORETICAL BACKGROUND

Chapter 1

Body-Mind Psychotherapy
in Context

Body-mind psychotherapy (BMP) draws its theory and techniques from diverse fields and integrates the body into psychotherapy. The standard practices of psychotherapy form the ground. The body of literature on somatic psychology and current innovations in the field have added basic techniques for working with the body. Many diverse approaches to working with the bodymind have offered particular jewels. Here we will review some of the major influences to the BMP approach.

PSYCHOTHERAPY

Psychotherapy is a broad term, signifying a vast and diverse field that is difficult to pin down. Thumbing through a series of basic primers on psychotherapy, I find that most authors are passionate about their subject, but do not for the most part have a basic definition of the term. Those authors do attempt a definition use broad strokes, referring to such concepts as *an exchange of information* and the *resulting behavioral change*. These definitions are so broad that they are practically meaningless. *Webster's* (1983) defines psychotherapy as "the application of various forms of mental treatment to nervous and mental disorders." This is an adequate, but somewhat dry and unsatisfying definition with

3

a bias toward pathology. However, by breaking the word *psychother-apy* down to its constituents, the results are more satisfying. *Psyche* refers to the Greek nymph who became a goddess, and who was the personification of the human soul. Psyche is defined as "the mind . . . considered as an organic system reaching all parts of the body." *Ther-apy* is derived from the Greek verb *therapeuein,* which means to attend, guide, or serve. Defining psychotherapy as the task of attending, guid-ing, and serving the psyche suits both aesthetically and spiritually. It encompasses the pursuit of health and spiritual development, as well as the alleviation of pathology. Particularly important in this perspec-tive is the view of psyche as "the mind . . . reaching all parts of the body."

Exploring the history of the field is also illuminating. Though barely a century old, psychotherapeutic theory has developed a fair degree of subtlety. Phillip Cushman (1995) explored the history of psycho-therapy from the perspective of social anthropology. Cushman tracked the infiltration of psychological thinking and references to psycho-therapy in popular American culture. From the perspective of his anal-ysis, it is clearly a major cultural influence today.

The pursuit of psychotherapy began with the emergence of psycho-analysis at the turn of the 20th century. Prior to that, most psychiatric approaches involved working fairly directly with the body, either through physical interaction or hypnosis. With the advent of psycho-analysis, an understanding of intrapsychic phenomena and the impor-tance of *insight* regarding one's psychology, emerged. Insight continues to be one of the primary cornerstones of psychotherapy today. The study of psychological insight has developed into a complex theory base. Most psychotherapists today work from a basic psychodynamic model, meaning an understanding of the ways that past experiences and particularly family dynamics actively affect current behavior. Cog-nitive approaches offer us basic tools for working with mental pro-cesses. Both psychodynamic insight and cognitive processing are integral to most psychotherapy today.

Relationship was also a prominent aspect of psychotherapy even in its earliest stages. Psychoanalysis began to look at the importance of the therapeutic relationship through the concepts of transference and countertransference. The development of object relations theory and self psychology furthered our understanding of the therapeutic rela-tionship. Today, establishing rapport and creating a working therapeu-tic alliance are the fundamentals of even the most basic approaches to counseling and psychotherapy. On a more sophisticated level, many

branches of psychology have combined to offer a complex understanding of relationship. The theory and study of attachment has
helped us recognize the importance of early bonding (Ainsworth,
Blehar, Waters, & Wall, 1978). While our understanding of attachment
theory continues to develop (Cassidy & Shaver, 1999), many theorists,
most notably D.N. Stern and his colleagues in the Boston Change
Process Study Group (1998) have moved beyond the categorization
system that attachment theory espouses. Instead they are looking at
such intangibles as dyadic consciousness and cocreativity in relationship. The vast and sophisticated studies of relationship have allowed
psychotherapists to move beyond a rigid transferential model of the
client–therapist relationship while retaining the important emphasis
on the therapeutic relationship in all its subtle possibilities. These un-
derstandings have allowed more room for the "person" of the psychotherapist to interact with the client and not to be overshadowed by
therapeutic technique.

With the advent of family therapy and its fruitful interaction with
systems theory (Bateson, 1972), psychotherapy opened up to a much
wider *context*. Understanding the role of the individual within the family and within society allowed psychotherapy to move beyond psychopathology and into functional analysis. Multicultural techniques
have expanded our awareness of multicultural context. Feminist psychology has brought awareness of gender issues. Ecopsychology placed
human psychology in the context of environment. And evolutionary
psychology has awakened us to the biological and evolutionary context of human issues. Today, most psychotherapists are more prepared
to understand the familial and cultural contexts of an individual's situation. While the study of biopsychology and biological psychology
have been active since the 1970s, these fields have traditionally been
of somewhat limited influence. We are just beginning to understand
the biological and evolutionary contexts of human behavior. BMP attempts to offer a simple and applicable framework for understanding
the biology of human nature. An overall awareness of context can
move us toward a general sense of the evolution of human experience.

Finally, with the explosion in the 1960s of encounter groups and
various experiential approaches to therapy, many psychotherapists
have integrated various types of nonverbal *experience* into the psychotherapy context. Simple tools such as role-playing, emotional expression, breath awareness, drawing, movement, meditation, journaling,
stretching, and visualization are being utilized by many psychotherapists in a practical, nontheoretical approach to support awareness, re-

duce stress, and promote change. It is within this group of experiential therapies that we find many body-mind approaches being utilized. While BMP draws from all of the aspects of psychotherapy described above, it is these body-mind approaches and their integration into psychotherapy that form the unique contribution of BMP. This identity locates BMP within the overall field of somatic psychology.

SOMATIC PSYCHOLOGY

Somatic psychology is a fairly recent term for a branch of psychology that has been present since the inception of psychology. Somatic psychology can be most simply defined as including all psychological approaches that focus significantly on the role of the body. *Somatic* is a term first utilized in therapeutic context by Thomas Hanna (1988). Drawn from the Greek word *soma* (body), Hanna utilized *soma* to denote the conscious experience of our bodily selves, as opposed to an unconscious, disembodied, or mechanistic awareness of the body. Somatic psychology, is generally synonymous with the terms *body psychotherapy* and *body-centered* or *body-oriented psychotherapy*.

The entire field of psychology began with a fairly organic view of the relationship of body and mind. As stated earlier, prior to the emergence of psychoanalysis, most psychiatric approaches were primarily physical. Pierre Janet's (1932) early work in the late 1800s with **dissociation** and his study of psychological force uses physical energy as a primary point of departure. Similarly Sigmund Freud began his career as a neurologist and his "Project for a Scientific Psychology" (1895/ 1966) attempted to initiate a search for the neurophysiological basis of psychology. Freud's development of psychoanalysis also began with an integrated respect for the body. He stated in *The Ego and the Id* (1923/1961, p. 14) that the ego is "first and foremost a body-ego." Throughout his earlier career, Freud grappled with the integration or lack of integration between body and mind. However, as Freud's psychoanalytic theory and technique developed, it became more and more solidly ensconced in the body-mind dualism prevalent in European culture of the time. Freud resolved the seeming conflict between id and ego through the superego's successful control over the id. Several generations of psychoanalysts have cultivated this hierarchical view.

Freud's psychosexual stages and drive theory might be described as entirely body-based. Furthermore, by using the couch in psychoanalysis, he was moving the patient out of their familiar posture for verbal communication, thereby inviting unconscious material (H. Stern, 1978). The use of the couch could be seen as an initial means of including bodily awareness. Freud's understanding of hysterical symptoms as the expression of unconscious psychic material which the forces of repression are engaged in repelling from consciousness paved the way for the whole field of psychosomatic medicine. His understanding of the indivisibility of body and mind held an important role in his theory of pathology.

Freud's former associate, Wilhelm Reich, began as early as 1935 to work toward developing somatic approaches to psychoanalysis (1935/1972). Reich's work has continued to be developed by several generations of students and is fundamental to the entire field of somatic psychology. In addition, Carl Jung moved beyond his work with Freud and developed expressive techniques that have led to body-centered approaches to psychotherapy. In addition to these Reichian and Jungian lineages, somatic psychology has been influenced by Eastern religions, most notably through yoga and meditative approaches, as well as the arts, both dance and theater. Beginning with Reich, we will go on to review a few of the major theorists in the Reichian lineage, then move to the contributions of Jung and the theories that derive from his work. Finally, some independent theorists will be introduced. This will not be an exhaustive review of these influences, but the following thumbnail sketch is offered to orient the reader and provide a basis for extracting major principles of somatic psychology.

Reichian Somatic Psychology

Wilhelm Reich probably contributed more to our understanding of the body's role in psychotherapy than any other person. His work with character analysis led him to view "character" as a biophysical phenomenon. He defined emotions as manifestations of "plasmatic movements of tangible bio-energy" (Reich, 1935/1972, p. 356). From his observations and experimentation in natural science, he developed a theory of character armor, which sought to understand the ways in which we inhibit our libidinal flow by means of our muscles. His writings cite observations of amebas flowing toward healthful stimuli and away from noxious stimuli; dragonflies' mating postures (head and tail ends bowed toward each other anteriorly); and the rhythmic movements of the ringed worm (passing waves of excitation longitudinally by the sequential contraction of the latitudinal rings). From such natural and clinical observations, he surmised that "the movement of the proto-plasm is expressive of an emotion" (p. 359), that muscular holding habituates into "armor"; and that the basic function of muscular armor is that of preventing the orgasm reflex, which is essentially surrender to outer and inner forces (Reich, 1935/1972). His clinical work

included breathing and postural exercises, massage, catharsis, intentional gagging, as well as verbal analysis. His therapeutic goal was to
restore a flow of streaming energy within the body. As his work developed, this came to mean restoring the ability to undulate through the
spine from the cervix to the coccyx (Lowen, 1975). Reich's work is
the basis for many approaches to somatic psychology that exist today,
and it is probably safe to say that his work is an influence on all
approaches. His direct exploration of biological science provided a
rich and fundamental basis for his clinical work.

Alexander Lowen was the most prominent proponent of Reich's
work. He continued Reich's work and developed it further in both its
verbal and nonverbal aspects. Still working clearly within a psychoanalytic framework, he reemphasized the importance of verbal interpretation and insight, elements that Reich had moved away from. He
generalized orgasmic energy into the pleasure principle (Lowen,
1975). Beyond this, Lowen developed a systematic mapping of particular neurotic complexes onto particular body parts. His work in bioenergetics created further postures and exercises, in some cases more
extreme and cathartic than Reich's, to release body armoring. Vocal
expression became more prominent in his work.

Stanley Keleman, perhaps the most distinguished of the "third generation Reichians," brought a poetic language and a visionary view to
the work: "Those of us who do not inhabit our flesh, who do not have
the deep satisfaction that our bodies can give, are always banging at
the door of ourselves . . ." (Keleman, 1975, p. 31). Whereas Lowen
adjusted Reich's work to the reasonable scale of everyday life, accepting the tension between inner and outer forces, Keleman (1975) went
a step further to view this tension, its rhythmic containment and release, as the formation of life, propelling both individual and collective
evolution. This view led him into the study of anatomy, evolution,
and human development. In his book, *Emotional Anatomy*, he stated:
"Life makes shapes. These shapes are part of an organizing process
that embodies emotions, thoughts, and experiences into a structure.
. . . Molecules, cells, organisms, clusters, and colonies are the beginning shapes of life's movement. . . . Human shape is marked by love
and disappointment" (1985, p. xi). Like Reich, Keleman led us back
to a phenomenological study of natural science.

Ron Kurtz (1990), whose work is known as *Hakomi*, is another significant third generation Reichian. We see in his work the development of subtlety in several technical areas: how to "turn people
inward," how to observe and interpret physical expression, and how
to work simultaneously with physical release and analysis. His way of

working might be said to proceed more slowly and thoughtfully than that of earlier Reichians. Still, he has worked with the same basic theory of inhibition and release. He has added very helpful concepts of "taking over," assuming the function of the client's physical or verbal inhibitions and eliciting "the child" state in order to contact the original assumption of postural armoring.

A number of other methods have grown out of the Reichian lineage and contributed greatly to the field of somatic psychology. One of these is integrative body psychotherapy (IBP), the work of Jack Rosenberg and Marjorie Rand. IBP clarified the Reichian notion of charge and discharge through refining issues of containment of energy and the importance of interpersonal boundaries. When their book *Body, Self, and Soul: Sustaining Integration* (1985) was published, it provided a stabilizing and professional influence on the field of somatic psychology.

Carl Jung's Influence on Somatic Psychology

To leave the Reichian lineage and enter the world of Carl Jung is to leave the very earthy realm of the body and enter the psychic realm of symbols and images. Nonetheless, Jung's work in no way denied the body. In fact, his work included a mode of analysis that involves bodily expression. This method is called **active imagination**. Jung described its genesis:

> "I therefore took up a dream-image or an association of the patient's and, with this as a point of departure, set him the task of elaborating or developing his theme by giving free rein to his fantasy. This, according to individual taste and talent, could be done in any number of ways: dramatic, dialectic, visual, acoustic, or in the form of dancing, painting, drawing or modeling." (quoted in Hochheimer, 1969, pp. 87–88)

None of these activities could take place without active participation of the body. Furthermore, Jung stated that the archetypes dwell in the body. He discussed the inseparable polarity of instinct and image, which teeters on the edge of the body-mind duality (Jung, 1969). Although his clinical work did not address the body frequently or directly, it left the door open to his students who were more explicitly inclined to do so.

Arnold Mindell stepped through this door most wholeheartedly. His work with the *dreambody* explored the parallel expression of the unconscious in dreams and in bodily experience. His clinical work was rather outrageous in its physical activities. For example, he described working with a little girl with a tumor: "she lay on her stomach and

started to make flying motions with her arms . . . 'Oh, Doctor, I'm flying—it's such fun,' she laughed. I amplified the flying movements of
her arms and we 'flew' together. She squealed with delight and told
me we were going over a cloud" (Mindell, 1985, p. 12). His theoretical work has focused on the various "channels" through which
psychological material is expressed. These channels are **kinesthesis**,
proprioception, **visualization**, hearing, relationship, and awareness of
the world (Mindell, 1985). His clinical commitment was to follow the
client's psychological process into whatever realm emerged as relevant.
Often this led to kinesthetic or proprioceptive awareness of movement
or sensation. His work, now called process-oriented psychology, is a
very inspiring example of willingness to engage nonverbally.

Mary Whitehouse was a dancer in San Francisco who underwent
Jungian analysis in the 1940s. Through this experience, she developed
a process of psychological exploration called **authentic movement**,
which she came to think of as active imagination in movement. She
encouraged her clients to go into their psyches and their bodies and
"be moved" by a "specific inner impulse having the quality of sensation" (Whitehouse, 1963, p. 3). Whitehouse is considered to be one
of the two founders of the dance therapy movement. Several generations of dance therapists have been influenced by her work and
through her, indirectly, by the Jungian approach.

Independent Tributaries

Without Reichian or Jungian roots, Eugene Gendlin discovered the
body in the course of studying therapeutic success rates. Gendlin and
his colleagues discovered that it was not the type of therapy or the
therapist, but the patient that determined a successful outcome. Their
studies painstakingly constructed what the successful patient does "inside themselves" (Gendlin, 1981). This process, which developed from
their studies, was named **focusing**. This process involves what Gendlin
termed the **felt sense**, which he described as "a special kind of internal
bodily awareness" (Gendlin, 1979, p. 10), that imparts a sense of
meaning and can guide and influence our lives and help us reach personal goals. Furthermore, the felt sense will shift if you approach it
with awareness and when your felt sense of a situation changes, you
change, and, therefore, so does your life. Focusing employs a very
simple, but powerful way of attuning the conscious with the unconscious, as it is experienced through a bodily felt sense. This notion of
the felt sense has provided an extremely helpful tool that is being
utilized throughout the field of somatic psychology.

The field of dance therapy arose, as noted, from the work of two people working independently. Mary Whitehouse and Marian Chace, the latter moving directly from the world of modern dance into using dance in a clinical setting. Unlike Whitehouse, she was not influenced by a major psychological theorist. Rather, she spontaneously "began to be aware of the needs these people were expressing through their bodies" (Chaiklin, 1975, p. 15). Chace began working at St. Elizabeth's Hospital in Washington, DC, in 1942, and a dance therapy program continues there to this day. As a result of Chace's and Whitehouse's work, the field of dance therapy has developed into a significant force in the field of psychology. As a method within the field of somatic psychology, dance therapy serves as a reminder of the importance of expressive movement.

Peter Levine's studies of ethology and animal reactions to danger and life threat have brought a much greater awareness of the physiology of trauma and the importance of using the body to resolve rather than retraumatize in therapeutic work. Sensorimotor psychotherapy, the work of Pat Ogden, has taken this understanding of the importance of attending to the body in working with trauma and integrated it into a cogent psychotherapeutic container (Ogden, 1997; Ogden & Minton, 2000).

Many approaches to somatic psychology have arisen out of a unification of body-mind integration techniques and basic psychological theory. The physical education tradition of Europe is the source of much inspiration. Physical education in Europe in the first half of the 20th century began to move in the direction of postural and breath awareness. Out of this base, Lisbeth Marcher of Denmark developed *bodynamics*, an approach to psychological development based on early motor development and a thorough study of the muscles. Likewise, BMP developed primarily out of body-mind centering, a United States approach to body-mind integration that utilizes experiential anatomy and physiology and early motor development. BMP and bodynamics similarly offer the field a more in-depth understanding of movement, anatomy, and early motor development.

The approaches mentioned here represent just a few of the influences that have shaped somatic psychology. Though inadequate to chronicle the history of the field, these few approaches provide an introduction to the issues current in the field. It is significant to note here that an international association of somatic psychology exists in loose federation between the United States Association of Body Psychotherapy and the European Association of Body Psychotherapy.

Through these and other forums, the field is coming into focus. Despite the existence of somatic work in the field of psychology since 1935, the field has yet to develop a clear basis of unifying theory, though there are some general principles that are common to most approaches.

Principles of Somatic Psychology

Fundamental to somatic psychology is the practical view that *the body reflects the mind, and the mind reflects the body*. There is tremendous neurological, physiological, and even philosophical complexity behind the search for a true understanding of the body-mind relationship. Furthermore, there is the issue of definitions. What is mind and what is body? For the purposes of this text, we will explore some of these issues of definition and the neurological and physiological background in Chapter 2, while knowing that there is a great deal that is unresolved at this point in our scientific explorations. The best minds in philosophy have grappled with the mind-body issue for centuries. A variety of solutions have been put forward, from Descartes's dualism to Spinoza's monism (Clarke, 2003; Morgan, 2002). However, most observers of these philosophical debates would agree that we have yet to arrive at a solution, and that perhaps there is no solution to be found via philosophic debate. The philosophical mind-body problem may be fundamentally an issue of experience, similar to the conclusions arrived at by Whitehouse. Perhaps the most practical course is that voiced by the Zen teacher, Roshi Suzuki, "Our body and mind are not two, and not one" (1970, p. 21).

Various schools in the field of somatic psychology take different sides of the philosophical debate between body and mind. However, there is general agreement regarding the idea of mutual feedback loops—the state of the mind influences the body and the state of the body influences the mind. Furthermore, there is a consensus that in working with the body-mind, we affect both. Bonnie Bainbridge Cohen (1993), founder of Body-Mind Centering (BMC), has said that the body is an excellent lever for working with the mind. How we use our bodies—our posture, our movement, our cognition, our speech—reflects our state of mind. And similarly, the state of our bodies—our posture, movement, breathing, head position, muscular tone—both limits and anchors our state of mind and its potential for change and creativity.

This recognition of mutuality has manifested itself in a diverse range of theories and techniques within the field of somatic psychology. Reich delineated a series of character types with concomitant postural styles. Character analysis has been continued and modified by later Reichians. In addition, there is the more individualized approach of body reading, articulated initially in bioenergetics. In BMP, the emphasis is on clients' self-awareness of their unique style, as opposed to any typology. The development of clients' awareness is assisted in a process of self-discovery regarding sensation, posture, and movement, and the relationship of those to mental and emotional states. This is articulated in BMP as **positional functioning theory**—a recognition that the posture and movement range that a person is utilizing has a direct impact on functioning and the possibilities of making behavioral or emotional changes. In addition, BMP utilizes the stages of early motor development to provide a framework for correlating physical structure and character structure. By grounding diagnosis in early motor development, there is an indication of the direction of future development within the present structure.

The link with early development leads to a second important premise fundamental to many approaches to somatic psychology. Our earliest development forms the templates for later stages of development, and early development is primarily nonverbal, so *working through the body provides direct access to early developmental, nonverbal, and implicit behavioral issues*. This idea is one of the key contributions of somatic psychology. It does not preclude cognitive exploration of early experiences, but rather, the somatic context provides increased substance to those explorations. Some approaches to somatic psychology, though not all, have emphasized the nonverbal over the verbal. For example, later in his work, Reich worked with clients on a table, focusing on involuntary undulation of the spine. This involved the earliest of neurological movements, and thus would involve early psychological material. However, in Reich's later work, there was less and less verbal psychoanalysis involved and more and more focus on the physical movements and breathing. As the field of somatic psychology matures and integrates into the mainstream of psychotherapy, there is far less of this exclusive focus on the body. BMP stresses the importance of observing the client from a body-mind perspective, and through that, the skillful integration of verbal and nonverbal awareness, explicit and implicit memory, and cognitive and somatic processing.

Similar to the access provided to early developmental material, *working through the body allows access to the physiological aspects of autonomic neurological regulation, so necessary in the treatment of posttraumatic stress, dissociative processes, depression, and anxiety*. Recent research into the physiology of trauma clearly indicates the profound impact of autonomic dysregulation upon the persistence of symptoms. However, understanding the physiology is not enough. Here, as with the exploration of early developmental issues, training therapists in the subtleties of nonverbal attunement is particularly important. As mammals, we all have an innate capacity to read certain key aspects of others' physiology. However, we have allowed this ability to be somewhat obscured through overemphasizing the verbal aspects of communication. In addition, we have not cultivated the translation of nonverbal observations of others' bodily states into verbal consciousness. By not making this translation, we relegate this information to the realm of the subconscious, thereby losing access to the raw data and often mixing that data with emotional projection. In the end, we call the whole cocktail *intuition.*

Most analyses of human communication judge over 80% of communication to be nonverbal. It is possible to cultivate our ability to consciously observe the physical communication of others in far greater detail than our culture acknowledges. In BMP, the ability to observe nonverbal behavior begins with clinicians' development of their own body awareness through the study of experiential anatomy and early motor development. Through this training, clinicians' sensitivity to their own bodies is vitalized and naturally generalizes to an increased sensitivity to observing the nonverbal experiences of others. Furthermore, in BMP **embodiment training** (discussed in Chapters 5 & 6), the therapist's responsivity as well as sensitivity are cultivated. In this way, our ability to attune to the client's experience adds a new dimension to the client-therapist relationship.

This physiological level of attunement allows us to work more authentically with the development of positive affect states, as well as the other areas mentioned. As the area of positive affect becomes of greater significance in the psychological world, it is important to find more meaningful techniques to address this. *Somatic approaches articulate concrete methods of cultivating and sharing positive affect within the therapeutic dyad.* In BMP, there is a natural progression toward accessing greater vitality as awareness of physicality develops. The ability for self-care and self-regulation can often increase a general sense of well-being. For the clinician, self-awareness and self-care are a constant focus that then provides modeling of self-care and self-regulation for the client. With increased levels of vitality, the cultivation of positive affect becomes much more accessible within the clinical relationship.

Finally, *somatic approaches provide concrete access to behavioral change.* These changes might be as simple as how we stand or walk, how we reach toward others or push them away, or as complex as sexuality, parenting, and group dynamics. Understanding the subtleties of sensation, posture, and movement, allows the therapist to interact with their clients intimately through awareness of subtle contradictions or lack of motivation.

These principles are basic to all forms of somatic psychology. In BMP they are mined through a precise attention to the body-mind relationship. For clinicians, this leads to an ongoing path of cultivating their own **embodiment**—their own bodily sensitivity and responsivity. Out of this, a deep physiological attunement with the client develops, and, beyond this, particular techniques of facilitating somatic and cognitive integration arise. However, it all begins with the recognition of the relationship between body and mind, and the fundamental connection of that to healthy human functioning.

BODY-MIND INTEGRATION

The field of work that addresses body-mind integration is even more extensive than the field of psychotherapy and it predates it by a couple of thousand years. The ancient traditions of yoga, meditation, and tai chi are all thousands of years old, yet alive and well today. Their purpose is to guide the practitioner toward an optimal integration of body and mind, and thus an optimal utilization of the self. Beyond these ancient traditions, there are a great number of modern Western approaches that address the bodymind: techniques of working with breathing, movement, posture, and body awareness. All of these approaches may be used to integrate the body and the mind or they may used more mechanically for fitness. This is an important distinction.

In my book *Natural Intelligence: Body-Mind Integration and Human Development* (1998), I distilled six principles which underlie body-mind integration in any context. These principles are: **respect, full participation, inclusivity, dialogue, sequencing**, and **development**. Without these attitudes, we are merely using our bodies to perform mechanical functions and thereby contributing to body-mind desynchronization.

In approaching the body with *respect*, we shift out of regarding it as a machine and approach it with more humility; we move from an attitude of *changing* it toward an attitude of *listening* to it and allowing it to express itself. As we listen we discover a variety of resources, qualities, intelligence, and experience within ourselves. Important parts of ourselves emerge with different strengths and needs. We can shut down the unfamiliar aspects of ourselves and maintain the status quo, or we can intentionally invite more of ourselves to be felt and expressed. Through *inclusivity*, we tap into our full range of resources. Each part of us can emerge as an important piece of the whole. Rather than attempting to control part of ourselves, we can move toward

TABLE 1.1 SIX PRINCIPLES OF BODY–MIND INTEGRATION

Respect:	appreciation for the intelligence of the bodymind, its motivations, emotional tone, and responses
Full participation:	empowerment of each aspect of the bodymind to shift in and out of initiatory and supportive roles as appropriate
Inclusivity:	cultivating participation by all parts and aspects of the bodymind
Dialogue:	cooperative communication between parts and aspects of the bodymind
Sequencing:	the uninhibited flow of energy within all parts and aspects of the bodymind and between ourselves and the environment
Development:	a recognition of the ability of the human organism to continue to develop throughout the lifespan

a more integrated teamwork approach. Through *full participation* of each aspect of ourselves, we shift from a static top-down hierarchy of commanding the body, to a model of shared leadership. In this approach to teamwork, there can be room for shifting leadership, with each part stepping forward to contribute its strengths. The vehicle for this teamwork is *dialogue.* By communicating both verbally and nonverbally between different aspects of ourselves, we open up communication among parts. As this develops, our breathing, movement, and physiological connections between parts become an open and continuous sequence of communication. Through intentionally practicing somatic *sequencing*, we extend this communication into a functional connection so it all works together. Practicing sequencing means to intentionally track a movement until it moves all the way out of the body, say from the chest, through the arm, and out the hand. Until a movement has moved all the way through the body, it is not complete.

By taking a developmental approach, we recognize the inherently growth-oriented nature of the human being. Some species seem to be characterized by development throughout the lifetime of each individual. In evolutionary theory, these species are described as *neotonous,* drawing from the concept of **neotony** which involves extending the characteristics of growth and development into the whole lifespan. Humans are neotonous creatures. In other words, we don't just reach sexual maturity and then stay the same for the rest of our lives. We have, at least, the potential to continue to grow and develop throughout our lifespans. Taken altogether, these principles of body-mind integration move us toward listening to the body and allowing it to express its intelligence versus relegating it to the role of mindless machine. As it turns out, this mechanical approach leads to increased difficulty and disease as well as limited resources. Body-mind integration is fundamental to BMP.

Any modality that works with the body can embrace these principles of body-mind integration, and many do. While this is not an appropriate place to review individual modalities, I would refer the reader to Michael Murphy's *The Future of the Body* (1992) for the ultimate review and Mirka Knaster's *Discovering the Body's Wisdom* (1996) for a basic introduction. Approaches for working with the body are practiced in a manner that ranges between the mechanical and the somatic ideal of integrated awareness.

BODY-MIND CENTERING

The mission of Body-Mind Centering (BMC) acknowledges and supports the integration of body and mind, literally *centering* the mind in the body. BMC is an approach to movement reeducation and repatterning created by occupational therapist Bonnie Bainbridge Cohen. In addition to occupational therapy, Bainbridge Cohen drew material from the world of physical therapy, modern dance, and Japanese body-mind approaches, including the martial arts, to name a few. Through these studies, Bainbridge Cohen developed a theoretic base to support her unique and innate talent to perceive the bodily experience on a microscopic level. She was able to literally perceive what was going on in the physiology of both herself and others. What was even more remarkable was that she was able to teach others to do the same. In 1973, she founded the School for Body-Mind Centering, and since that time has offered professional training in BMC. These studies include an in-depth and experiential study of anatomy and physiology, down to the cellular level. In addition, Bainbridge Cohen has brilliantly synthesized studies of early motor development into the system of basic neurological actions that form the basis of the energetic development work in BMP (Chapter 10). In 1993, Bainbridge Cohen's book *Sensing, Feeling, and Action: The Experiential Anatomy of Body-Mind Centering* was published. This book introduces many basic aspects of her work through a series of articles on topics as varied as dance and infant development.

I will now present an overview of some general BMC principles.

Several basic principles of BMC are central to BMP. The first is *self-knowledge through direct experience*. BMC invites one to directly experience any aspect of oneself and any detail of one's functioning. This is done through exploring the body, but also recognizing the *quality of mind* that one encounters in any particular aspect of anatomy. Through the experiential study of anatomy and physiology, BMC creates a way to recognize *how* one is doing whatever one is doing. For example, if someone has a back problem, the BMC practitioner will teach the client about all the anatomy and physiology involved. This study is not just intellectual, the individual is given the opportunity to experience—to touch, to feel, to visualize, and to attend to—each detail. The person comes away feeling directly involved with the back problem. BMP takes this approach into the psychological realm. For example, in understanding a particular obsession, one might examine the physiological and neurological patterns and mechanics involved and learn to recognize the states that prime one for an obsessional state of mind. In addition, one might delineate the postures that support and perpetuate the state. Finally, one might look to the rest of the body for resources that allow the process to unfold in a different direction.

Second, BMC presupposes a *functional integrity of body and mind*. When one immerses oneself in physiology at the level of molecular behavior, body and mind become indistinguishable. In the BMC approach to experiential anatomy and physiology, this functional integrity is illustrated to the client palpably. Whatever the task or handicap, the client gets a good look at how they are using their bodies and how this use is affecting the problem. This gives the client a sense of empowerment and responsibility—moving beyond a sense of being pathological or having a fixed pathology.

Through the study of early motor development, BMC rests on two important principles that are central to BMP: The first is that *development continues throughout the human life span*. Bainbridge Cohen taught adults to perform early developmental movement that they had not performed as infants, and they reported overall changes permeating their movement habits. BMP uses early developmental movements as a template for basic interaction with the world and includes emotional patterns as well. Second, the BMC study of early motor development reveals a basic reality: *support precedes movement*. In learning to crawl, the infant must be strong enough to support herself on one hand and one knee before she can reach her other hand forward and move through space. This is clearly true in the psychological realm as well—an individual must be able to care enough about himself to want to improve his life before being able to move toward more positive choices. In BMP the interaction between physical support and emotional support creates a rich ground for concrete experimentation.

BODY-MIND PSYCHOTHERAPY

While BMC stands on the unshakable foundation of body-mind wholeness, its basis falls within the parameters of anatomy, physiology, kinesiology, and early motor development. In order to apply BMC to psychotherapy, the mechanics of human psychology had to be more thoroughly factored in. Out of this synthesis, I was able to develop and synthesize simple techniques for integrating bodily awareness into the practice of psychotherapy. These include embodiment training (Chapter 6) and the **interaction cycle** (Chapter 5). All other BMP techniques are aspects of these two.

BMP's unique contribution is to view psychological processes through the tissues, fluids, and cells of the body. This approach is derived from BMC. As well as a somatic view, BMP takes a contemplative approach to psychotherapy by cultivating a deep awareness of the body-mind.

The foundation of BMP is the thorough training of clinicians to experience themselves very completely and deeply on a somatic level. By studying the psychology, energy, and sensations of all the major tissues and fluids of the body, as well as the cellular level of experience, BMP practitioners deepen their own bodily experience. This forms the foundation of presence, understanding, and interaction within the therapeutic container. Out of this depth of self-awareness comes the sensitivity of deep physiological witnessing of another, the ability to hypothesize about the physiological states and changes occurring within another person, a process that greatly enhances the diagnostic process. To the therapeutic exchange, BMP brings the ability to facilitate embodiment, energetic sequencing, and physiological state changes in the client. These are the specific contributions of BMP. However, BMP is less about utilizing particular techniques and more about the clinician's thorough grounding in the body for personal resources, diagnostic insight, and genuine interaction.

All of the principles of psychotherapy, somatic psychology, body-mind integration, and BMC described above are essential to BMP. In addition, BMP has developed its own foundations, techniques, and approaches. Before delving into these, it is important to understand the mechanics of the brain-body partnership in order to understand these principles at a more concrete rather than purely abstract level.

Chapter 2

The Body-Brain Partnership

It is not only the separation between brain and mind that is mythical,
the separation between mind and body is probably just as fictional.
The mind is embodied, in the full sense of the term, not just embrained.
— Antonio Damasio, *Descartes' Error*

In speaking about body and mind, we are speaking colloqui-
ally. The task of actually defining mind and distinguishing between
body and mind is a complex one. The word *mind* derives from the
Anglo-Saxon *gemynd* and was originally primarily about memory, as in
bringing to mind. From that root, the word *mind* generalized from memory to a more inclusive sense of attending to, as in *minding*. This, then,
expanded into a sense of perceiving which easily translates to our current sense of *mind* as mental activity, specifically thinking. This thinking function clearly connects to the brain, specifically the prefrontal
area of the cerebral cortex (Figure 2.1), the aspect of the brain that
consciously processes ideas. For the most part, when English speakers
use the word *mind* it is nearly synonymous with the prefrontal cortex,
as when experiencing difficulty with a concrete cognitive function,

FIGURE 2.1 PREFRONTAL CORTEX

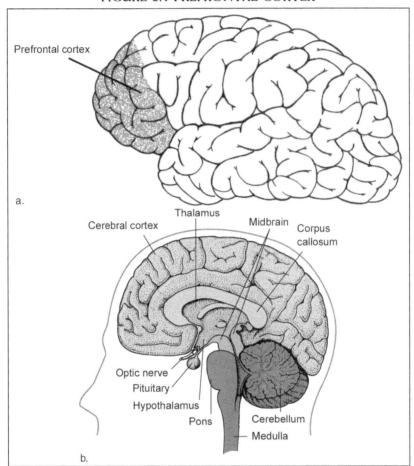

A lateral view (a.) of the cerebrum (with the brain stem, and the cerebellum removed). The cortex (bark, *latin*) of the cerebrum is a thin outer layer to tissue. The term neocortex (new cortex) refers to the cortex of mammals, and is often used synonymously with cortex. The prefrontal cortex is the rostral (most anterior) portion of the frontal lobe of the cerebrum. The cerebrum is divided into several lobes, (frontal, temporal, parietal, and occipital) based on proximity to cranial bones of the same names. (Figure 2.1b is reprinted by permission. "Figure 3643a," from *Biological Science, Sixth Edition*, by James L. Gould and William T. Keeton. Copyright © 1996, 1993, 1986, 1980, 1979, 1978, 1972, 1967 by W. W. Norton & Company, Inc. Used by permission of W. W. Norton & Company, Inc.)

"My mind isn't working well today," or when preoccupied, "My mind is somewhere else."

This correlation between mind and cortex extends fairly well into philosophers' inquiries into the nature of *consciousness*. In the case of modern Western philosophy, consciousness is nearly always viewed as the self-conscious aspect of our thoughts and perception, whereas in the philosophy of other cultures, consciousness and mind are often seen as transcendent qualities extending beyond the individual. This transcendent view of consciousness clearly goes beyond the brain. From this point of view, the brain is only significant in that it is able to consciously conceptualize the idea of a transcendent consciousness, a truly remarkable aspect of the human brain. Brain involvement in self-consciousness extends beyond the prefrontal lobe and conscious thought. Our entire cerebral cortex includes areas which are integrating awareness of other aspects of the organism, such as a conscious experience of integrated sensory input, an awareness of the existence of the self in space and time, and an awareness of the position and state of the body (Figure 2.2). *Principles of Neuroscience*, a standard introductory neuroscience text, states that "Consciousness represents the summated activity of the cerebral cortex" (Kandel, Schwartz, & Jessell, 2000, p. 897). While this perspective seems to accurately illuminate our self-awareness on a neurological level, the whole line of thinking lends itself to a number of confusions.

First of all, a distinction needs to be made between conscious thought, which cognitive neuroscience has exposed as only the tip of the iceberg, and the prolific, nonconscious cognitive processes that must support each conscious thought. LeDoux wrote, "States of consciousness occur when the system responsible for awareness becomes privy to the activity occurring in unconscious processing systems" (1996, p.19). Thinking is a form of cognitive processing, but most cognitive processes are irrevocably nonconscious and occur outside the prefrontal lobe. Nonconscious cognitive processes are distinctly different from subconscious thoughts. Subconscious thoughts refer to thoughts or experiences that are sublimnal, not fully called into consciousness, but able to be, and therefore clearly, cortical activity. By contrast, nonconscious processes cannot be made conscious by any means. These nonconscious processes include various stages of perception, memory, and association. All cognitive processes are tremendously subjective.

By the time we arrive at conscious thought, the final product, there has been vast room for error and subjectivity, which reminds us not to believe our mental contents so readily. Within all the basic brain

FIGURE 2.2 CEREBRAL CORTEX

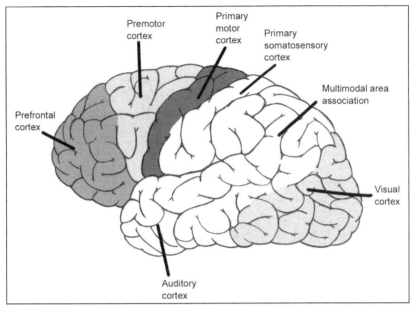

Prefrontal Cortex—Modulates social conduct, judgement, emotional responses, motor planning, language production, working memory

Premotor Cortex—Coordinates motor planning

Primary Motor Cortex—Directs movement of particular joints

Primary Somatosensory Cortex—Receives sensory input throughout the body including, touch, pain, temperature, position, vibration, two-point discrimination

Multimodal Association Area—Receives information from all sensory modalites, and can regulate all motor functions

Visual Cortex—Receives and coordinates visual input

Auditory Cortex—Receives and coordinates auditory input

processes of perception, association, and memory, there is so much subjectivity and manipulation of the data, that many neuroscientists view brain functioning as more akin to a closed system than an open one. Understanding the nervous system provides strong arguments against our basic tendency to *believe* the contents of our consciousness. This perspective can be helpful in promoting psychological change.

Second, the correlation between mind and prefrontal lobe naively ascribes the origination of our thoughts to our prefrontal lobe. In fact, all information reaching the cortex arises elsewhere. The prefrontal lobe is called upon to articulate deeply held feelings or beliefs gleaned from experiences elsewhere in our being. Therefore, we may be mistaking the translator for the speaker. Ezra Pound (1969) translated Confucius as saying that it is the brain's job to articulate the subtle tones coming from the heart. When we speak our deepest mind, while our prefrontal lobe is actively articulating, the basic experiences underlying the thought are arising elsewhere.

These misconceptions about the brain are embedded deeply in our cultural worldview. To clarify that confusion, I prefer to speak about the brain and specific areas of the brain when referring to cognitive processes. Throughout this book, I will reserve the terms *mind* and *consciousness* to refer to some larger aspect of experience, one that perhaps transcends the brain.

BODY-MIND DUALISM

The concept of body-mind dualism was first clearly articulated by the rationalist philosophy of Rene Descartes at the beginning of the 17th century. Descartes's proclamation of body-mind dualism and subsequent relegation of the body to a mechanical artifact, resounded clearly through 17th-century Europe. His articulation was new, but clearly the idea was readily accepted by society, and therefore arose as a crystallization of the worldview prevalent at that point in the evolution of human culture.

Prior to Descartes, human civilization had been increasingly fascinated by human capacity. As crop cultivation and domestication of animals took place, human dominion over nature grew and in time the use of science and technology expanded that dominion. As science developed, it both sparked the growth of religious institutions and challenged them as well. During Descartes's lifetime, the battle between science and religion was mounting, with both sides contributing toward the fragmentation of body and mind. Post-Descartes, in the 18th century, the first steps in industrialization reinforced the concept of body-mind dualism.

Throughout the development of human cultures, as visions of how to live grew more complex in some parts of the world, in order to manifest those visions, industrialized nations came to dominate more of the natural world—including other humans. Body-mind dualism is part and parcel of this domination. In the act of dominating, we forgot our bodily connection with the *other*. In the act of being dominated, we become fragmented, losing touch with the vitality of our own subjectivity. This fragmentation increases cyclically; it is far easier to dominate a fragmented creature, be it human or animal or plant. We overlook the ensuing pain by moving ahead toward our newest ideas. We have become increasingly fascinated by our prefrontal lobe's ability to envision, plan, and create. Our fascination has led us to a narrow-minded pursuit of what is possible, what we *think* of, to the exclusion of what *feels* right to the rest of our bodily selves. We have recklessly implemented our visions, and thereby manipulated ourselves and our environments. We have differentiated ourselves from nature—living more and more complexly, developing technology, philosophy, and religions that set us apart from the rest of nature. The net result is that we have nearly divorced ourselves from own bodies as well.

On the other hand, there are movements in the other direction toward body-mind integration. Although Cartesian philosophy began a crystallization of our cultural movement toward body-mind dualism, that movement was immediately challenged (Clarke, 2003). As soon as the philosophy was articulated clearly, the fallacy of it became apparent to some. Most notably, Baruch Spinoza countered Descartes's dualism with a solidly monistic view, which saw human functioning as relying on both body and mind together; and rationality depending on the body and emotion. Spinoza claimed that no real distinction existed (Morgan, 2002). However, Spinoza was not supported by the intellectual culture of his time. Since then, the voices that support integration have continued to be a fairly quiet minority.

BRAIN PLUS THUMB PLUS TONGUE EQUAL CULTURE

Despite some recognition of integration, human culture has continued to evolve in an increasingly dualistic manner. In a certain sense, this process could be seen as the coming of age of the brain. The modern brain is approximately 100,000 years old. The potency of our brain is completely dependent on our hands and our tongue, and their subsequent extensions—technology and language. Early hominid hands allowed us to create tools. This not only extended our reach in controlling nature it also stimulated our intellect, thereby causing the brain to develop further. Furthermore, the development of tools and other technology stimulated our communication processes. There was more to communicate *about*. The development of modern mouth, teeth, and tongue allowed us to articulate in so much detail that we could free up our hands even further. We could now speak and do at the same time, which again furthered brain evolution. This synergy of brain evolution with speech and manual dexterity combined to begin the acceleration of human culture that continues today. The more we do, the more we communicate, and the more our intellect is stimulated. This is a circular process that is continually accelerating. This process has allowed us to really test our brain's abilities. In a certain sense, without this cultural development, we could not fully experience our brains' potential. We had to practice using our brains and they became more able through practice and more sophisticated use. The human brain's functioning improved as its range expanded. From this point of view, it took us these 100,000 years to get our brains fully up to speed.

Unfortunately, this 100,000-year developmental burst has been a bit one-sided. We have been absorbed by experimenting with our burgeoning ability, and there has been no tempering influence. Perhaps we have become simultaneously smarter and less wise. In a certain sense, this 100,000 years has been an adolescent phase in the development of the human species, and as is often the case with adolescence, things have run a bit amok. We have had a whole planet to play with and no sense of our own mortality. Voices of temperance have been readily overpowered by exuberant curiosity. Somehow this appears to be the natural developmental course of our species. The hopeful perspective is that this adolescent phase is coming to an end. We are starting to wake up to our own mortality, the need for sustainability, recognition of the interdependency of the whole planet, the desire for physical peace and well-being. But the timeline from here is quite unpredictable. How able are we as a species to shift into a more adult version of human culture? How quickly can we turn the momentum of our gargantuan culture? How easily can we reintegrate our brains with the rest of our bodies? Regardless of the answers, there is growing awareness of these issues, and one of them is manifested in our growing understanding of the human brain. With this better understanding, the possibility is that we can mine the brain-body partnership rather than continue with body-mind dualism.

BRAIN-BODY INTEGRATION

Throughout the ages, the human brain has fascinated us. Not only are aspects of the human brain among the newest, most exciting evolutionary toys on the planet, it is a gorgeous structure. Its visible delicacy and detail are unparalleled by other organs of the body, except perhaps the heart. Nonetheless, the brain's fascinating qualities have seduced us into exaggerating its role over the last century or so.

We have come to regard the brain as the master of the body and the sole holder of intelligence. Fortunately, science is slowly divesting us of these delusions. First and foremost, we must remember: *The brain is part of the body*. It functions as part of each body system with which it engages and has a relationship of mutual feedback loops with those systems, giving and receiving input. In fact, it is dependent on the rest of the body for feedback, because *the brain has no sensory nerve endings*. It cannot feel; its data is secondary. The nervous system is an extension of the various body systems. As Cohen (1993) says, "The brain is the last to know."

Beyond this, we must remember that *intelligence extends far beyond the human brain*. Life forms developed and evolved intelligently for 3 billion years prior to the emergence of the first primitive nervous system. During this phase, single-celled organisms created such innovations as colonies of cells, photosynthesis, and aerobic respiration. Each of these innovations was a brilliant adaptation to physical challenges. For example, 2 billion years ago photosynthesis rapidly filled our atmosphere with a new and alien gaseous poison—oxygen. This created a global crisis of pollution, at a concentration level 200 times greater than the air pollution we struggle with today. At that point, cyanobacteria responded by developing aerobic respiration, the cornerstone of modern animal life, ingeniously rebalancing the atmosphere and the planet's life forms. Life reinvented itself so that poison became nourishment. This was a highly intelligent solution. As Lynn Margulis cellular biologist said: "Show me any definition of consciousness, and I'll show you a protist [single-celled organism] that can fit it" (quoted in Mann, 1991, p. 381). Similarly, Candace Pert, neuroscientist and former department chair at the National Institutes of Health, stated that, "The mind exists in every cell of your body" (quoted in Moyers, 1993, p. 183).

In fact, it might be a better model to see the *brain as a modulator and coordinator* rather than controller of the various body systems. Because so many bodily functions are modulated by feedback from the brain, we often assume that the brain is controlling these functions. However, much of what we consider to be control is actually modulation. An obvious example of this is heart rate. The heart generates its own impulses in the sinoatrial node (Figure 2.3). These impulses are modified by input from the brain stem through the vagus nerve. The vagus nerve has both afferent and efferent fibers and is carrying information in both directions, from brain to heart and from heart to brain. Therefore, this particular connection, like most others in the body is actually a *mutual feedback loop* connecting the brain to individual organs and body systems. In all physiological responses, even when the brain sends the initial signal to instigate a physiological shift, the brain is also monitoring and responding to the bodily input. These body-brain communications are both continuous and vast, coming from each system in the body, each organ, each tissue or cell group, and every cell.

FIGURE 2.3 SINOATRIAL NODE

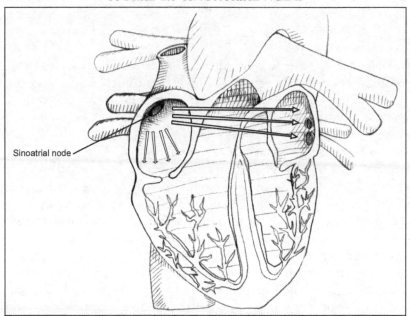

Sinoatrial node

The Sinoatrial node acts as the pacemaker of the heart by generating electrophysiological impulses thereby controlling and synchronizing cardiac muscle contraction.

KEY TO THERAPEUTIC CHANGE

This mechanism of mutual feedback is the key to integrating cognitive processing and somatic processing in a therapeutic context. All psychophysiological states are created and either perpetuated or defused by interactions with the many feedback loops between various brain centers and bodily systems. At each point in a feedback loop, the exchange can either augment or diminish a pattern. Therefore, intervening in the output of various components of the system can either augment or diminish a body state. This is true in extreme cases, such as severe depression, anxiety, trauma, or psychosis, as well as in more mild sorts of confusion and malaise. Likewise, it is true for positive and negative states alike. The brain and body can work together to enhance or minimize any body-mind state.

To illustrate these mutual feedback loops, let us analyze the development of a state that originates predominately from the body—fatigue. When the prefrontal lobe notices a state of physical fatigue, it can react in many different ways. Suppose a person has a history of depression and a resulting fear of falling back into depression. Receiving input about the fatigue state, the prefrontal lobe might begin a subliminal thought sequence around the theme of "Uh-oh. This might be depression. Depression is bad." This valuation of the physical state, like any valuation, though inconclusive, is immediately conveyed to the limbic centers (Figures 2.4a & 2.4b). They react conclusively, solidifying a negative, fearful response. This limbic shift is conveyed to the brain stem (Figure 2.5), the center of autonomic functioning. It shifts to a negative, fearful mode and sends this message to all body systems. The fatigue begins to shift into a depressed state.

In working with this state as with every other state, potential change is most easily accessed through areas of conscious awareness. We can be consciously aware of both our thoughts and our bodily sensations. Both thoughts and bodily sensations may be subconscious and therefore require some effort to bring to consciousness, but both are ultimately accessible. Much of modern psychotherapeutic technique has focused on accessing and working with our thoughts.

However, as we have seen, there is a massive amount of very complex subconscious and unconscious process, feedback loops, monitoring systems, and many other internal checks and balances, and these are not so easily brought into consciousness. To move beyond this, we must rely more on the body, and the main functioning and messaging of the body is not in thought but in sensation. Most of this book will therefore focus on accessing and working with sensation. For now, let us create a thumbnail sketch of how the two work in this example of mild depression.

Starting with an awareness of the subliminal thought process that reacted to the fatigue, we begin with recognizing and restructuring those thoughts—the common technique of working with *self-talk*. We shift out of the "Uh-oh, depression is bad" mode, and into, "It's okay. I'm just tired from overactivity. I don't have to get depressed." If issued repeatedly, this message will eventually reach all the components of the feedback loop.

The other component is awareness of the bodily sensations involved. This awareness can allow the sensations and their physiological activity to develop without feedback from the brain instructing them to shift toward depression. There are multiple ways of interacting with sensations, but they all begin with a simple awareness, "What do I feel in my body right now?" From there, rather than projecting past fears of depression on those sensations, we can meet them with present moment awareness and allow them to complete their normal physiological cycles in the most beneficial manner.

The above example deals with a relatively mild state that began in the body. The mutual interaction of feedback between brain centers

FIGURE 2.4a LIMBIC CENTERS

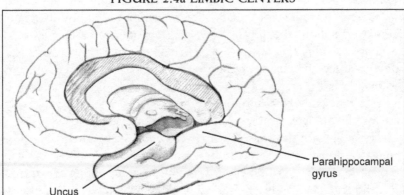

Medial dissections of the cerebrum showing surface structures of the medial temporal lobe.

FIGURE 2.4b LIMBIC CENTERS (AMYGDALA)

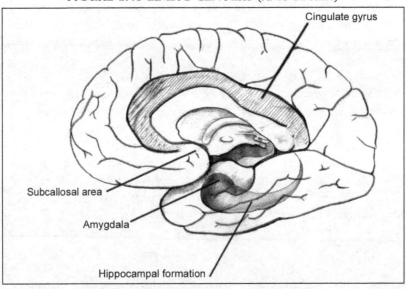

Medial dissection of the cerebrum showing two structures (the amygdala and the hippocampus) that rest within the temporal lobe.

The limbic lobe refers to the gray matter that forms a *limbus* (border, *Latin*) around the brain stem. There is no general agreement regarding inclusion, but the subcallosal gyrus, the cingulate gyrus, the parahippocampal gyrus, and the uncus are included. The limbic system generally refers to the limbic lobe and other cortical and subcortical structures related to it, including: the septal nuclei, the amygdala, the hypothalamus, the thalamus, the reticular formation of the brain stem, neocortical areas shown, the olfactory cortex, and ventral parts of the striatum.

FIGURE 2.5 THE BRAIN STEM

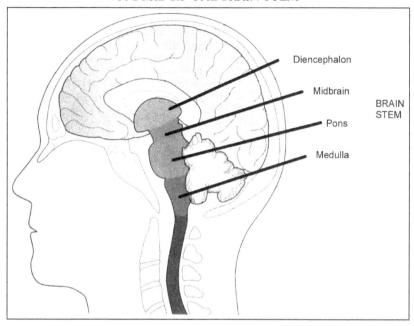

Diencephalon

Midbrain

BRAIN STEM

Pons

Medulla

and body systems can begin anywhere. To explore the variety of possibilities, let us examine a more extreme state that begins in the brain—a sympathetic arousal in the brain stem. Suppose that the client has a deadline to meet at work that has initiated the sympathetic arousal. His heart rate is elevated, his neuromuscular system is ready for action. And let us further suppose that the client has a posttraumatic stress disorder. This would mean that his bodily systems are easily triggered into an autonomic stress reaction—fight, flight, or fright reactions are in a hair-trigger state of readiness.

Due to their prior conditioning, as soon as the limbic brain structures notice this sympathetic arousal, the amygdala overreacts (Figure 2.6), sounds the alarm, initiating a full-out traumatic response. This message goes back to the brain stem, which alerts the rest of the body. The body systems respond rapidly and dramatically. Heart and respiration rate shoot up; muscle tone increases; digestive processes are shut down and speeded toward completion. The prefrontal lobe becomes flooded with thought fragments and images, none of which are complete, but all of which are frightening. When working with anxiety or traumatic response, if the client remains focused on the spontaneous mental contents—whatever mix of cognition or emotion is occurring—escalation is more likely to occur.

FIGURE 2.6 THE AMYGDALA

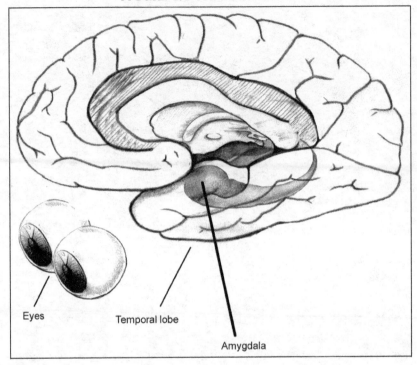

Eyes   Temporal lobe

Amygdala

The amygdala lies within the temporal lobe approximately one inch deep inside of temples, directly behind the eye sockets. Loctaing it in your own cranium provides a more concrete reference point: Place your fingers at the outer corner of your eyes and then move them back about an inch. The amygdala lies about an inch inside your cranium.

Again, awareness, clarity, and self-talk can order the thought processes, as in "This is a traumatic response. Everything is really okay out there. I'm OK." With these messages soothingly and repetitively in place (as much as is possible), the client's attention can now be shifted to the level of pure sensation. Through shifting awareness to sensation, as in "How do you experience that in your body right now?" and, then maintaining that attention, it is possible to allow the physiological reaction to complete itself. The neurohormonal responses shift back to a baseline. The muscular readiness can be relaxed through reengaging with the environment. In various ways, all the physiological responses can complete themselves and sequentially move out to the periphery of the body. This stops the cycle of continual reinitiation of the physiological reaction, which occurs as the lower brain continues to react to frontal lobe content, such as fearful thoughts, via limbic system commands.

By delineating distinct players in the mutual feedback loops—prefrontal cortex, lower brain centers, and the rest of the body—we can work more appropriately with each player to stop the escalation of the state and eventually learn to diminish the intensity as it arises. This possibility involves shifting between cognitive, emotional, behavioral, and somatic interventions, restoring a relaxed, alert neurological state.

The same interaction of mutual feedback loops is true for positive states as well. Richard Davidson and colleagues at the University of Wisconsin (Davidson and Kabot-Zinn, 2003) have articulated the idea of emotional set-points, brain initiated states of baseline moods. In their Laboratory for Affective Neuroscience, they have used meditative techniques of mindfulness to shift these set-points. These techniques include a cognitive component, the intent of which is to be mindful and adhere to a meditation form. In addition, within most meditative techniques, awareness of sensory experience automatically increases. Mindfulness and awareness can be used in psychotherapy and in the course of daily life to shift into more positive affective states.

Clearly the brain is central to many psychological issues. However, our brain is not designed to function in either isolation or as unilateral leader. Therefore, it is helpful to recognize how completely and dependently the brain interacts with the rest of the body and be able to work directly with the partnership between the two. In this way, the clinician can assist in optimizing the brain-body partnership. Much of this work counteracts the cultural influence of body-mind dualism, which has created some unrealistic and dysfunctional interactive patterns, most importantly that the brain is "in charge." Restoring the balance and integration between brain and body is central to the BMP approach. Understanding some basic research about intelligence and brain functioning can assist the clinician in leading clients toward this integration.

THE EVOLUTION OF INTELLIGENCE

As noted earlier, culturally we have a half-conscious, primitive belief that the human brain is the sole intelligent agent in our world. This singular notion of intelligence breaks down under scrutiny. *Webster's* (1983) definition of *intelligence* is the ability to learn or understand from experience. *Intelligence* is derived from Latin, *inter*, between, and *legere*, to gather, choose. From this we apprehend a central meaning of *discernment*. Again we can see discernment as a strategy available to even the simplest of creatures.

Our understanding of intelligence appears to be highly subjective, based on personal and cultural biases. Asian cultures have traditionally seen the heart as the source of wisdom and therefore the central location of the mind. In most Asian languages, the words for *heart* and *mind* are synonymous.

Howard Gardner's (1993) work with multiple intelligences opened up our thinking about a broader context for intelligence. Daniel Goleman's (1995) popularization of the idea of emotional intelligence has similarly expanded our views. In *Natural Intelligence* (1999) I introduced the idea of a synergistic intelligence that combines all the creative resources of every tissue and fluid in the body down to the cellular level. From this perspective of **natural intelligence** every body system has its own unique abilities to perceive and respond, which contributes to the overall intelligence of any particular behavior of the organism, including thought. This idea will be evolved throughout this book.

Cellular Intelligence

The perspective of natural intelligence makes more sense when one considers the evolution of the nervous system as based on the evolution of various communication systems within simpler organisms. The most basic organismic communication system is the cellular membrane of the unicellular organism. The cellular membrane receives chemical, electrical, and mechanical input from internal cellular functioning as well as such data in the external environment as fluid dynamics, chemical makeup of the surrounding fluid, electrical variations, and pressure from contact with solid entities. Based on this input, the cellular membrane makes decisions regarding what to take into the cell, what to discharge, what to retain, and what to exclude. These four decisions are obviously central to all organismic functioning and can be applied to even the most complex, psychological decisions of any animal. Furthermore, the cellular membrane signals the internal structures of the cell, including the nucleus, to respond in a particular manner, most notably the production of proteins in the nucleus and the production of adenosine triphosphate (ATP) in the mitochondria. Finally, the cell membrane ushers out the cell's chemical response to the environment around it. The fundamental molecular components of this dialogue are the same for single-cell organisms as well as cells within a multicellular creature. The cell membrane is an incredibly complex structure that discerns choices, makes "decisions," and responds on the order of thousands of interactions a nanosecond.

In the human body, there are some 100 trillion human cells. Each cell has some 100 different types of receptors. There may be as many as 10,000 to 1 million individual receptors of each type (Figure 2.7). Obviously, cellular processing is a huge vehicle for communication. Ultimately everything that happens within our bodies physiologically happens on the level of the cells. Even communication with the outside environment is not complete until an exchange occurs across a cellular membrane. On this most basic level, the outside environment is represented in the contents of the fluid that flows around our cells.

The ramifications of cellular intelligence will be explored further in Chapter 11. For now, it is important to view this vast reserve of intelligence as a primary mechanism of the brain-body partnership. It was this chemical intelligence alone that was the physical mechanism behind the innovations of early life forms mentioned earlier, such as photosynthesis, aerobic respiration, and multicellular colonies.

Advances in neuroscience have led researchers to recognize the importance of chemical intelligence. The original discovery of neuropeptide receptors in immune cells led to the advent of psychoneuroimmunology. Neuropeptides are proteins intricately involved in the neuronal exchange across synapses. They have been regarded as the

FIGURE 2.7 THE CELL MEMBRANE

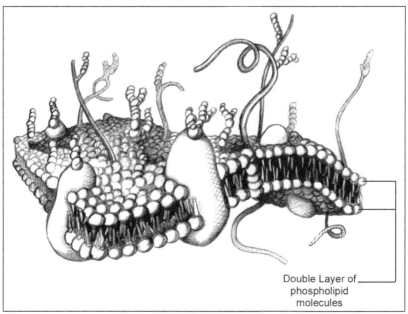

Double Layer of phospholipid molecules

The cellular membrane is composed of a double layer of phospholipid molecules. Within that are various types of receptors which communicate with the fluid outside the cell.

chemical analog of thought or emotion. The initial discovery of peptide receptors in immune cells revealed the intricate relationship between the nervous system and the immune system and implied a
potential effect of thought and emotion upon our immune function.
Since the discovery of neuropeptides in immune cells, we have found
that virtually every cell type in our bodies can both receive and synthesize neuropeptides. Acknowledging this, Pert (1997) has jokingly
suggested that perhaps we need to redub psychoneuroimmunology to
reflect our expanded understanding of peptide functioning. The result—
psychoneurocardiomyogastroendoimmunology—though more accu-
rate, is unwieldy. The fact that neuropeptides are being generated and
received throughout the body is truly a basis for the statement that
"The mind exists in every cell of the body." With our revised understanding of their widespread involvement throughout the body, we
are realizing that much of what we regarded as neurological intelligence and emotional complexity is actually chemical intelligence.
Miles Herkenham, a neuroscientist from the National Institutes of
Health, has estimated that only 2% of neurological activity occurs
across the synapse (Pert, 1997). The remaining activity occurs at the
level of the cell membrane throughout the body, the oldest form of
physical intelligence.

Vascular Intelligence

As cellular life evolved from colonies of cells to multicellular organisms, a new form of communication evolved—vascular communication. While still relying on chemical messengers, vascular systems
provided organized, fluid channels of communication that both sped
up and directed the communication process within an organism (Margulis & Sagan, 1986). Our circulatory systems are still fundamental to
communication within the human organism. As living systems, they
also interact with the information exchanged rather than purely transport it. One method of interaction occurs by means of dilation and
constriction of vessels and membranes throughout the body that direct the flow of circulation, thereby affecting the volume and speed
of communication. The vascular system also monitors and is directly
affected by the chemical and molecular mix that it carries. At various
points in the system, fluids and substances are added and subtracted.
Dilution and concentration and enrichment are other processes of interaction and communication. The development of vascular systems
allowed life to move out of the ocean and onto land. Vascularity is a
stepping stone in the communication process and provided a foundation for the development of the first nervous system.

Neurological Intelligence

Six hundred million years ago, the first invertebrates with simple nervous systems evolved. These basic nervous systems were designed for locomotion (Figure 2.8). Their function was to coordinate the movement of limbs separated by distance. This is an important fact to remember in understanding the nature and functioning of the nervous system. *Nervous systems were originally and fundamentally coordinators of muscular activity.* In this sense, neurological intelligence is the intelligence of a coordinated motor response. The human brain is still rooted in this reality. All nervous systems retain the basic framework of sensory data coming in and motor responses going out. Our unique self-consciousness and emotionality are interesting by-products of this basic function. Here again is another important reminder of the brain-body partnership and another basic argument for the importance of expressing psychological change through the body.

Rodolfo Llinas (2001) explained the progression from movement to consciousness by the principle of *predictability.* Movement became more refined and effective in order to predict the completion of the organism's own movements as well as the external movements in the environment. For the fish, this external movement may be some plankton drifting in the currents. For the frog, the external movement may be a mosquito buzzing past. The human parallel has expanded to our attempts to predict long-term economic trends, weather patterns, and the like.

THE EVOLUTION OF EMOTIONS

Human emotions are biologically-based neurological functions that evolved from simple organismic behavior. Single-celled creatures move toward nutrients and away from noxious stimuli. Reptiles are able to freeze and hide to avoid predators. These behaviors are the foundations of mammalian emotions and behavior. Mammals built on these foundations, adapting behaviors and neurological circuits, and adding unique components for nurturing offspring.

Emotional Operating Systems

Jaak Panksepp (1998) identified innate psychobehavioral processes possessed by all mammals. These basic **emotional operating systems** involve the whole brain and body. Each of them sets up unique, fundamental brain-body states and involves specific movement behaviors. The primitive emotional operating systems are *seeking, rage, fear,* and *panic.* In addition to those four, Panksepp identified three more sophis-

FIGURE 2.8 SIMPLE NERVOUS SYSTEMS

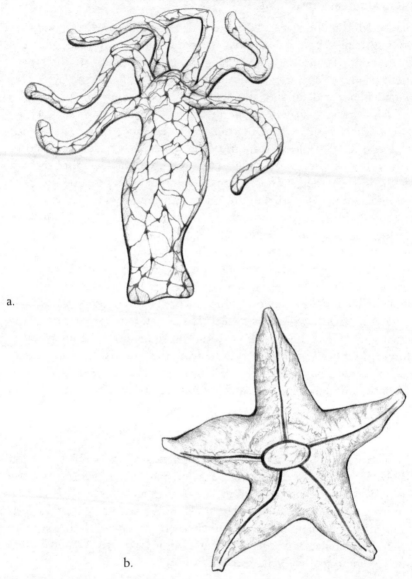

a.

b.

The hydra (a) has the simplest type of nervous system, the cnidarian nerve net. Stimulation at any site spreads to cause movements of the entire body. Similarly the sea star (b) like other echinoderms has coordinated movement initiated at any arm.

ticated and specific socioemotional systems—*lust, care,* and *play.* These are whole body states that form the basis of intention for all behavior. Panksepp has delineated the brain-body mechanisms of these systems and has thereby established a neurological and evolutionary mapping of emotion and psychobehavioral coherence.

Remembering the biological basis of emotions can allow us to work with them more skillfully. Panksepp's model helps us to understand some of the neurobiology of each of the primary emotions. First, the basic emotional mandate must be honored whether it is seeking contact, defending territory, or avoiding fear. Second, the bodily processes that have been engaged must be physically completed in some creative manner. Finally, the whole emotional process must be experienced within its functional context. Comprehending the biological basis of emotions facilitates a much more functional approach to emotions.

In addition to these basic emotional operating systems, evolutionary psychology helps us remember the biological roots of more secondary emotional behaviors. For example, some of our sexual behavior and gender differences are more understandable when one remembers basic biological realities, such as the relatively short period of human female fertility, 35 to 40 years, and the contrasting period of male fertility that potentially lasts the whole of their adult life span (Wright, 1994). Evolutionary psychology provides many such helpful biological explanations of human behavior.

As clinicians, recognizing the biological basis of emotional behavior allows us a unique perspective on human nature, placing rational consciousness in its rightful seat relative to our instinctual behaviors. Rational consciousness most naturally plays the role of a bemused spectator and commentator with occasional veto power and some possibility of mentorship. This mentorship grows out of a deep and realistic understanding of the whole self, including the biological self. With this organization, we can begin to cultivate the natural intelligence of our whole self rather than having the rational brain futilely attempt to control the rest of the body.

When we understand emotions as the basic operating states of the bodymind, then we realize that our fundamental emotional mode is perhaps the most powerful force in our beings at any given time. At any given moment, it is possible to recognize the strongest motivation guiding our behavior. Are we operating out of seeking intentions or rage or fear or lust or care or play? How do these strategies blend to create temperament? Thanks to modern neuroscience, we are getting closer to being able to answer questions such as these from a neurological point of view, by looking at the activity of various brain centers.

The Amygdala

A great deal of neuroscience research has focused on the importance of the amygdala (see Figure 2.6) in regulating emotional responses. Jerome Kagan and his associates (Swartz, Wright, Shin, Kagan, & Rauch, 2003) in the psychology department at Harvard University completed a long-term study of inhibited or shy children. As 2-year-olds, these children showed more amygdalar activity in reaction to unexpected sights than did other children. Twenty years later, this group was more behaviorally variant. Some no longer exhibited noticeably fearful behavior; however, their amydalas continued to react more to new or unexpected sights than others in the group. While this study needs further replication, one might tentatively conclude that some of the subjects had learned to work more effectively with their reactive brain responses and therefore overcome their shyness or inhibitions, while others had not. One might presume that this group of 22-year-olds, who were no longer behaving in a shy or inhibited manner, had employed effective body-mind strategies to learn to overcome their brain tendency.

Working with amygdalar reactions is not an easy task. As we have come to understand the amygdala and its role in fear and other emotional reactions, we have recognized that it can receive and react to pertinent sensory data before the prefrontal lobe has had time to completely receive and process the input. In other words, before we recognize the stick in our path as not being a snake, we have already jumped out of its way. Our lower brain functions recognize that this stick could be a snake. It is adaptive to jump first, evaluate later. Not only does the prefrontal lobe receive and respond to the sensory data more slowly as it is further away from the sensory input with many more synaptic connections to complete, it also has a relatively weak ability to control the amygdalar response. The prefrontal lobe has fewer and slower connections into the amygdala than the amygdala has to the prefrontal lobe. This makes the effect of the amygdala on the prefrontal lobe both quicker and stronger than the effect of the prefrontal lobe on the amygdala.

Understanding this brain circuitry helps explain why our emotional intensity can easily overcome our rational perspective. The degree to which this is true seems to vary with individuals and is a fundamental aspect of temperament. Furthermore, this mechanism can be strengthened in either direction through practice and experience. This tendency for emotional intensity to overcome the rational frontal lobe is especially salient in dealing with posttraumatic stress disorder (PTSD), psychosis, addictions, and adolescence. In these situations, the prefrontal lobe is already operating at a disadvantage. Thus, the emotional intensity generated by the amygdala can more easily overpower it.

Polyvagal Theory

In the evolution of emotion, mammalian behavior is distinct due to the centrality of bonding and parental care. Some argue that this evolutionary legacy has placed relationality at the center of our emotional processing. Stephen Porges (1995), director of the Brain-Body Center at University of Illinois, has developed a **polyvagal theory** of autonomic nervous system regulation (Figures 2.9a & 2.9b) that places the roots of social engagement in the brain stem, at the very foundation of our neurological regulation.

According to Porges's theory, human autonomic regulation has three tiers of operations. The earliest and most primitive form of autonomic regulation to evolve is an extreme parasympathetic state controlled by the dorsal (posterior) aspect of the vagus nerve. In addition to normal parasympathetic functions, the dorsal root is able to shift the organism into an extremely slow metabolic state. This extreme state was used by reptiles to preserve oxygen under water and in a variety of other situations. Mammals use this state under life-threatening circumstances in which there is no perceived escape. In this state of extreme dorsal vagal tone, heart, respiratory rate, and muscle tone are low, and the mammal has very little ability to think or respond to the world. For simplicity's sake, we will describe this state as **immobilization**. When this occurs in the laboratory animal, the animal stops moving, goes limp, and defecates.

The next higher tier of autonomic regulation is the high **sympathetic arousal response** of fight or flight. This occurs when the organism is in danger yet has the possibility of escape. In this state there is an elevated heart and respiratory rate and high muscle tone. The freeze state is also one of high sympathetic arousal as well. In the freeze state, the animal is not moving, but has a high heart and respiratory rate and high muscle tone. This is distinctly different from the immobilization state, which has the opposite physiological profile. The freeze state may occur by choice to hide from predators or feign death, or, as occurs most often with humans, the animal may be frozen because he is unable to respond, but still maintains high sympathetic tone. The popular notion in trauma theory is that the freeze state results from high arousal in both the sympathetic and the parasympa-

FIGURE 2.9a THE AUTONOMIC NERVOUS SYSTEM

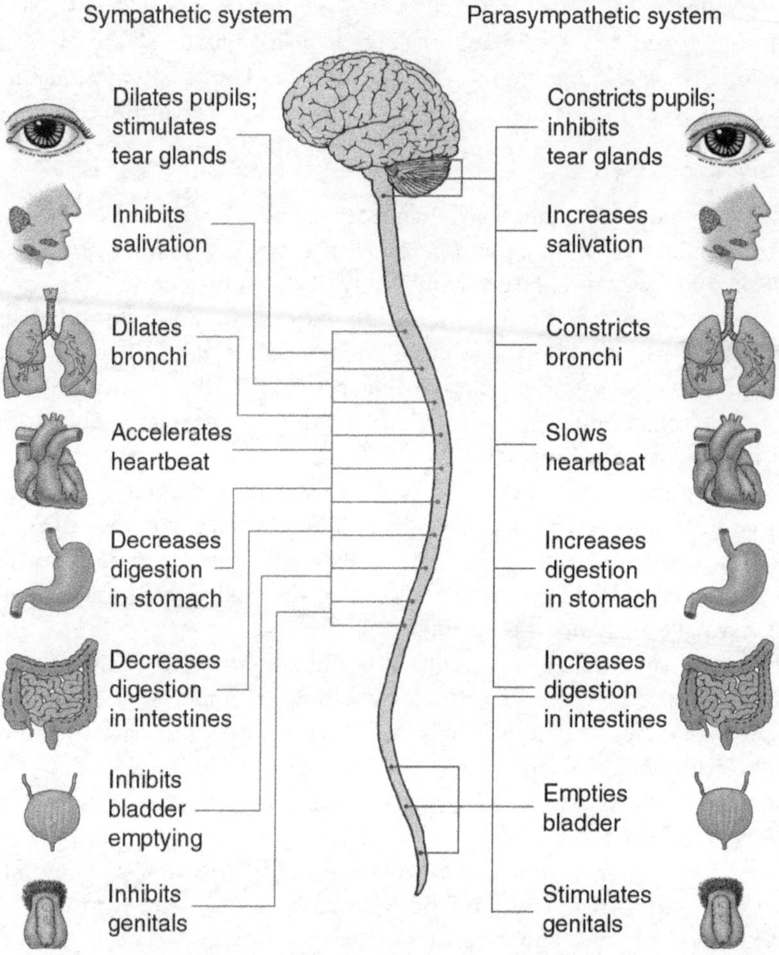

Sympathetic system   Parasympathetic system

Sympathetic system	Parasympathetic system
Dilates pupils; stimulates tear glands	Constricts pupils; inhibits tear glands
Inhibits salivation	Increases salivation
Dilates bronchi	Constricts bronchi
Accelerates heartbeat	Slows heartbeat
Decreases digestion in stomach	Increases digestion in stomach
Decreases digestion in intestines	Increases digestion in intestines
Inhibits bladder emptying	Empties bladder
Inhibits genitals	Stimulates genitals

The autonomic nervous system includes the sympathetic and parasympathetic sections. This diagram of one side of the body shows the parasympathetic functions to the right and the sympathetic functions to the left. (From *Abnormal Psychology, Fourth Edition*, by Martin E. P. Seligman, Elaine F. Walker, and David L. Rosenhan. Copyright © 2001, 1995, 1989, 1984 by W. W. Norton & Company, Inc. Used by permission of W. W. Norton & Company, Inc.)

thetic nervous systems simultaneously. From the perspective of autonomic neurological functioning, this kind of coupled high arousal state is physiologically unlikely.

Finally, the polyvagal theory recognizes a third and most evolutionarily recent strategy of the autonomic nervous system, the **social en-**

FIGURE 2.9b THE BRAIN STEM

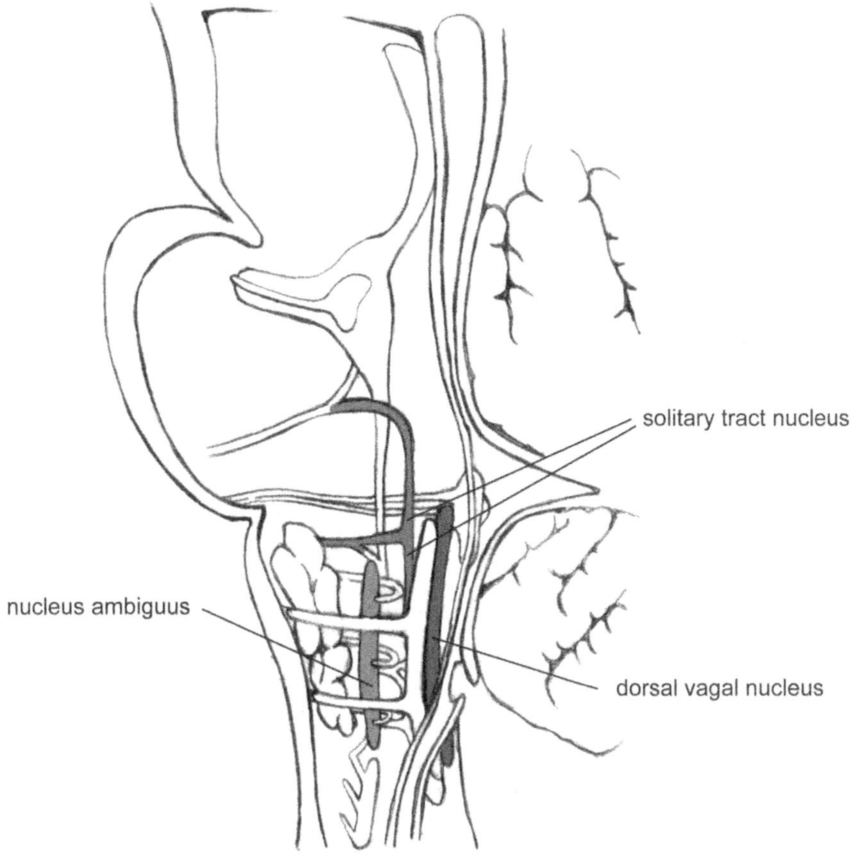

solitary tract nucleus

nucleus ambiguus

dorsal vagal nucleus

Polyvagal theory associates the dorsal vagal nucleus with what is generally seen as more traditional parasympathetic functioning. The nucleus ambiguus along with nuclei in the brain stem associated with cranial nerves V, VII, and IX form the social engagement system.

gagement system. This system involves the ventral root of the vagus nerve as well as aspects of other cranial nerves. Together these nerves and their respective nuclei in the brain stem control bonding and engaging behaviors, such as facial expression, vocalization, listening, and sucking. In a state of social engagement or high ventral vagal tone, heart and respiratory rate vary, speeding up and slowing down with an interaction. Imagine the lab rats above engaged in a group social experience. Each rat moves in and out of engagement with other rats, approaching, sniffing, withdrawing. As they do so, their heart rates go up and down, the tone of their facial muscles varies, their eyes, noses, and ears move toward and away from each other. They have the ability to respond with a variety of behaviors. This variability is essential to engagement. It could be seen as a fundamental aspect of responsivity or attunement. To recognize the roots of social engagement, responsivity, and attunement as residing in the brain stem is to recognize that emotional relationality is at the very foundation of human nature.

Interactive Psychobiological Regulation

Schore (1994) has synthesized a great deal of research about this fundamental relationality as it occurs in early development. Schore examines the interface between psychological development and brain development. His thorough review of brain development leads the reader to understand that at birth the infant is reliant on adult interaction for soothing, and without this soothing can easily go into shock as a response to many common stimuli such as hunger, discomfort, or being alone. The infant requires the mother to act as an "auxiliary cortex" interactively modulating the infant's arousal level. Schore quoted Trevarthen (1990) as saying, "'The intrinsic regulators of human brain growth in a child are specifically adapted to be coupled, by emotional communication, to the regulators of adult brains'" (cited in Schore, 2000, p. 269). Immature and mature brains enter into a long program of communication that is fundamental to healthy psychological development. Put simply, without adult soothing, the infant is unable to modulate affective arousal and will move into distress. This phenomenon can result in a continuum of states from tired and wired to distraught to shock.

The interactive process between infant and caregiver occurs through sequential nonverbal exchanges including physical contact, eye contact, and vocal tone: the rhythmic attunement processes have been studied diligently by Beebe and Stern (1977), and many others. Through this process, "not only the infant's overt behavior, but its covert physiology and thereby its internal state are directly regulated by the mother" (Schore, 1994, p. 4). The mother and infant are interactively regulating each other through the exchange of emotional affect. This includes exchanges dealing with both positive and negative emotions.

In order to learn to ride the curves of sympathetic arousal and enjoy the exchange of positive emotion, the mother provides the infant with healthy play opportunities. The good-enough mother (Winnicott, 1965) tunes her activity level to the infant during periods of social engagement; the more she allows him to recover quietly in periods of disengagement, and the more she attends to the child's reinitiating cues for reengagement, the more synchronized their interaction. This exchange occurs through short face-to-face interactions in which eye contact and vocal tone are key. However, Schore points out that the interaction in which the mother and infant share the infant's rhythmic tempo of crescendo and decrescendo of sympathetic arousal is physiological in nature. In the disengagement phase, the infant's sympathetic arousal decreases and there is a moderate increase in parasympathetic tone. The infant returns to a restful, alert state. Once the infant is satisfied with her time alone, she can shift once again into interest, then potentially into play, and finally into joy, then into restful disengagement, then back into restful alert. When this arousal curve occurs in an optimal rhythm and within an optimal zone, the baby learns to value excitement and interaction. When the arousal is fear laden, overstimulating, or prolonged, the baby goes into distress. When the baby is in distress, the caregiver can assist the infant to regain sympathetic-parasympathetic equilibrium, either through disengagement or soothing depending on the infant's needs and preferences.

In pathogenic situations, caregivers may negatively shape infants' patterns of arousal. Through not responding to the infant's cues for engagement (i.e., not enough positive play in the baby's own rhythm), the caregiver does not allow the infant to develop a resilient relationship to sympathetic arousal. This may result in a low capacity for joy. Similarly, by not responding to the infant's cues for disengagement (primarily gaze aversion), the caregiver patterns the infant into a distressed sympathetic arousal. Interaction is overwhelming at best, terrifying at worst.

Schore proposes that the right orbitofrontal cortex (OF) ultimately mediates this infant–caregiver exchange. The right hemisphere is dominant for the processing of affective material and the OF is a convergent zone between the conscious prefrontal cortex and the preconscious limbic areas and the hypothalamus which relay emotional and somatic information.

The right brain is dominant during the first two years of life (Schore, 2000). Additionally, the right brain is dominant in affective response and autonomic nervous system control, and the right OF is the hierarchical apex of these systems. Descending projections from the prefrontal cortex to subcortical structures are known to mature during infancy. Schore proposes that mother–child interactions are essentially right brain to right brain. During mutual gaze transactions, the infant can be observed to track the caregiver's pupils, "the visible portion of the mother's cerebral nervous system" (Schore, 1994, p. 75).

Schore proposes that the affective exchanges between the mother and infant during the first two years of life concretely impact structural brain development, particularly of the right hemisphere, which is experiencing its peak structural development during this early period. Thus, in addition to the genetic influence of the parents, environmental influences translate into concrete physiological patterns, manifested not only in chemical tendencies, but in patterns of brain tissue growth.

Schore describes this process as **interactive psychobiological regulation**. He proposes that healthy self-regulation includes both independent regulation and interactive regulation. Furthermore, healthy independent regulation is dependent on the establishment of healthy patterns through interactive regulation in infancy between caregiver and infant. In other words, the human brain is designed to regulate through interaction with other human brains, and this involves whole body experiences and interpersonal interactions. Clearly this is important information for psychotherapists.

Schore is confident that psychotherapists also function as interactive psychobiological regulators, even in working with adult clients. He is a strong advocate for the importance of psychotherapy as a brain reorganizer. Brain reorganization can occur on both functional and structural levels. Psychotherapy can impact the brain on both levels. Lewis Baxter, at the University of California, Los Angeles, has documented structural brain changes as a result of psychotherapy (1992). Unfortunately, there is minimal funding for such research.

Taken as a whole, this information regarding the evolution of emotion points toward working with the person as an integrated whole, in which brain and body are working together within a context of relationality. This integration provides important directions and implications for psychotherapy.

Somatic Marker Theory

This integration is echoed in Damasio's work with patients who have suffered ventromedial prefrontal lobe injuries. Damasio (1994) observed an interesting relationship between rationality and emotionality in these patients. While they could still perform analytical cognitive processes, such as mathematics or verbal skills, these patients' lives were falling apart. They alienated their families and friends, lost their jobs, and generally made poor decisions about the most important aspects of their lives. Damasio came to realize that due to their injuries, they were unable to connect their decision-making processes to the information they were receiving about their bodily states. Measuring heart rate and galvanic skin responses, Damasio discovered that their bodies were giving them cues, but that those cues were being ignored. As Schore has pointed out, this ventromedial cortical area connects rational thought with both affective and autonomic lower brain structures. Thus, the frontal lobe was not receiving the affective and autonomic information. This explains why the somatic cues were being ignored. It also points to the importance of emotional and somatic information in decision making.

Out of this research, Damasio developed **somatic marker theory** which credits our brains with learning and using gut feelings to guide rational thought. Damasio has used neurological research to redefine our understanding of the relationships between both intellect and emotion, as well as mind and body.

EMBODIED PSYCHOLOGICAL CHANGE

All of this research points to the importance of an integrated approach to psychological change. Recognition of this importance is growing throughout the psychological world in research, theory, and practice. Fundamental to our integration of nonverbal behavior is our understanding of habituation, states, traits, and implicit memory. The neurological basis of these phenomena is the old but still correct theory of neuronal learning articulated by Donald Hebb in his 1949 neurology classic, *The Organization of Behavior*. Hebb's basic concept was that behavioral patterns are learned by repetition and association. He saw that neurons which fired together were much more likely to fire together in the future. Furthermore, he saw that their dendritic connections (Figure 2.10) grew and remained robust. This basic understanding of neuron functioning laid the foundation for understanding more complex connections within the brain. Neuronal connections link together to make circuits, which interact as networks, and networks combine to make systems, as in the emotional operating systems discussed earlier. All of this forms the neurological basis of habituation.

Schacter and Singer developed this thinking further with the concept of implicit memory (1986). Explicit, or declarative memory is generally verbal, visual, or auditory, and carries with it a conscious experience of recollection. This is the kind of memory that psychotherapy has previously based itself on. However, the importance of implicit memory is beginning to overshadow explicit memory in its psychotherapeutic importance. Implicit or procedural memory, brings no conscious awareness of remembering. Instead, we unconsciously associate a state or a behavior with a stimulus. Implicit memory is fundamental in remembering how to ride a bicycle after years without practice. Implicit memory is also the way in which we are induced

FIGURE 2.10 NEURON, AXON, DENDRITES

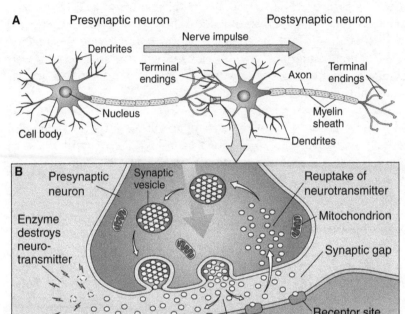

(From *Abnormal Psychology, Fourth Edition*, by Martin E. P. Seligman, Elaine F. Walker, and David L. Rosenhan. Copyright © 2001, 1995, 1989, 1984 by W. W. Norton & Company, Inc. Used by permission of W. W. Norton & Company, Inc.)

into a familiar emotional pattern when visiting our family of origin. Implicit memory pervasively affects our lives and is fundamental to habits, patterns, and persistent states. As Bruce Perry and associates described it, familiar states often become personal traits (Perry, Pollard, Blakley, Baker, and Vigilante, 1995), particularly early in development. The younger the brain, the more receptive it is to learning.

Understanding how completely habit and implicit memory are unconsciously dictating our behavior necessitates working with our states of being in order to achieve psychological change. Furthermore, understanding the system of mutual feedback loops supports us in changing behavior to support brain changes. Stephen Porges' work serves as a reminder of the importance of using "peripheral input" to influence brain states. Finally, current research is begging us to stop believing so much in our ideas about ourselves, and start attending to our basic body-mind states. Beatrice Beebe (1999), a psychoanalyst who has contributed greatly to attunement research, implored psychotherapists to expand the playing field of treatment to include nonverbal behavior to teach ourselves to observe ourselves and our clients. This intention is the basis of BMP and in order to achieve it one must delve deeply into the realm of the body, both to experience and reclaim its resources.

Chapter 3

Bringing Together Biology
and Human Consciousness

Fundamental Principles

of Body-Mind Psychotherapy

W e are animals: We grunt and moan when giving birth;
we shudder when we die. And yet, we are human animals who study
the stars, contemplate the origins of the universe, and wish for peace
on earth. In the last 500 years or so of Western culture, we have
attempted to transcend our animal, bodily selves. To these ends, we
have bent every aspect of nature we can reach. When our primitive
impulses make their presence known, we try our best to ignore them
away. Nevertheless, they do not go away. So long as we have bodies,
certain basic impulses such as lust, greed, aggression, and submission
will linger. This is not to say that we cannot work with these impulses
because we can respond to them in a creative way. But to do this, we
must recognize that they exist. As we integrate our bodily impulses
with our philosophical aims, we gain a great deal of natural intelligence and grace—groundedness, centeredness, authenticity, flow, true
compassion, vitality, spontaneity, earthiness, sensuality, contact—wonderful qualities all of which flow out of our bodily selves.

Unique to our human animal selves are these marvelous intellects,
which have not only allowed us to access language and abstract
thought, but also art, science, and spirituality. In the last few centuries
our intellectual and spiritual pursuits have led us away from the body.

50

We have polarized our physical selves and our spirituality. Often we equate spirituality with bodily transcendence. This seems to end up in a morass of contradictions: virtue versus selfishness, charity versus greed, religiosity versus sensuality.

On the other hand, embodied spirituality allows a continuum between our bodily selves and our spiritual longings. We feel our selves and find the continuity between self and the desire to give and serve. We recognize our human animal nature and allow that to blossom into a larger perspective. Embodied spirituality is based on reality rather than pretense, on what *is* and what is *becoming*, rather than jumping ahead to what *should* be.

There is a story of two monks on a pilgrimage. They reached a fast-moving stream where a frail woman sat wet and forlorn. She told them that the stream was moving too quickly for her. She waded out and had to return to the bank. She was unable to get across. The monks watched the current, and felt confident that they could ford the stream. As one monk began to wade across, the other monk turned to the woman and invited her to climb on his back. He crossed the stream, set her down on the other shore, and continued on his way. The other monk was outraged. As they continued along, he upbraided his companion, "You touched that woman's body. You broke our sacred vows. How could you do such a thing?" His companion looked up calmly and said, "I set her down on the other side of the stream. Why are you still carrying her?"

Body-mind psychotherapy (BMP) embraces this integration of human nature, in which all levels of ourselves, from the sacred to the earthy work together, support each other, and create a full spectrum of humanity. There are seven fundamental principles of BMP, each of which practically supports the body-mind connection.

Each of these seven principles arises out of basic realities that connect all levels of human nature. The ripples from each principle overlap with the ripples of the others. Nonetheless, each of these principles merits independent articulation.

EMBODIMENT

The sort of human difficulties that bring an individual to therapy always have some connection with our cultural imbalances. Our culture is seriously disconnected from nature, spirit, and humanity. These disconnections are interrelated. This quality of disconnection is not inherent in every culture. In an interview about healing, Sorbonfu Some (2000), a Dagara shaman from Burkina Faso lecturing in the United States, was asked how her people dealt with chronic mental illness.

TABLE 3.1 SEVEN FUNDAMENTAL PRINCIPLES
OF BODY–MIND PSYCHOTHERAPY

Embodiment	Fundamental to human development.
The Present Moment	Healing occurs only in the present.
Accepting reality	Leads to appreciation, compassion, and effective change.
Energy and Basic Goodness	The energy of life is basically good.
Conditioning and Essence	Differentiating between conditioning and essence allows choice in development.
Development	All humans have the potential for continual development throughout the life span.
The Self-in-Relationship	Awareness of self and self-in-relationship are fundamental to adult development.

To paraphrase her response, "We don't have it. If there is a problem that emerges in childhood, we take care of it then. Whenever difficulties arise, we take care of them." Obviously, we have a different kind of dynamic in our culture. This fundamental sense of disconnection is nowhere more vivid than our disconnection with our own bodies. Through recognizing this lack of synchronization of body and mind, we have the possibility of reintegrating in a unique and unforeseen manner.

Brian Swimme, an astrophysicist (Swimme & Berry, 1992), proposed that the human being is the self-aware function of the universe, to witness and appreciate the universal splendor. If this proposition is correct, then in order to fulfill our function within the universe, we must fully regain our senses. We must fully develop our ability to sense and respond to the universe. Fundamental to this is the task of reintegrating our bodies and minds. This is a task that must occur within each of us individually and between humankind and the rest of the planet. On an individual level, we could call this task embodiment.

Embodiment is the moment to moment process by which human beings allow awareness to enhance the flow of thoughts, feelings, sensations, and energies through our bodily selves. Embodiment requires the creative ability to allow the life of the universe to move through our bodies, be colored by our unique perspective, and move back out into the world. Embodiment implies an unencumbered flow of life through us. Life comes into us as food, air, liquid, sights, sounds, and more organized experiences. Embodiment also implies the elegant and creative integration of these elements into the totality of our being. Embodiment means that these elements are thoroughly processed and expressed in our unique relationship with the world. The world comes in, we process it, and through the processing we find ourselves in a whole new relationship to the world. Embodiment, then, is a grounding and flowing relationship between ourselves and the rest of the world.

Embodiment is fundamental to most contemplative approaches to life. Buddhist meditation is seen as the synchronization of body and mind. From the simplest point of view, we might ask "Are my body and my mind in the same place at the same time?" I might be physically here, but my mind is halfway around the world, far into the future, or stuck in the past. Difficulties arise when we are unaware of this desynchronization, or we are so habituated to it that we are unable to "be present."

Embodiment enters into the task of psychotherapy in many ways. For the client, as a member of our fragmented and dualistic culture, there is always some aspect of every dilemma which is related to body-mind dualism. By recognizing the deeper cultural roots of an individual problem, we might discover more fundamental ways to rectify it. We might also be simply relieved to see our personal issues from a larger perspective.

As therapists, the more deeply we embody ourselves and our place in the world, the more fully present we are for our clients. Presence is a matter of degree. How present are we in this moment in this body? How much of this body is actively available to respond to the present moment? What aspects of my whole being and body are dancing with the flow of information and energy that is coming into it? And, in terms of output, how much of therapists' being is available to understand, respond to, and facilitate clients' processes? As the therapists' own embodiment deepens, her understanding and skill in interacting with clients will simultaneously deepen as it draws from a wider range of resources.

To state all this simply: Embodiment is fundamental to the development of any aspect of a human being. Embodiment allows the psychotherapist to be present with understanding and skill. As a teacher and trainer of psychotherapists, I constantly observe myself as I work with clients. I do this so that I can teach my students and trainees how to do what I do. While I can articulate various conceptual guidelines for my decisions, the quality with which I do things and the timing that I use often defy conceptualization: They just *feel* right. This ability to feel your way through the world and to integrate feelings and thoughts with elegance is a hallmark of embodiment, a seemingly infinite process. It is infinitely possible to become more sensitive, more articulate, and more fluent in our abilities to listen to our bodies, express ourselves with our bodies, and process more energy more precisely.

THE PRESENT MOMENT

Healing occurs in the present moment. Anything that happens can only happen in the present. If we forget this reality, we become lost in the past and future. We meander through our memories and dreams and forgot that we are missing out on living *now*.

To the extent that healing involves a relationship between two people, there has to be a moment of meeting. There is no such thing as a hypothetical relationship. To support each other in healing, we must touch each other through mutual presence in a particular moment in time, at a particular place. Chogyam Trungpa, Rinpoche (1985), a Tibetan Buddhist teacher said that healing occurs through the meeting of two minds.

Few things prepare us better for staying in the present moment than meditation. Although there are many approaches to meditation in different cultures, what is common to all meditation practices is the cultivation of mindfulness—the ability to maintain attention toward a particular object or field of awareness. As mindfulness develops, some approaches to meditation cultivate awareness as well. The term *awareness* refers to a larger, more open state of presence, with less fixed attention than pure mindfulness. Meditation practices that include open eyes and open attention translate more easily into psychotherapy than do meditation practices with closed eyes and fixed attention. It is the continual practice of sitting within the present moment that prepares us to remain present for clients without wavering in the face of challenging energy. While this may seem very basic relative to the sophistication of psychological theory, it is often the most difficult aspect of actually doing psychotherapy. Embodiment supports presence most clearly when we are witnessing intensity in our clients. Our ability to work with our perceptions and responses and allow them to move through our bodies can support us to stay present rather than dissociate in the face of intensity.

ACCEPTING REALITY:
NONAGGRESSION AND COMPASSION

Out of this ability to stay present, we begin to dissolve our aggression toward our world and ourselves. We stop arguing with reality. "No, I want to be bigger or stronger or richer or calmer. I want to be loved more. I want to have bright, shiny new things." As we spend less time arguing with reality, we become more curious about things as they are. We look more deeply into the nature of our lives. Who are we really? What is this world all about? We feel the softness of the spring breeze. We stop to smell the roses—and the skunks. I received a great lesson about skunks from my neighbor, Mr. Henderson, when I was a little girl. He told me "They don't smell bad. They just smell." He said this with a twinkle of delight in his eyes. To this day, I am able to slow down when I habitually react against the smell of a skunk. I can appreciate the richness and the power of the smell.

As we stop arguing with our lives, we become curious about things we might have automatically rejected. In this way, delight can grow. We come to marvel at life, at the nature of human beings, at ourselves, at what a strange and challenging thing it is to be alive in this world. We develop appreciation. Through intentionally allowing ourselves to love the world, we cultivate compassion. This is not love for what is good and beautiful alone, but love for the whole human journey. We have learned that hating it does not make it go away. And we have learned that loving it sometimes does help it heal.

When nature rears its savage head, when people die in mudslides or we watch a wildcat slaughter a young deer, we can accept that these are the ways of nature. But so many of our human atrocities seem so unnecessary, so unnatural, and yet they exist. If they are un-necessary, then we must heal the confusion that created them. In order to do that, perhaps our compassion is necessary. Perhaps, however, some of our human foibles and even atrocities are part of human na-ture. Learning to accept our greed and lust, for example, may be part of learning about human nature. This does not necessarily imply a laissez-faire acceptance, but becoming realistic about human nature may actually allow us to work with these primitive parts of ourselves more creatively. This is an important aspect of BMP, supporting clients in learning to accept their own natures, with all the implied complexities and contradictions. From that ground, we can develop certain qualities within ourselves, such as maturity, wisdom, and com-passion.

Compassion, in this case, is not idealized. Being compassionate does not involve ignoring our primitive selves, our selfishness, or our greed. Compassion is not some kind of saccharine sweet, overgeneralized policy of being nice to everyone: Trungpa, Rinpoche described such an approach as *idiot compassion*. Rather, compassion comes out of an open relationship to the world. Through keeping our minds and hearts and eyes wide open, through practicing nonaggression, we tap into a natural compassion for all that we experience.

The privilege of the psychotherapist is to be intimate with some of the more glorious and nasty aspects of humanity. We may witness the joy of someone learning to love and the pain of someone who was sexually violated as an infant. We may listen to ecstatic dreams and watch an ugly addiction relapse. This is a great privilege. It is impossible to forget the highest and lowest tones of the scale of humanity, and yet it is so tempting to pick and choose. Can we not have all the beauty and ignore the pain? In the therapist role, this tempts us, and as we stand on the threshold of our own healing processes, we ask ourselves this. My clients often say to me, "I don't want to feel that," or "I don't want to go through that." I know, I understand, but it is a package deal. Life includes birth and death, pleasure and pain. If we want more life, we have to open up to more reality. Holding compassion for our clients requires accepting their lives, not wishing too strongly that their lives were different. It is possible to feel deeply sorry that someone is suffering without cultivating the illusion that this suffering should disappear.

More particular than accepting all of reality is the act of accepting our own lives and our own beings. This particular life with all its good and challenging qualities is the only life we have. Often, we attempt to cast our lives away. We denigrate them, compare them disfavorably to others, and wish they were different. It is a powerful gesture to accept our particular lives and our personal natures, to hold them as if cradling them in our hands, "This is what I have to work with."

ENERGY AND BASIC GOODNESS

Opening up to reality connects us to a basic sense of energy. On the simplest level we can relate energy to life force, or on a broader level to nature itself. From a scientific point of view, we don't yet fully understand energy. Physics recognizes four categories of energy: gravity, electromagnetic energy, strong nuclear energy, and weak nuclear energy. On a biological level, we understand changes in elements that bind and release energy resulting in life processes: photosynthesis, respiration, oxygenation, and metabolism. However, we are still unable to define the nature of life itself. We can characterize it, but we are not quite able to pin it down. We can say that living forms are able to replicate themselves. Nonetheless, we all have a direct experience of life and more specifically of human life. What is the fundamental nature of life? What is the fundamental nature of human beings? Are we evolving? What are we becoming?

Again, opening up to reality requires that we accept ourselves as we are. What if nature and life and human beings are basically good, just by nature of their existence? The sun rises and that is good. What if there is a goodness that goes deeper than what we like and dislike? What if the sun is good even when it is causing drought. Is it possible that as human beings we are still good even when we are angry or greedy? What if these energies are parts of our natures? What if experimenting and becoming aware of these difficult human energies are part of the totality of nature? Can we trust our biologies? We have in our biologies naturally lustful, slothful, and territorial energies. Are we bad because of these? An innate feature of our biologies is nurturing and creative energies. Are we good because of these? Or is it a matter of creatively integrating all these energies into a whole self.

Both somatic psychology and many spiritual, contemplative approaches regard our fundamental energy as basically good. While some behavior may be destructive or confused, perhaps the energy or impulses from which they arose are not basically bad. Perhaps bringing more attention and awareness to challenging feelings and behaviors is more effective than judging them as bad and wrong. In the process of psychotherapy, it can relieve people tremendously to recognize the basic biology of their behavior. Looking at the biological bases of certain behaviors removes a certain level of shame. Everybody is dealing with some degree of greed, lust, and territoriality. It can also be helpful to recognize our particular physical nature. Some people are just biologically more aggressive than others. Some people will naturally be more intellectual or more feminine. Each individual life form has its unique energetic qualities. Perhaps none are bad or better than others. Perhaps again, it is a matter of integration and manifestation. On the other hand, clearly human energy can become confused and twisted. Murder is a twisted expression of rage or fear. When my clients question why someone behaved in a certain way toward them, we look at their confusion. The person behaved as they did because they were confused. Recognizing the basic energy of life that exists underneath confusion can free us from both hopelessness and condemnation. Working directly with energy can allow us to change patterns without cutting off aspects of ourselves.

CONDITIONING AND ESSENCE

This brings us to the tricky process of discerning our innate nature from our conditioning. The nature versus nurture issue has always been central to psychology. To what extent are we genetically determined and to what extent is our behavior learned? Now that we have invested many decades in this debate, we are starting to recognize how the two factors interact on many levels. Our environment signals certain genes to activate. Simultaneously, particular individuals elicit particular kinds of reactions from the environment. So the environment and our genetic nature both shape each other. The more we know about this, the more complex it appears to be.

Nonetheless, it can be very helpful within the process of psychotherapy to entertain the question, "What is my true nature? Who am I fundamentally? What is essential to who I am?" Looking at the other side of the issue, we might ask whether a particular behavior is learned and is not fundamental to our innate nature. While we can never answer these questions empirically, to ask them may begin to empower us and to create the space in which to grow and change and move beyond our conditioning.

DEVELOPMENT

This ability to grow and change may be a hallmark of human nature. Creativity seems to be at the root of the entire world. Imagine our whole universe unfolding from the big bang or the primeval fireball, as Swimme and Berry (1992) called it. Each phase of the history of the universe is a creative event. Creativity, development, and evolution are inherent in our universe. Evolution is constantly occurring within every species of life. However, some species seem to be characterized by more evolutionary changes during the lifetime of each individual. Humans are such neotonous creatures; we change and develop throughout our life spans. On a biological level, there are major brain changes that occur in mid life and enhance our potential. So we do not just deteriorate, we can potentially play with creating ourselves all the way into the moment of death. Consciously holding this view of continual development is a tremendous challenge to our view of life. It challenges us to go beyond stability and comfort as life goals. It offers us the possibility to work and play our way toward our own enlightenment and the possibility of global harmony.

THE SELF-IN-RELATIONSHIP

What is a self? What does it mean to have one or to be one? Awareness of self and self-in-relationship are fundamental to adult development. First we need to know that we have a self, then we need to know its habits. Finally, we need to cultivate a relationship to the self that is creative and healthy.

There is some affiliation between our selves and our bodies. The awareness aspect of our selves generally seems to hover in the vicinity of our bodies. Embodiment involves the integration of our bodies and our fields of attention. There is a relationship between having a strong sense of self and embodiment. The ideal of embodiment is that our attention is centered in the core of our bodies, the central pathway from the head through to the pelvic floor. In an embodied state, as our attention goes out to the environment, it extends out from the center. Our attention can expand so that it includes our bodies and the external environment, creating a flow of communication between the inside and the outside (Figure 3.1). However, the high level of stimulation in the world outside of us frequently pulls our attention out of our bodies altogether. In this case, our attention is figuratively thrown out of our bodies and into the outer world. Our attentional field is not large enough to include both our bodies and the environment. Often in engaging with others, we lose our awareness of ourselves in this way. When we are not literally feeling our bodies, we cannot make self-informed decisions. We must operate on logic alone. This logic may be based on the needs or desires of others. Or we may base an action on an internalized image of proper behavior. This state of affairs precludes a strong relationship with oneself or intimacy with others. On an individual level, we lose access to much of our intuition, creativity, and internal developmental impulses. On a relationship level, dependency, codependency, and lack of individuation are the result.

In BMP, there is tremendous emphasis put on feeling oneself. BMP trainees spend long hours practicing feeling their bodies while attending to and engaging with others. In this way embodiment and self development come together inseparably. Then this training is offered to the client in a different form. In BMP, therapists track their clients' attentional fields and continually encourage them to come back to themselves. "Now come back to you. Take a breath, feel yourself. And then begin again from there to examine your life situations or relate to other." Most adults in this culture need this kind of training. Without feeling ourselves, we cannot directly contact others because our experiences will occur by proxy. In order to truly communicate with others we must bring ourselves into direct contact with them. Thus, as psychoanalysis has been telling us for decades, a sense of self forms the foundation for intimate relationships. Embodiment offers a fresh

FIGURE 3.1 FOUNTAIN

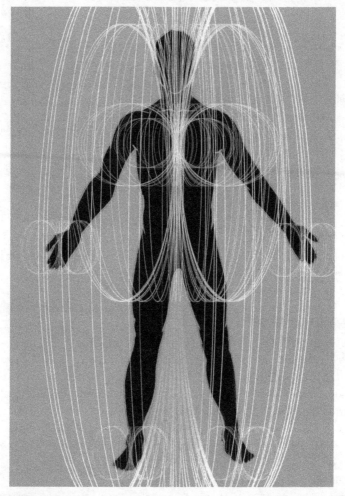

Information via sensory perceptual experiences move through the body connecting inner and outer attention.

perspective and vehicle for strengthening and cultivating a sense of self. Embodiment is the foundation of self-development, the practical basis for it.

Human beings are basically pack animals. We want to relate to others, yet we do not want to lose ourselves when we do so. Although we have enough biological diversity so that we may choose to live as hermits, we have over a million of years of communal life in our genetic heritage. This legacy thrusts us strongly into relationship with other human beings.

A major factor compelling us toward relationship is our postnatal gestational period. We gestate for nine months in utero and then by some reckoning, another nine months postnatally. We are dependent on other humans for our nurture for years. At the very least, out of this, we develop the habit of relationship. In fact, it seems we are hard-wired to do so.

Our intellectual ability allows us to see beyond our immediate experience and into an awareness of our interconnectedness with other life forms, the planet, and even the stars. We have conceived of the idea of ecosystems, communities, and intergalactic communication.

All of these factors make it impossible to deny the importance of relationship in human life. We love each other, teach each other, and complement each other. We are rarely self-sufficient beings. Yet, modern culture is encouraging us to live less and less intimately. For many people, psychotherapy is a means to heal the rifts that have formed between our selves and others. Are the boundaries between us too permeable or too rigid? How do our relationships with others affect our sense of self? How does our relationship with ourselves affect our connections with others? There is a constant dynamic interplay between our selves and those around us. Many early approaches to somatic psychology were so focused on the flow of energy through the body that the relational aspects of psychotherapy were ignored.

As the field matures, this imbalance is being rectified. In his book *Bonding* (1986), Keleman described the basic physical bonds that underlie our energetic exchanges. He sees these as uterine, mouth-breast, genital, and full-bodied. Daniel Stern's recognition of attunement as a preverbal dance between primary caregiver and infant is documented in his book, *The Interpersonal World of the Infant* (1985); this makes a strong case for the importance of the body in bonding. Likewise, Schore (1994) documented some of the ways that both mothers and therapists can serve as "interactive psychobiological regulators." All of these psychological sources recognize the inherent link between interpersonal bonding and the body.

Similarly, some spiritual paths focus primarily on liberating the self. However, many religions, spiritual paths, and approaches to meditation see serving others as the ultimate purpose. In Buddhism, one vows to support all sentient beings to attain enlightenment. Psychologically, there is a complex set of issues here: sense of self, boundaries, communication, and intimacy. Ultimately, growth in each of these areas supports growth in the other areas. In BMP the balance between individuation and relationship is seen as reciprocally supportive. The more we differentiate from others, the more deeply intimate we can be. It is only on a conceptual level that these two polarities may seem conflictual. On a body level, we can feel the mutuality of these two aspects of our being.

These seven principles—embodiment, the present moment, accepting reality, energy, development, conditioning and essence, and self-in-relationship—form the basis of body-mind psychotherapy.

PART II

TASKS AND FORMAT

Chapter 4

Charting the Course

Tasks of Body-Mind Psychotherapy

The tasks of psychotherapy can be mapped out in various ways. As discussed in the preface, psychotherapy is a sprawling and changing landscape difficult to define. In order to introduce BMP technique within the overall landscape of psychotherapy, we look at the three general tasks of psychotherapy: (1) healing developmental deficiencies; (2) resolving trauma; (3) supporting further development. These three tasks are not truly distinct from each other; they form stepping stones for one another. They grow out of each other and into each other. Nonetheless, for the sake of articulation, let us begin by discussing them individually. For each of the three areas, case studies illustrate different facets of the tasks. BMP diagnostic and facilitative techniques are presented in later chapters, so the cases in this chapter are presented in general ways without technical details. The intent is to introduce general BMP techniques and illustrate how these techniques can interface seamlessly with standard techniques of psychotherapy.

HEALING DEVELOPMENTAL DEFICIENCIES

Donald Winnicott (1965) introduced us to the concept of the good-enough mother. Yet, this concept still contrasts poignantly with the concept of a perfect childhood. Of what would this perfect childhood consist? We would be understood by our parents, teachers, and community—our strengths appreciated, our foibles mentored. We would find ourselves in the right family, in the right place, at the right time, with just the right balance of support and challenge. From a conventional psychological perspective, I might conclude that I have never seen this reality. In contrast, from a universal, spiritually encompassing perspective, one might say that every childhood is "perfect" in the sense of perfectly reflecting the individual's soul and preparing one to meet one's future. These two perspectives mark extremes on a continuum. However, adopting any fixed position on this continuum is fraught with moralistic judgment and the potential of minimizing either health or pain.

The practical reality is that as we develop, we are faced with aspects of ourselves constructed in the past that must be dismantled, reorganized, rehabilitated, or fundamentally recycled in order to go on with our growth as human beings. Our earliest experiences are foundational—becoming templates for our concepts of who we are, what the world is like, and what relationships are like. These templates are fundamental to our behavior, our beliefs, and our perceptions. As we grow and change, our behavioral, conceptual, and perceptual templates must grow and change as well.

The following case study is offered as an example of healing developmental deficiencies. Simple BMP techniques are utilized. While these techniques are detailed later, they are presented briefly here as an introduction. The techniques utilized in this case are: (1) identification of feelings as they are located in the body; (2) awareness of the breath; and (3) intentional breathing into a specific location in the body.

Jim was struggling with anxiety and isolation. While outwardly he was very mild mannered and soft spoken, inwardly he experienced himself as possessing a hidden power that he believed was central to who he was. Over a period of months in psychotherapy, he began to have dreams including images of wild animals and powerful human figures. In therapy, he was able to recognize feelings of power, intensity, and passion in his body. He experienced this as a sense of warmth and power radiating from his chest. Over time, he became better able to tolerate these feelings within the therapeutic container—he was able to sustain the feelings for longer periods. As he began to desire to manifest his own personal power in the world, his anxiety reasserted itself. He experienced it most prominently as a knot in his solar plexus area.

Within a particular therapy session, he worked with breathing into this knot. As he did so, he moved into a more upright, less constricted posture that he identified as "being powerful." Within moments, he hunched back over into his knotted, anxiety position. I asked him what happened. He gestured with his hands over his head, as if they were pushing his head down. He said that it was as if something was saying, "Don't do it, don't do it." I asked, "Where did you hear that, where did you learn not to do it?" "Well, no one ever really said it to me, but somehow I learned from my father not to do it," Jim replied. "Breathe, and feel in your body how you learned not to do it." Jim closed his eyes and reflected inward, "I can see my father's face. He looks at me, and then it's as if I suddenly don't exist. He looks down, not at me." As Jim does this, he tucks his chin back, looking quite stern. I mirrored this back to him, and he said, "Yeah, like that. It was just his subtle little message of disapproving."

Jim's father was basically loving, and he had always treated him in a kindly fashion. There was no history of trauma or any major developmental deficiency, just a subtle message that he was going a bit too far if he expressed his intensity too overtly. Jim's situation is an example of an extremely subtle developmental deficiency. Jim needed approval to feel powerful. In order to pursue further development, this developmental deficiency must be addressed. The old message, "Don't do it," needed to be dismantled, and a new message internalized. In this case, Jim's growing awareness supported by the therapist's ongoing encouragement allowed him to experiment with including his passion, power, and intensity in his daily life. Jim recognized that these were real and important parts of him that were in some way more essential than the conditioning which had taught him to suppress them. Expressing his power relieved the anxiety which he identified as pent-up energy and allowed him to reach out to others with his passion to relate. As a child, Jim did not receive enough acknowledgment and encouragement to express the more powerful aspects of himself. This deficiency caused him to avoid developing these parts of himself until, as an adult, their absence became painful to him, as anxiety and isolation. All of these stages in Jim's psychotherapy are standard in most approaches. The BMP use of bodily awareness and working with breathing facilitated those processes and allowed the new experience to be firmly rooted in the body.

The following case illustrates a more extreme deficiency. In this case, as with the last one, standard psychotherapeutic techniques are integrated with body-oriented techniques. Verbal explorations and body awareness are utilized together as a way of accessing emotion. Dreams are explored both verbally and through the sensations they evoke. Conflicting emotions are integrated through somatic dialogue.

Marjorie's children were grown, and her husband of 25 years had left her a year earlier. Quietly terrified of almost everything, until now she had managed to cope within a very quiet, controlled lifestyle. As a young mother she had avoided even driving a car. When her children became older, she forced herself to learn to drive within a prescribed range from home, taking them only to their various activities and back. Now, living alone in her small apartment was one long panic attack. She had never lived alone. Her children convinced her to see a therapist. After a long period in therapy of examining her dreams, bringing awareness to her breathing, and stretching her body, she awoke from the sleep of her containment, and she was mad: She was mad at her husband for leaving her, but mostly mad at her mother for never really looking at her, or holding her, or listening to her.

Marjorie described her mother as quietly seething with an icy rage. The family, in turn, avoided disturbing her mother, in an equally quiet manner. Marjorie, as the oldest child, had been the first assault to her mother's fortress. Marjorie was not sure how her mother had taught her never to have any feelings. As a child, Marjorie remembered going into her closet and pursing her lips until a feeling went away. Marjorie deeply needed to be seen, to be appreciated, to be the center of attention, to have her feelings acknowledged and validated, to get her way. Fundamentally, Marjorie needed to feel deeply held by a maternal love. As she breathed into an angry image from one of her dreams, she would begin to tremble and then clench her jaw. In therapy, we would focus together on being kind to both the fear and the rage— not rejecting them, not shutting them down. Bit by bit, she came to feel more and more of the fundamental aloneness with which she had always lived. She shut me out emotionally and talked about terminating her therapy, but she couldn't quite go through with it. I stayed aware of my body, my breathing, and my feelings, and continued to invite her awareness and kindness toward the pain inside her. She railed against me and questioned why she could feel so relentlessly alone. I kept breathing in her rhythm and affirmed how important it was to feel the abandonment that she had never felt as an infant or child.

Slowly she began to realize that she was beginning to feel somewhat safe in her apartment. Her son came for a visit, and she was relieved to have her peace and quiet back after he left. As she put it, she was beginning to "find" herself. During the most vivid moments of this she would cry and hold herself while I would speak quietly about being there with her and encourage her to stay with herself, to not abandon her sadness as it had been abandoned before. She talked of spiritual love. I asked her whether she was willing to imagine being held in that spiritual love, to feel immersed in love, to allow our attention to her to become emissaries of this love. I asked her how this felt in her body. As this became easier, we could imagine her as a baby and as a child. We would send love to those young parts of her.

Marjorie had a major deficit in the early bonding between herself and her mother. While there had obviously been some bonding that had enabled her to marry and raise children, there had not been enough to support her to feel safe when she was alone, and to feel capable of supporting herself. In order to face the basic tasks of an independent adult life, she needed to immerse herself in mothering herself and internalizing the maternal acceptance that the therapeutic container embodied. Furthermore, she needed to allow those feelings to penetrate into the oldest, most primitive parts of herself—parts that had long ago given up hope of ever feeling loved.

In resolving any developmental deficit, it is really important for the new experience to permeate all the way to the original wound. To do this, it is important to identify the feeling of the deficit in the body. During the process of becoming familiar with this deficit, an internal witness or internal parent is developing. The therapist is modeling healthy parenting, and the client is developing an aspect of herself that is able to acknowledge, be with, and eventually, minister to the old needs. As the client learns to give to herself and to receive from the therapist and others, do these new feelings permeate all the way to the part of the body that felt deficient? This permeation can literally feel like anointing a wound, or warming a cold area, or filling an empty area. When the client is able to experience a new possibility in their bodies, it has become real to them. In Marjorie's case, she conceptualized this new possibility as "divine" love. As she was able to feel the old pain and this special love at the same time, she was able to bring that feeling of special love directly into her heart and belly, where she felt the original abandonment.

This is the **healing edge**, the direct experience of a meeting in the body of the old pain and the new possibility. On a bodily level, Marjorie experienced this special love as a warmth that flowed over her skin and slowly saturated her from the inside out. As she allowed this feeling to mix with her feelings of rage and sadness at being abandoned, she felt her heart open and her belly soften. Eventually, she felt warm through to the core. At this point in the healing process, the initial phase of healing has taken place and the client has a new conception of herself. The work is then to integrate this new self into

the more outward aspects of the client's life, such as work and relationships. While the original version of self may never wholly disappear, healing occurs as it is eroded bit by bit and replaced with new
experiences. In BMP it is an essential principle to appreciate the growth
and development even when it is not fully complete. I often speak of
not stepping on tender young seedlings that are just beginning to
grow; otherwise, how will they ever mature? Another principle, parallel to appreciating new growth, is the process of staying open to further healing and development as one desires it. This is essentially the
process of turning impatience into appreciation and desire. These processes are essential to integrating new aspects of oneself.

The stages of healing a developmental deficit include preparation,
core healing, and integration. The preparation may consist of many
aspects: the initial desire to change, an understanding and acceptance
of one's history and the people and dynamics involved, and a deep
feeling and recognition of the old pattern and pain. The core healing
experience consists of staying on the healing edge by bringing the old
pain in contact with the new experience—feeling this in the core of
the body, the heart and the belly (in Marjorie's case). The therapist's
presence and the client's internal parent must work together to offer
what is needed. The new experience must really permeate all the way
to the core of the old pain. In the final integration phase, the client
uses awareness and intentionality to observe her fluctuations between
old and new behavior, concepts, and perceptions.

RESOLVING TRAUMA

Trauma is significantly different from a developmental deficiency in
that the central nervous system is conditioned to produce an intense
physiological reactivity (van der Kolk, 1996), including the flight,
fight, and freeze responses that are biologically anchored into the central nervous systems of all vertebrates. These responses can be triggered by any sensory phenomenon resembling the original trauma.
Coping mechanisms for trauma responses combine various degrees of
numbing and arousal in the central nervous system. While trauma is
generally thought of as resulting from an external event of a certain
degree of intensity, the individual's response to the event determines
whether or not the event is actually traumatizing (van der Kolk, 1996).
Like other animals, we respond to crisis in a physically adaptive manner, by running, fighting, or freezing. Once the crisis is complete, the
autonomic nervous system may regulate itself through adaptive bodily
responses such as breathing, shivering, or crying. As adult humans, we
are able to repress both our adaptive defensive responses to

trauma—as in not fleeing or fighting back—as well as the physiological responses that allow posttraumatic recovery—as in not shaking or breathing freely. When these bodily responses are not fully expressed and the autonomic nervous system does not complete its physiological process, posttraumatic stress is exhibited and the nervous system subtly or grossly maintains and repeats the traumatic cycle over and over again until it is resolved. In psychotherapy with individuals who have posttraumatic stress, the tasks involve creating basic coping skills, supporting healing and development without reactivating the trauma, and, when sufficient healing and development have occurred, allowing the trauma to be slowly and safely renegotiated. The ability to track the client's physiological responses requires that the therapist be well versed in the subtleties of neurological overload and understand the potential effects of trauma on all bodily functioning.

Dissociation is a related issue. While definitions of dissociation vary tremendously, the fundamental condition is one in which the central nervous system is limited in its ability to perceive, process, and respond to current stimuli in a constructive manner. Dissociation is a hallmark of posttraumatic stress. In BMP we track dissociation not only in the nervous system, but throughout the entire body. There is a subtle continuum between embodiment and dissociation. We are always moving in and out of being more or less present in our bodies.

The following is a case of mild trauma that was interwoven with childhood developmental issues, and recapitulated in an adult relationship. The first step was to help the client to recognize the bodily state of posttraumatic stress. The second was to begin to allow the body to regulate itself using conscious awareness of the breath and allowance of bodily movement when this response occurred.

Denise began therapy as support during a divorce. She had recognized a similarity between her relationship with her husband and the harsh judgmental treatment she had received from her father as a child. There was always a quality of fear in her eyes when she felt that she might be judged. She would hold her breath and get very still. As she learned to recognize this state and how it stopped her from asserting herself in any way, she began to work with breathing into the stillness in her head and eyes and thawing it. (**Breathing into a body part** refers to directing the movement of the breathe in a particular direction, in this case Denise's head and eyes. A more detailed discussion of breathing takes place in Chapter 6.) Denise used the energy she accessed through breathing and awareness to role-play various scenarios with her landlord and prospective employers.

As her new life unfolded and her confidence in herself grew, she still dreaded running into her ex-husband. She had nightmares of such a meeting. She said she feared being "overpowered."

I asked her to say "overpowered" again and feel how it felt in her body. Her heart began to pound, her eyes opened wide, and she got into her still and frozen state. This was the most extreme version of her traumatized state that she had manifested within the therapeutic context so far. Yet, over her time in therapy, she had developed an ability to move through similar states into a feeling of empowerment using her breathing as a bridge. I asked her to breathe into this frozen fear state and feel how she wanted to respond. "How dare you, how dare you?" she said over and over, her breath full and strong, her eyes afire with anger. "How dare he what?" I asked. Denise froze for a moment and began to sob. I stayed with her and monitored her ability to tolerate the feelings she was having. While they were strong feelings, she appeared to be allowing them to move through her body without becoming frozen, panicked, or dissociated. As her crying softened, I asked her how she was doing. She nodded. "What happened when I said, 'How dare he what?'" Her crying increased a bit as she said, "I just remembered how much he used to scare me. He'd lock me in the bathroom sometimes when he was mad and yell at me through the door. Or I'd wake up out of deep sleep, and he'd be standing on the bed, towering above me, yelling at me. Sometimes he'd punch at my face and barely stop himself before he hit me."

*She began to sob again. I encouraged her to stay with the feelings and allow them to sequence through her body. She lay down and breathed deeply as she sobbed. She stretched her arms and legs a bit and I encouraged her to include her hands and feet in this, so that these feelings really got to move all the way out. As her crying died down, she began making sounds with her exhalation, "Whew." (All this activity was based on movement **sequencing** skills that she had practiced previously in therapy. Sequencing will be discussed in Chapter 5.) As we were nearing the end of the session, I asked her to stand up and walk around a bit before she left. "How are you doing?" I asked. "Good," she said, "I feel better." "I can't believe I took all that crap from him." I asked, "Would you do it again?" She shook her head as she looked at me. I suggested she face herself in the mirror and say that out loud to herself. As she did this, her eyes narrowed and teared. She spoke in a strong and angry voice with her arms poised by her sides as if readied to defend herself. "I will never, ever take that kind of crap from anyone again."*

At our next session, Denise was ready to keep going with her work. When I asked her what she would do differently now if her ex-husband approached her violently, her breath stopped for a moment, and then she took a quick breath and her round, soft face flushed and hardened and she said she would tell him to stop! She would call the police. She'd divorce him right away. Her breathing was full, and her arms and trunk were more prepared for action. I encouraged her to stay with this self-protective energy and let it move through her body. I told her to keep going with this, let her body get used to feeling this way. I asked her if she wanted to stand up. She stood up and fumed a bit. I asked whether there were any words to go with this state. She blustered a bit, but couldn't really find any. I reminded her that the previous week she had said, "Don't you dare," and asked if she wanted to try that again. She tried it, and I asked what she would do if he were coming toward her as if to punch her. Her hands rose up in defense, but a bit weakly. I asked whether she wanted me to move my arm slowly toward her so that she could feel herself being vigorously self-defensive. She nodded. I moved my forearm slowly toward her. Her hands came up more strongly. I coached her on a stronger position. We slowly increased the speed and intensity of this as her confidence grew. By the end, she was breathing hard, sweating a bit, and she had a big smile on her face. We ended when she felt fully capable of blocking his punch. I asked her to walk around a bit and see how she felt. "Who are you now? Breathe and feel that, and look out the window and imagine yourself out in the world and see how that feels." "I feel good," she said, "I feel strong."

Later as we sat to talk, she said that for the first time she felt really glad she was divorced and that her old feeling of seeing divorce as a failure wasn't present at all. She was excited to be a single woman making her way in the world. We talked about her father and how she had learned from her relationship with him to be both a victim and dependent. She felt exhilarated as she left, and she had a good week following that session.

Denise had been mildly traumatized by her experiences with her ex-husband. Nevertheless, the trauma was strong enough to encourage her to repress the experience through forgetting and maintaining secrecy. The trauma dovetailed with a developmental pattern of victimization and dependency established with her father. By working developmentally on her ability to assert herself, she gained the resources she needed to confront the trauma. Generally, when trauma has been repressed, it comes forward either when it is reactivated or when there is sufficient strength to resolve it. Through Denise's work on her developmental issues and self-assertion, she developed a variety of strengths that allowed her to reexperience her trauma in a constructive way. She had a strong, cognitive commitment to her own healing and basic goodness. She understood the dynamics of codependence and victimization that disempowered her, and she knew how to allow sensations to move through her body without dissociating.

If a client begins to dissociate, they may suddenly seem less present and vital. Their eyes may become less focused. In BMP, the therapist will inquire as to what just occurred. This may reestablish the client's ability to remain present. If not, it maybe necessary to ask him or her to stand up, walk around, or perform some activity that allows them to come back.

This ability to sequence energy is an aspect of embodiment. In the nonhuman animal world, when an animal is startled or traumatized, it visibly shakes off its response when the stimulus is over. With a mild startle, this appears as a shiver, a headshake, or a skin twitch. With a full-blown trauma, this may be rolling, shaking, moaning, and bellowing. Through acculturation, adult humans learn to freeze around intense sensation and suppress our natural responses. When our sequencing responses are shut down, we can get stuck in some phase of the trauma response. To resolve trauma, we must learn bit by bit to allow our trauma response to sequence through our bodies without maintaining the freezing phase. This can be accomplished by going slowly, learning about sensation and movement, and becoming comfortable with intensity. The key is to be able to stay present during the intensity.

Catharsis and Dissociation

Catharsis is important in the history of psychotherapy. *Webster's* (1983) defines the psychological meaning as the alleviation of a complex by bringing it to consciousness and affording it expression. The first definition is *purgation*. In clinical psychotherapy practice, catharsis has come to mean intense emotional reexperiencing. In working therapeutically with a traumatic response, if there is not sufficient ability to stay conscious, sequence this energy out of the body, and hold the intention of healing, a cathartic experience can be retraumatizing. The original experience of trauma involves being literally overwhelmed, unable to respond in a way that restores safety or well-being. In such a case, there is a lack of sufficient resources to respond effectively. The point of reexperiencing trauma clinically is to resolve it through effective response. To do this, we must first establish sufficient resources to respond. Then we must slowly renegotiate the trauma with the intention of resolving it through allowing our bodies to sequence the energy and to respond protectively and effectively. Peter Levine (1997) pointed out the need to proceed slowly and thereby titrate the traumatic response, dissolving it into restored autonomic flow. **Titration** involves the smallest amount of activation that is manageable. When there is an intense cathartic release, this intensity may overwhelm the nervous system and cause dissociation. **Dissociative catharsis** is retraumatizing. This possible danger has generalized into a fear of intense expression in general. However, this danger can be handled responsibly through systematic development of the client's ability to sequence energy while monitoring for dissociation. There are many factors that enable the therapist to spot dissociation: loss of eye contact, a diminished or exaggerated range of movement, and the loss of verbal clarity. The most fundamental aspect of avoiding retraumatization is staying present with a **healing intention.** In the heat of an emotional expression, one may get lost in the emotion and lose sight of the therapeutic context. In this case, the emotions may overpower our intention to heal ourselves. It is possible for the client to express intense emotions and stay present and clear about the healing intention. Here, the catharsis will be a healing experience. It is the therapist's responsibility to assess if this is the case. It may be necessary to ask the client questions about the experience and intention in order to anchor the client's ability to renegotiate intensity.

In a traumatic disorder, our neurological functioning is disrupted. In addition to resolving the central traumatic response, it may be necessary to reintegrate more peripheral functions. These might include basic autonomic regulation, such as digestion, cognition, and motor reflexes. In Denise's case, she needed to reestablish a reflexive ability to defend with her arms. Other people may need to reestablish defenses with their voice (the ability to scream), or with their legs (kicking and running). In reestablishing these reflexes, the therapist monitors the client for neurological overwhelm. With more severe trauma it tends to take longer to be able to renegotiate these responses. The client's ability to sequence energy, commitment to healing, and ability to stay present must be even stronger. The stronger the trauma response, the more easily it is reactivated. While Denise experienced mild traumatic stress, Michael, whose story follows, clearly suffered from posttraumatic stress disorder (PTSD). His trauma was easily reactivated and therefore required greater care to renegotiate. In this case, BMP techniques of sequencing movement are especially important.

Michael was an extremely intelligent, slight, young man who came to therapy because he was determined to "do better," than he had in past relationships. He had been in therapy off and on since he was a teen and his parents had divorced. He had vague visual memories of being anally abused by his father. He believed this began in infancy and continued intermittently until about age 2. He had always had these memories and had first discussed them in therapy as a teen. During this period he researched abuse, trauma, and the recovery process with the help of his therapist. Also with his therapist's support, he shared his memories with his mother who intuitively felt that they might be true. She confirmed that his father was often home alone with him during that time because he worked in the evenings. When Michael was 2½, his father had taken a job that kept him traveling much of the time. This was consistent with Michael's sense that the abuse had occurred only at a very young age. All of this was put together during his stint in therapy in his teens. Much healing had taken place during this period of therapy, extraordinarily so for such a young boy.

Now Michael found himself in his first homosexual relationship with any potential for commitment. In the past he had gone through the motions of relationships with women. When they had gotten too close, he had increased his abuse of alcohol and marijuana. Through substance abuse and neglect of the relationship, he always managed to have these women reject him. When he began to experiment with relating to men, he felt more intensity, but was only able to be sexual when he was intoxicated. Donald, his current partner, was the first man with whom he had developed a friendship as well as a sexual intimacy. Donald and Michael both wanted a committed relationship, but Michael was very frightened. He felt that his fear stemmed from his early abuse. He stated that he "couldn't stand being close to an erect penis without being high."

I asked Michael to think about his impulse to begin a new course of therapy and to allow that thought to develop fully in his imagination. I suggested he close his eyes and allow the thought to float around in his body. He squirmed a bit; I encouraged him to take a deep breath and stay with it a moment longer. His face flushed slightly.

Therapist: So what are you feeling?

Michael: At first it felt kind of good, I felt kind of excited to do this, and then it felt scary and like it was too much. My heart is pounding.

I heard this as a parallel of how his relationship with Donald felt, exciting at first and then building toward reactivating his trauma. The challenge is always to learn to support the excitement and gather strength to move through the trauma. With that intention, I suggested:

So feel your heart again and look for some way that you can support it to stay with the excitement and not get overwhelmed. His attention turned inward for a moment, and then he looked up, "I don't know." As he said this, he squirmed, sort of an impatient rock back and forth with his pelvis. I did the same movement and said, "Let's take that squirming movement to be your body's answer to the question. So, maybe your lower body can help support you to stay with the excitement." I avoided using the word pelvis, because I felt it might be somewhat reactivating. "Feel yourself seated on your cushion. Take a deep breath. Imagine your heart feeling really safe and supported from below." This image definitely settled him down a bit, but it also seemed to quell his excitement. In order to reinvite his enthusiasm and also to move into safer territory, I said, "So Michael, I really heard how important this relationship with Donald is to you, and I believe that working slowly with yourself, you can make intimacy feel safer, bit by bit. So what's the hardest part of relating to Donald?" As this first session proceeded, I asked questions about the relationship and as he answered, I coached him to take a deep breath and feel the support of his body.

The next few sessions proceeded in a similar fashion. We did an educational piece on the pelvis: its importance as the base of the spine, how it is involved ideally in every movement, and how we are culturally indoctrinated with fear about the pelvis. This helped to disarm any superficial triggering that the word *pelvis* may have had.

I asked Michael how things were going sexually with Donald. "I don't know. It's going okay. It doesn't seem that important to either of us. We don't do it very much. When it seems like it's up, I slug down a couple of beers and just kind of get through it. It's okay." Michael's voice seemed flat, his vocabulary limited; his eyes were downcast. He continued to talk about sex, but flipped into an intellectual mode. As he continued it got more feverish. "Whew," I inserted into a gap, "that's a lot of pressure. Do you want to focus on this?" "Hell no," he replied, "I don't want to do it. I hate it. I hate the whole idea of sex." "Slow down, breathe, feel what's happening in your body right now." He slumped down, breathed deeply a couple of times, and shook his arms a little bit. His eyes teared up. He looked at me, "What do we do now?" I smiled at him, "Let's just be here together for a minute. Michael, you've been working with yourself in a very sensitive way, so feel your body and your breath. Find the support of your pelvis underneath you. Really take the time to connect to the wisest part of yourself. From this place, ask yourself the question, 'What do I want right now? Where do I want to go from here?'"

Michael sat quietly with his eyes closed, breathing deeply. Finally he looked up, his eyes were misty, but strong and clear, "I'm not ready." I acknowledged his ability to know that he wasn't ready.

Over the next couple of months we discussed what it would mean to get ready. This gave us an opportunity to talk about sex in a general, almost theoretical way, and to learn to be comfortable with each other. We discussed bringing Donald in when Michael was ready. During this period Michael's relationship with his own body got stronger. He began working with his breathing more consciously and energetically in our sessions and on his own, as well as reconnecting to riding his bicycle energetically a couple of times a week, which also encouraged deep breathing.

When Michael felt ready, he and Donald talked about their sexuality and what they wanted. Donald shared more of his own fears and sexual issues. Together they developed a set of goals of what they wanted for their sexual relationship. I asked Michael how he would like Donald to support him if he had an anxiety attack while they were making love. They developed a plan. Michael would let Donald know whether he got anxious, and Donald would ask periodically how Michael was doing. If Michael were anxious, Donald would hold his hand very firmly, look into his eyes, and say, "Do you want to breathe together?" They practiced that in my office together. I suggested that they talk some more together about both their histories and how they had affected their sexuality. We agreed to meet again together.

When we met again, Michael wanted to lie down and breathe while Donald held his hand. They did this together while Donald told Michael that he loved him, that he wanted to be there for him if Michael needed him, and that he wanted him to feel safe with him. I asked Michael whether he was willing to imagine feeling safe with Donald. He said yes, smiled softly, and breathed more deeply. Then he began to whimper. This quickly escalated into full sobbing while Michael gripped Donald's arm. Michael's eyes were wide open. Afraid that he might be overwhelmed and dissociate, I leaned over into Michael's field of vision and asked him to stay in his body "Feel your feet. . . . What's your intention?" (We had talked about the importance of maintaining a healing intention toward oneself.) "I want to heal." I felt reassured that he was not dissociating, but encouraged him to put his feet on the wall and push to stay grounded. He breathed more deeply with his crying. He began to grit his teeth and twist and turn. He seemed right on the edge of dissociating. I told him to use his feet. He began to pound the wall with his feet. I asked whether there were any words. He began yelling, "No, No, NO, NO." I told him to use his hands. He began to pound the futon underneath him, yelling and stamping and pounding while he twisted and sobbed. I coached him to keep going, feel his body, feel what wants to happen next. He was able to make good clear eye contact with both Donald and myself. He struggled to his feet, flailing his arms and legs and screaming "No, I hate you. I hate you." I kept saying "Stay in your body, feel what wants to happen next." As a slight lull began to arise, I said, "Is he [meaning his father] still here?" Michael looked slightly to his right and nodded as he panted. I said, "Get him out of here. You get him out of here now." Michael began yelling "Get out," and charging the spot he had looked toward. Finally Michael, sweating and panting, said, "Yeah, he's out." I encouraged Michael to feel his body and let it recuperate. He breathed and shook and stretched. Donald joined him. Finally, Michael lay down again and began a soft gentle crying. Donald was right beside him, crying a bit himself, and touching him and kissing his head. Michael looked up at Donald, "Thank you." He looked at me as well, "Thank you." I said, "You

are so welcome; I am so happy for you. You did great." Michael cried some more.
We talked about taking it very easy that week. I asked him to call me the next day
and let me know how he was doing, and we ended.

This was a great turning point in Michael's life and in Michael and
Donald's relationship. Michael was able to integrate this traumatized
part of himself. He remained stable in his life. They went through
similar episodes on their own a few times, but the episodes died down
in less than a month. Michael was able to achieve his goal of making
love without alcohol. Michael and I continued our work together for
about a year longer, and then Michael and Donald moved to a new
city. I encouraged Michael to connect to a therapist in his new city
and to be prepared to take care of himself if his trauma were reactivated in the future.

In Michael's case, the ground was carefully prepared for trauma renegotiation. One fundamental piece was teaching Michael how to
work with intense sensations and use his breath, intention, and movement to sequence the energy through in a positive way. The other
fundamental piece was creating an atmosphere of trust in which Michael trusted his own judgment about what he was ready for, and in
which he trusted himself with me and with Donald without giving up
his own autonomy. Because of this foundation, we were able to successfully renegotiate his trauma. In a situation like this, I am constantly
monitoring the client's ability to stay present and not dissociate. This
monitoring takes place through eye contact, verbal contact, and observing the degree of spatial orientation in the client's movement. As
I monitored these with Michael, I assessed that while he was experiencing tremendous intensity, he was doing it in a very conscious way
which could lead toward healing. If a client appears to dissociate, even
slightly, in the middle of such intensity, I immediately move in to
slow things down and insist on grounding the energy. I do this through
insisting that they maintain eye contact, that they talk to me, and by
directing their activity. It is sometimes possible to reorient and go on
from there, but at other times it is necessary to totally change direction. In this case, I ask the client to walk around, look out the window,
whatever it takes to come back to present reality and feel safe and
grounded. Obviously, while preparing to renegotiate trauma and integrating that change into one's life, tremendous healing and development take place. In Michael's case, he healed his relationship to
sexuality and developed the ability to live intimately with a partner.
Again, healing and development are always interwoven into a larger
process with renegotiating trauma.

SUPPORTING DEVELOPMENT

The final task of psychotherapy is that of supporting development. In some rare situations, a developmental issue presents itself with no impinging deficit or trauma involved. Even if trauma or deficits are involved, it is important to differentiate between those and a normal developmental process. In supporting development, BMP begins with assessing and acknowledging a person's strengths, what they have achieved in their lives, and normalizing the desire for support. Human beings are social animals. We all need the support of other humans. At critical junctures in our development, psychotherapy can act as a support for a normal developmental process and might not relate to pathology in anyway. If we do not acknowledge a person's strengths and accomplishments, the desire for further development can begin to be seen as pathological in some way. This pathological view undermines confidence and appreciation for the life process. It is the therapist's job to detect any self-pathologizing that may be occurring and challenge it. I find it helpful to repeatedly review, "Look what you have already done in your life. Look at the challenges you have overcome. Look at the resources you have within your basic being." I do this in a very specific way with each client, specifically acknowledging individual strengths. With one person it might be courage, with another creativity, with another intelligence, with another kindness, but whatever the person's strengths, it is important to evoke them as sustenance for their future journey.

The process of preparing for a new developmental stage is akin to the phase in many mythical tales in which the hero or heroine prepares for their journey by visiting a magical kingdom or power spot of some sort. Generally before the journey, the heroes and heroines bask in the very best of themselves for a period of time. They rest and eat well and enjoy nature and entertainment. This phase is usually followed by their being given some aid to help them along the way. In BMP, the therapist finds out what support clients need and want, and then creates a way for them to use their bodies, breathing, and movement to tap into that support. These bodily activities act as both a tool and a talisman, corresponding to the magic nectar, or arrow, or shield that we find in mythology. Often in these journeys, the hero or heroine forgets to use their power objects; they lose the sense of why they had set out on their journey. Someone or something must remind them so that they wake up, remember their intention, their strengths, and their power object, and then of course they triumph in the end. The psychotherapist serves to remind the client to wake up and stay with their journey rather than to drift off into the gray mist and become lost.

Education is often an important aspect of supporting development. In preparing for a developmental journey, education about body-mind integration can give clients basic tools to assess and work with their own state of mind. Education about the normal tasks and challenges of various developmental phases can reassure clients that their developmental tasks are not pathological. Education about communication skills and systems dynamics can support them to change their behavior more easily and effectively. The following case illustrates this process.

Anne and Brian were a young couple in their early 20s. Their two-year relationship had been a tumultuous one, including several break-ups and reunions. They had read books on intimacy and relationship skills together and worked through many issues on their own. Faced with continuing their educations in different states, they were torn between following their individual dreams, and their deep belief that they were soulmates and that it was important to protect and preserve their relationship. When I checked to learn what options they had explored, they reviewed the various compromises they had looked at and decided against, such as one of them postponing their education, or one of them attending a school that was not as favorable. They had ruled out these compromises as unacceptable.

I asked them whether they were there to get help in making a choice. "Yes, uh huh," they both agreed. And I asked them if they'd ruled out these compromises and asked what choice was left. They looked at each other with rueful eyes. Were they here to get help accepting a choice they had already made? They sank even lower in their chairs and looked at each other again. Had they talked about their fears and concerns that came up around the idea of a separation? Silent nods. Had they agreed on how to handle things like communication, vacations, and meeting new people? Big sighs, and more nods.

"So, how about if you each take a quiet moment with yourselves and feel what's going on inside you right now?" They both settled back in their chairs and looked down. "Good, take a breath, close your eyes if you want to." They each sat quietly for a few moments. "Look for the thoughts, the emotions, and the feelings in your body." I waited another few moments. "So, what did you find?" Brian said, "Sad."

Therapist: How does that feel in your body?

Brian: Heavy.

Therapist: How are you doing Anne?

Anne: I'm scared and I feel guilty.

Therapist: And how do you feel that in your body?

Anne: I feel real tense and knotted up in here [pointing to her belly].

Therapist: That's great that you are so aware of what's going on with you. Take a minute to breathe and be kind to those feelings. Maybe if this idea you have about being soulmates is true, than your relationship can keep going or even begin again after school. I agree with you that it would be wrong to compromise your individual dreams too much, especially at this age. During this they each continued to breathe. Anne had her hand on her belly.

Therapist: What do you think? [Anne nodded thoughtfully, and Brian made a face of resignation as he nodded.]

Therapist: So keep breathing and staying with your feelings in a kind, respectful way, and see what you want to say to each other right now?

They turned toward each other, moving closer. Brian reached out toward Anne. She leaned her head against his. They cried a little bit, said the simple basic things like "I love you. I'm scared. I know. I'm sorry."

I told them that they could feel very proud of themselves individually and the relationship they had created. These exceptional young people just needed some encouragement to make their decisions. They needed validation, and they needed an outside perspective to reflect their strengths. They had already created for themselves the guidelines and touchstones that they needed for their journey.

Developing further is always challenging. Whenever we move into new territory, it is, by definition, unknown. This is always true about development. Otherwise, it wouldn't be a new development, but just a new expression of something that we had already developed.

While development always has a very personal, solitary aspect, there are many ways in which other people are needed. We may need other people to witness our strengths, offer encouragement and outside perspective, or to validate our decision-making process. We made need further education or tools. This was the case for Robert, whose story follows.

Robert was a successful insurance agent. He had raised a family and was happily married. He had never considered psychotherapy before. Now his 80-year-old father had suffered a stroke. Robert and his brother were setting up home health care for his father. Robert was the older child and had always gotten along well with his father, working at his father's business for several years as a young man. They had played golf together most Friday afternoons for decades. Robert's brother, Alan, had always bristled against his father and Robert. There were no major problems, but Alan was not especially close with either Robert or his father. Now the two brothers were having to work together to help their father. There were arguments between the two of them. Robert began having nightmares and losing sleep. His wife suggested that he talk to a counselor.

Robert came in somewhat nervous and uncomfortable. He began talking about all of the tasks and decisions involved in his father's care. He talked about his and Alan's disagreements, and expressed frustration about ways that he thought Alan was making things more difficult than was necessary. I suggested a three-way meeting with Alan so that they could both discuss how they wanted to handle their shared role. Robert was surprised by that possibility, but ultimately agreeable.

With that decided, I asked him how he felt about the sudden change in his dad. Robert sighed with force, "Well, when you put it that way. Yeah. You know, my dad and I have always had a great relationship. He and Alan had trouble, but I never found my dad too restrictive. He was a good guy, I mean, he is a good guy. Wow, I can't believe I said was."

Therapist: Maybe that's your way of saying that part of him is gone now, and you don't know how much will come back. [Robert nodded his head as he stared bleakly at the floor.] Whatever happens in the future, right now you've just experienced a major loss. Take a minute to let that reverberate. Notice how you feel inside. [I saw his head nod slightly, and he took another deep breath.] Good. Notice the sensations in your body that go with these feelings. [His chest collapsed.] Yes, what do you feel in your chest?

Robert: Heavy and sad. And I don't like this.

Therapist: When we don't like something, we often feel anger. [Robert looked up at me a bit startled.] Anger is a normal feeling to have when we lose something. It's not about being angry with somebody. It's just our way of protesting against the event. So, take a deep breath and give yourself permission to be as mad as you want to be that this has happened to your dad, and to you.

It was close to the end of our time, so I gave him some homework to explore his feelings more in writing and with others.

At the next session Robert reported talking to his wife about his feelings. I shared some studies about the positive effects of emotional sharing and awareness. "So to deal with your dad's needs effectively, you're having to learn some new skills. You are not being a baby." Robert agreed and said that this would all take some getting used to. I said that it sounded as if his wife were really there to help him, and so was I. I asked whether he had any male friends that he could talk to about this. We discussed talking with them, and then we examined his writing about feelings. He had done a good job with this and

captured many nuances of feelings, such as being angry because he
was having to act like a parent to his dad. I simply acknowledged the
universality of these feelings and applauded him for being aware of
them. I acknowledged how much adjusting he had to do and how
much giving he was having to do even while there were tumultuous
feelings happening inside him. I asked him what would keep him going through this. He thought for awhile and mentioned his wife, "I
don't know. Love. I guess it boils down to love."

*Therapist: That's really a great thing to be aware of. It's almost like love is the
fuel that keeps anyone going during a rite of passage like this. If we're aware of it,
then we can keep refueling. Whatever that looks like, going to a beautiful place,
going for a walk with your wife. Take a moment to think about love and really let
the idea come alive right now, how do you feel it in your body?*
Robert: Well, I feel. [He gestured to his heart and paused.]
Therapist: Your heart?
Robert: Yeah, I feel my heart sort of swell up.
*Therapist: Good, keep thinking about love, let the idea come alive, and really
feel it in your body. [My voice was soft and quiet so that it would not interfere
with his process.] We continued with this exploration for the rest of the session.*

Overtime, Robert developed a practice when dealing with Alan or
the doctors or any other situation that he found difficult. He would
close his eyes for a moment, take a deep breath, and give himself an
infusion of "love." We had our meeting with Alan and, as is so common in family therapy, both brothers shared things that were unknown to the other. They cleared up some misunderstandings, and
Alan resolved to talk to his dad about their relationship.

In any developmental process, there is a balance between focusing
on future goals and resting into what is really happening in the moment. By feeling the pain, sadness, and anger, which he was feeling in
the present moment, Robert could move toward the healing power of
love. This is the healing edge. By immersing himself in the feeling of
love, Robert found the strength and resilience he needed to go
through this important developmental stage of *filial maturity*, the process in which grown children develop the emotional ability to care
for their parents. There is a natural momentum toward development,
both in our biological selves and in the progression of time. Therefore,
the more we allow ourselves to feel our current feelings, the more the
next step naturally emerges.

In Robert's case, his practice of refueling with love became his
power source on the developmental journey toward filial maturity. For

different aspects of development, one needs different kinds of support. Creating a concrete, body-based way to support oneself can be a major focus in psychotherapy.

In most of psychotherapy there is a blending of the three tasks of healing developmental deficits, resolving trauma, and supporting development. Each of these tasks weaves into and supports the other. BMP emphases on development, brain functioning, and body awareness provide basic tools to facilitate these processes. In the next chapters, we will explore the details of the specific skills and techniques utilized in BMP.

Chapter 5

The Interaction Cycle

The Basic Format of Body-Mind Psychotherapy

In this chapter, we will examine the basic format of BMP, the **interaction cycle**, a four-step cycle that joins both clients' and therapists' awareness of how clients' developmental processes are manifesting in the clients' bodies at a particular moment. The interaction cycle is grounded in therapist's own embodiment. Therapists' ability to express their own experiences genuinely and appropriately forms the basis of the therapeutic container and all interactions. Within this container, the therapeutic focus is to support the clients' development, through attending to the developmental edge.

The **developmental edge** is the border between our strengths and our challenges. It can be identified as a place in the body, or more behaviorally as the limit of our current abilities, or as the distinction between behaviors that are mastered and behaviors that are untried.

As evolving beings, we always have a developmental edge. As a child, I once saw a tidal bore in the Bay of Fundy in Nova Scotia. A tidal bore involves a shift from an empty riverbed to a full one, based on the tides at the nearby ocean shore. Waiting for it, I had no idea what to expect. We looked across the big, muddy expanse of the waterless bay. In my memory I see a wall of water a yard high come chugging along up the river bed; there is a river in its wake.

TABLE 5.1 INTERACTION CYCLE

Step 1: Embodiment	Deepen into embodiment
Step 2: Desire	Identify the client's desire
Step 3: Awareness and Feedback	Point the client toward self-awareness and offer feedback (if necessary)
Step 4: Process	Facilitate the client's process through actual sequencing and resulting insights and intentions

For me, this is an ideal image of a developmental edge which, as evolving beings, we embody. We chug, we ooze, we flicker between who we were and who we are becoming. Mindell and Mindell described their view:

> An edge is a filter to what you are perceiving. It marks the limits of who you are and what you imagine yourself capable of. . . . Ask yourself if there's something that you want to do but cannot yet do . . . something in your life that you are almost able to do . . . in fact you do it occasionally. (1992, p. 43)

We all have developmental edges. Some are active, and others are dormant. We have edges that underlie all of our activity, and edges that are focused on a certain aspect of our lives, such as communication, sexuality, productivity, or spirituality. Picture an ameoba: its membrane is a three-dimensional edge. As it oozes out in any direction, its shape changes. If we add both expanding and reorganizing to this ameoba image, we have a primitive visual model of overall human development.

Unconsciously, our self-identity cordons off a field around our being with ideas about what we can and cannot do or be. Stanislav Grof (1988) has identified **sensory boundaries** around this field. If we extend ourselves beyond our prescribed self-image, we have sensory feedback that sends us back inside our familiar sense of self. These sensory barriers may consist of many different kinds of sensation, such as trembling, nausea, or dizziness.

It requires courage and motivation to move into a developmental edge and extend beyond both the sensory boundaries, as well as the boundaries of our self-concept, our habits, and the expectations of others. The interaction cycle taps motivation by beginning with the question of desire. What does the client want? How and where is she or he motivated? What is alive?

In any living organism, there is an indestructible link between life and motivation. Biologically, a living entity strives to stay alive. In organisms advanced enough to consciously experience desire, the desire becomes intertwined in a dance with life and motivation. Desire, aliveness, and motivation link arms in a dance that can direct us in some mysterious way toward our own development. This is the function of the interaction cycle.

STEP 1: INTERACTION CYCLE

The interaction cycle is grounded in therapists' relationships to themselves. Through self-awareness, breath, and the practice of allowing physical energy to circulate through their own bodies, therapists become finely tuned instruments which can resonate and respond to others.

Therapist's Embodiment

Deepening one's relationship to one's body is an endless path. One does not just reach a certain level and then conclude, "There, I am aware of my body now." Self-awareness is an ongoing path that stagnates without attention. There is a constant interplay between body and mind. As you become aware of new ideas and emotions, you can also become aware of the physical states that accompany them. As you become aware of the flow of energy through your body, you become aware of the emotions and concepts that stop that flow.

In order to really work with the body in psychotherapy, therapists must work with their own embodiment. All therapists' biological processes, including conceptualization, are allowed to fully sequence through their bodies. This creates a fullness of both presence and aliveness. It is out of this presence and aliveness that compassion and creative interventions arise. Thus, the first step and ongoing ground of the interaction cycle is to feel your own body and allow its process. The following exercise invites the reader to deepen into embodiment, the first step of the interaction cycle.

☐ ☐ ☐ ☐

Take a moment to rest into your body. Feel the sensations that move inside you. Allow your breath the freedom to come and go at its own rhythm. Open your mouth a bit to create this permission.

As you feel the sensations moving through you, recognize them as physiological events occurring within you. Every sensation is the result of the movement of your physiology. Within you are 75 trillion human cells, and they are all rippling with constant physiological activity. Take a breath as you acknowledge all of that life moving within you.

In addition to our human cells, we have approximately 10 times more nonhuman cells in each of our bodies. These primarily consist of bacteria. We are each an active biosphere. Again breathe with the awareness of the fullness of life inside you. We are biospheres in and of ourselves and we exist within the biosphere of this planet. The atmosphere of the earth, the body of the earth, and the web of life within that, create a womblike space which supports the life of each creature on the planet. Feel all the life of the biosphere humming outside you. We are in the womb of the biosphere. Again take a breath and rest into an awareness of the fullness of life moving inside you and the fullness of life moving outside you. And these two systems of life are exchanging with each other. The life inside you is spilling out into the world, and the life outside you is entering you constantly, in many ways, with every breath, with every movement, and every thought. What if you lived your life grounded in awareness of this flow of life?

□   □   □   □

To feel this flow of life is to embody yourself, and this is the basis of the interaction cycle. In practicing the interaction cycle, whenever you feel stuck, come back to this. Reestablish a feeling of flow in your body rather than flailing for something to do. Let your actions arise out of the flow of life energy within you.

Participating in this culture encourages a certain degree of dissociation from the body. In order to counteract that, one must proactively practice embodiment. The practice of embodiment involves simply giving yourself time to feel the sensations in your body and giving them permission to breathe, move, and sound in whatever way they want to. Later explorations of the body systems and developmental pathways fill out the details of embodiment, but this basic flow is fundamental. Most people find that an initial immersion in this practice helps it take root. Therefore, initially, taking some time to practice every day for a period of time is essential. Then one might spread it out as needed. How to do this varies from person to person. One person might begin with ten minutes a day. Another person might vary from 5 minutes to 45 minutes. This might extend for a week or three months. After some period of initial connection, one should be able to feel when formal embodiment practice is needed.

Using embodiment in therapy requires that one can continue to feel while listening, thinking, and talking. Cultivating this skill allows one to integrate logic and knowledge with bodily instincts and responses. One might think that everything a client is saying *sounds* good, but something doesn't feel right. Although it might seem elementary, the ability to be fully with oneself and with another is actually a very advanced skill. Practice the following exercise with a friend.

□   □   □   □

Each of you take some time individually to get in touch with your body. Attend to your sensations and give these sensations permission to breathe, move, and sound however they want to. Get in touch with the basic flow of life energy that is moving through you at this moment.

When you both feel ready, come together standing. Allow yourselves to look into each other's eyes. Feel the sensations that arise in your body as you do this. Continue to rest into the flow of energy in your body and continue to allow your sensations to breathe, move, and sound as they want to. Continue this for a few minutes.

□   □   □   □

In this exercise, the eye contact should increase the sensory activity in your body. As you allow these responses to move, you are sharing your internal process with your partner. This increases the level of intimacy. As the intimacy increases, this will again increase the sensational responses in your body. This cycle will support the basic ability to feel your own body as you communicate with others.

Embodiment in relationship is an ability that broadens and deepens with time. As you give yourself more and more permission, you can find more creative and constructive ways to express your energy. What previously felt impossibly outrageous could become simply helpful. Allow this focus on embodiment to continue throughout the later steps of the interaction cycle. Throughout the interaction cycle, the therapist's embodiment is always the foundation. Finally, the ability to feel while thinking and listening can develop into embodied speech—the ability to speak directly from your own bodily experience as you feel it the moment.

☐ ☐ ☐ ☐

Notice a particular feeling that you are having at this moment. Locate this feeling in your body. Let your attention settle into the particular sensations involved so that your attention is not focused on those sensations, but rather your attention is actually centered within the sensations. Keep your attention there as you speak of those feelings. Play with one simple sentence. What is the pitch, the pace, the vocal resonance that seems to come directly out of the feeling, so that the feeling is speaking for itself, rather than being spoken about?

☐ ☐ ☐ ☐

Practicing embodied speech is more difficult than it appears to be at first. We are so practiced in taking verbal short-cuts, indicating the basic gist. Over time, the innate ability of embodied speech is uncovered for moments and then covered back up by the speed of our acculturation. Embodied speech is perhaps the most difficult aspect of cultivating embodiment. The first task is to feel one's body and allow that to mix with awareness of what is occurring in the session. In the following case vignette the therapist uses her own experience to form the basis of a pivotal intervention.

This family hit a plateau in which they seemed to have all the skills that were needed to move out of a state of perpetual conflict, but it was not happening. Dad was expressing his deep sadness about this. His wife, two children, and I, as the therapist, listened as he sobbed and made some very poignant statements. Suddenly, I realized that I wasn't feeling at all moved. I felt very indifferent to his pain. My first thought was that I was being heartless, but when I checked my heart, it felt open but untouched. I looked at the others. They looked relatively neutral as well.

Looking at Mom, I said, "I'm not feeling anything. Are you?" She shook her head, "No, not really." I looked at his son, questioningly. He shook his head saying, "I hate it when he gets like this." As we explored this moment, we discovered that Dad was in a very self-absorbed state that looked communicative on a superficial level, but was actually quite encapsulated. Dad expressed his desire to communicate in a genuine way and asked for feedback from his family. This interaction seemed to jolt the system back into a state of change, which allowed them to move out of perpetual conflict.

In this interaction, the risk was in acknowledging what was felt but not spoken. This discrepancy was discovered through the therapist's self-awareness. By consciously observing my internal process, I decided that my internal process might indicate important information that could be shared. These kinds of moments are continual in the process of therapy. Many masters of psychotherapy acknowledge that much of the success of therapy depends on internal awareness informed by intuition. Cultivating awareness of the body and its expression is a very concrete way to cultivate intuition.

The other side of this ability to attend to oneself and another at the same time is the ability to stay in relationship. In psychotherapy, some approaches downplay the relationship between client and therapist and other approaches see the relationship as the essential part of the therapy. In BMP, the relationship is always important and bears constant attention, but it may move in and out being the primary focus. It is the therapist's attention to his or her body that can signal that shift. On a body level, the therapist may notice a desire to move toward or away from the client, to nurture or challenge. While the impulses must always be measured against the client's process, there is rich information in feeling them. **Staying in your body** and allowing your own process to sequence can become the ground for enhancing the relational aspect of the interaction cycle. Staying in one's body means remaining aware of a significant portion of one's bodily sensations from moment to moment. When you want to respond to the other person in some way, allow that to happen. Obviously, the therapist's process of embodiment occurs within the larger context of being in service to the client, attending to the client, and having a sense of what the client wants or is asking. But within that larger intention, follow your body as it moves toward and away from the client physically, as it is drawn to ask questions, give feedback, register emotions, and extend emotionally. Cultivating the ability to integrate these impulses in a safe and ethical way is a process that occurs with time. Embodied relationship deepens verbal sharing. Sharing your bodily response with clients can provide a very full communication. The following exchange illustrates this.

> Client: I feel like you must be repulsed by me.
> Therapist: I don't feel that at all. What I feel right now is a great deal of warmth and openness around my heart.

Compare that to the following situation in which the therapist might have the same feeling toward the client, but a different level of awareness.

Client: I feel like you must be repulsed by me.
Therapist: I don't feel that at all. I care about you a great deal.

By adding a description of current sensation, the client has a more graphic and convincing sense of what the therapist is experiencing. In this way the communication becomes physical and embodied, not just abstract.

Through embodying one's own emotional process, the therapist gains information about the client, maintains a full presence, allows compassion to arise, and can communicate more effectively. The ability to embody one's process is an ever-deepening one, which requires continual attention and intention as it unfolds and brings continually richer possibilities of relationship. The therapist's embodiment is the first step and ongoing foundation of the interaction cycle.

Client's Embodiment

The therapist always begins the interaction cycle by anchoring attention in her own embodiment process. In many situations this embodiment happens without acknowledging this to the client. However, at other times, it may also be useful to invite clients to also begin the session or a new phase of work by checking into themselves. Whether or not this occurs depends upon clients' level of comfort with introspection. If they are also comfortable with their bodies, therapists might invite them to attend to their breathing and bodily sensations as well. When clients are interested and able to begin a session with embodiment, this can allow the session to open with more of a sense of self-reference and self-direction. The therapist might invite clients to do any number to the following:

- Close their eyes
- Take deep breaths
- Feel the breath move through their bodies
- Notice the sensations in their bodies
- Allow those sensations room to move, breathe, and sound however they like

This process may take anywhere from a few seconds to the whole session. Most routinely, I might spend a minute here. This approach would not be indicated in a situation in which this might create anxiety, bewilderment, or alienation in the client. In such cases, the client may need to be more closely guided into awareness.

STEP 2: INTERACTION CYCLE

Step 2 of the interaction cycle involves finding out what the client really wants.

Deciphering Desire

As discussed above, finding out what is wanted is a way of enlisting basic motivation. Without this step, psychological inquiry can become an obligatory process of "doing what you know is good for you." We may inadvertently tap into curiosity within this process, but that can fade rather quickly without a strong motivation. Tapping into what we want brings us to some sort of vantage point at our development edge. However, it is an art to excavate the essence of a desire. Often people begin with a symbol of what they want rather than the experience, such as in the following conversation with a 15-year old boy.

> *Therapist: So what do you want in your life right now?*
> *Boy (eyes aglow, breath full in his upper chest): I want to get my license. I want to be able to drive by myself.*

We live in the illusion that what we want are material things and events, but the deeper reality is that we want experience of psychological, energetic states. This boy fundamentally wants ecstatic freedom. Sometimes children or lower functioning clients might not be able to articulate what they want. In this case, the therapist might have to imagine it for them. But it is always illuminating, if not essential, to ask. Then share that fantasy, "I would guess that you might want. . . ." See whether there is any affect change. Are you hot or cold? To continue the conversation with the boy above:

> *Therapist: Wow. That sounds so exciting.*
> *Boy: Yeah.*
> *Therapist: So what kind of car do you want?*
> *Boy: A yellow jeep.*
> *Therapist: You can go anywhere in a jeep.*
> *Boy: Yeah. [with an ecstatic glee]*
> *Therapist: Freedom, huh?*
> *Boy: [Nods, smiles deeply] I can't wait.*

"The Problem"

Often when exploring psychological issues, we begin with a sense of problem: What is missing or what is not working? Irvin Yalom (1989) liked to ask clients initially, "What ails?" This is what most clients are initially interested in communicating. However, at some point, the process of reviewing the problem is complete. You have looked at and thoroughly understood what isn't working. At that point, it can become a limitation to focus on the problem. To move toward what we want, we need to name it and open ourselves to it. Opening up this possibility within a therapeutic exchange is a matter of timing. Occasionally people need to unload their experience and concept of the problem before they are ready to continue. However, if this goes too far, the problem begins to grow in strength through the continual attention. Watching the flow of energy in the client's body can help the therapist assess this. While talking about the problem, does the body appear to be releasing unwanted experiences and thoughts, or does the body appear to be reinforcing patterns of negativity? Watching the client's movement sequencing out through the endpoints is one sign that talking is allowing an energetic shift. However, when the therapist observes that the client's breathing is not complete, or their posture is becoming more distorted, or that an energetic charge is building up internally without sequencing through the body, then these are signs that the talking is not productive at that moment. In either case, there comes a moment in which the therapist can ask, "And what is it that you want around this issue?"

Fleshing Out the Desire

There are so many different ways to open up this topic of desire. Inquiring into desire is tapping into the client's motivation. It is pointing to their growing edge. Ask, such questions as: What do you want in relation to this emotion, person, situation, or aspect of your life? What do you think you are trying to learn here? What do you see as the most positive possible outcome? What do you want in your life right now? What do you want out of our interaction? Who do you want to be when this is all over?

Opening up to this level of ourselves makes us feel vulnerable. Most of us have been wounded in some way around desire: We may believe it is weak, selfish, or even sinful to want. Desire may shatter our sense of self-sufficiency or invulnerability. If I want something, it might mean that I am weak. I might have decided never to want because it hurts to want if I can't have. I may perceive that it is shameful to want something I may not get, a sign of defeat or dishonor. Because of these wounds, it is sometimes necessary to work directly with finding permission and willingness to want anything. Some of our clients may not be feeling at all, and it is necessary to feel in order to want.

In some cases, education might be needed to open up to desire. In other cases, just a tiny bit of coaxing might do it, or reinforcement of their self-esteem. Whatever the case, it is important to remember how vulnerable desire is. There is something delicate, almost infantile about desire. It has been conceived, but not yet manifested. It is life that is newly budding. Staying present with your own bodily sensations can help with staying present in the delicate dance of inviting desire.

Whatever your client says about what they want deserves to be acknowledged and remembered. The stated desire becomes either a therapeutic goal, or, as with the driver's license, a symbol of the therapeutic goal. The goal may need some balancing or modification, but keeping the desire central to the therapeutic goal is what keeps the client motivated. The teenage boy wanting his drivers' license may need to realize that to achieve his goal, he must integrate grounded responsibility into ecstatic freedom. But, every time the therapist acknowledges the driver's license, the client's motivation will be roused. Grounded responsibility will seem more and more desirable.

This is true for all of us. Often, we need to get realistic about how to move toward what we want. For example, I might want an intimate relationship, but I am so angry about being alone that I push everyone away. In this case, if I really want intimacy, I may need to open up to it. The more concrete a goal becomes, the more distant and unattainable it may seem. If I want to become a famous movie star, the chances are fairly slim. However, if I can ferret out the essence of what I want to experience as a movie star, I may find goals that are more attainable. Being a famous movie star might symbolize engagement with the world, creative expression, feeling sexually desirable, feeling loved and wanted, or all of the above. When we clarify the experience we want, we can feel the basic energy of that experience. On an energetic level, any experience is readily available to us at any moment. We can support clients in beginning to open up to this, asking, if you had this how would it feel? "If you were loved and wanted how would that feel?" As they describe the sensations and images, the physiological reality is that, to a certain degree, they are experiencing being loved.

This energetic reality is something that we resist mightily. "But it's not real, I don't really have it." We have been trained to focus on the external symbol of attainment. However, so often that attainment does not bring the desired experience with it. How often do people realize a fantasy only to find it empty? In therapy, as we are exploring the energetic experience that we desire, it is necessary to tread lightly so as not to arouse resistance. However, on a physiological and experiential level, it is actually true that everything we ever want is swarming around us waiting to enter. This is a subversive idea, which may sometimes be appropriate to allude to or even to illustrate, but often it will arouse a strong defense. In those cases, just feel it yourself. Some people will be able to accept the idea that practicing feeling open to what they want will help them actually get it. If that concept seems difficult to grasp, one might simply offer that sometimes it helps. In any case, once the client has clarified the essence of their desire, then it is time to move on to the next step.

STEP 3: INTERACTION CYCLE

The third step of the interaction cycle translates the idea of what is wanted into bodily reality. This step points the client toward self-awareness. The basic question involved is, "How does that desire feel inside you?" With a question like this, we move from thinking about what we want, to feeling what it is that we want. At this point, one might feel the actual desire itself, or the feeling of having what is wanted, or the frustration or deficit of not having what is wanted. Any or all of these are appropriate.

Cultivating Awareness

Encourage self-awareness of how this desire-intention sequences through the body. For some people this awareness comes very naturally. Others need to be encouraged, "Slow down, take a breath. Feel your heart or your belly." Pick a particular spot, which you think might contain the most information for them; this could be based on their gestures or their posture or just common sense. Once the client is focused in a particular area of the body, be encouraging: "Now think about this thing you want." Name the desire as simply as possible. The body likes simple, short, personal words: *freedom, love, confidence*. Tell the client to pay attention while they think about it. What happens inside?

If the person is so terrified or nonplussed that they are not allowing this thought to sequence into their body, they might need some help with that. "Take a breath. Let your jaw or your shoulders go. Give your body a chance to imagine this thing you want, and feel it." If they are still rigid, perhaps they need to stand up or lie down, stretch a bit, move a bit, then try again. Perhaps they need a series of sessions educating them about living in a body.

Another approach that is helpful when it is difficult for clients to be conscious of feeling is to explore their issues and highlight moments when they are really emotional about something and say, "Now feel that, that's what it means to feel these emotions in your body."

Or one can imagine extremes if need be, such as, "What if you never, ever got that? Notice how that feels in your body." Or, "What if it showed up right now? What if it were absolutely perfect? Better than you could ever imagine. How does that feel? What if you were immersed in what you want?"

Eventually, this step would include their awareness of how the energy of both the desire and the old pattern moved and interacted in their body. The client is then able to feel their development edge directly and just needs to be supported in this awareness and to allow it to naturally sequence. At this point, the client might report, "I can feel the excitement of taking leadership all over, but especially in my chest, and my eyes feel really open. It's kind of tingly, but when I think about doing it in front of my boss, my stomach just clenches. I pull up. If I breathe into that, the energy moves back down into my belly and legs." The therapist's role is to support this process.

Feedback

Offer feedback on what has been observed. As clients observe their own process, they may be aware and able to articulate everything that is important about how this energy sequences through them. Or there may be aspects of which they are not conscious that are important in order to achieve their goals. If this is the case, it is important to support their ability to trust themselves and their own discovery process. Pick the simplest, most pertinent aspect of your observation. Introduce it initially as a question: "What do you feel in this particular part? How does that part feel about this?" If this doesn't bring their awareness to where you are pointing, try making a simple observation, "I see." Only offer comments as you sense they are helpful.

You might give feedback that is purely descriptive: "I see you really squeezing your arms together." If it feels as if they have dissociated from the emotional aspect of their experience, ask specifically about the emotions there. If they are unable to touch them, you might offer a menu: "Are you angry or sad or scared? contented or excited?" As a third and last option, offer your interpretation as an option, "The way you squeeze your arms together looks like maybe you're scared? How does it feel?" This step then requires further awareness and movement on their part to integrate the new information (Table 5.2). Checking in with themselves they might find out something new, such as, "No, I'm not scared. Actually, really I feel angry. My arms are pressing in so that I won't lash out." Or they might find that you were correct, "Yeah (shivering) I am scared. Gosh, I'm really scared of what she'll do." Having made these discoveries, there may need to be time to

TABLE 5.2 HIERARCHY OF FEEDBACK

Open Question	How do you feel? What do you think? How do you experience that in your body?
Focused Question	How do you feel-think about that? What do you feel in that part of your body?
Menu	Does your feeling seem more like sadness or anger? Do you want to stay or do you want to go?
Descriptive Feedback	When we talk about this, I see you shift back into your chair.
Interpretation as a Question	When I see you shift back in your chair, I wonder if you don't want to talk about this issue. What do you think?

breathe and move to allow these energies to circulate, and then it is possible there might be the need to check in again. "So, from this place, check in again and find out what you are wanting."

STEP 4: INTERACTION CYCLE

The fourth step of the interaction cycle supports the creative and developmental processes that arise from awareness. On a body level, we begin with feeling a desire. From there, we focus our awareness on our bodily process. This awareness of our bodily process naturally develops into a process of sequencing through the body into an action that moves toward the desired state or object.

Facilitating the Process

The therapist's role in this fourth step is to support the client in staying with his or her awareness and the process of sequencing. Beyond this, the therapist may lightly structure the creative processes that are emerging, highlight the insights that arise, and acknowledge the developmental aspect of the process.

Sequencing

Let us begin with the most basic aspect of this fourth step. In delineating the six principles of body-mind integration in Chapter 1, sequencing was defined as "the uninhibited flow of energy within all parts and aspects of the bodymind and between ourselves and the environment." What does this mean in practical terms? Sequencing can mean many different things depending on the energy being sequenced. If there is a complex thought process going on internally, sequencing may mean allowing the thoughts to complete their logical sequence or dialectic. If that thought process is preparation for communicating, sequencing may involve actual speech. However, because our bodies have been so dominated by our minds, the concept of sequencing has developed primarily as an attempt to encourage other functions of the body, beyond thinking and speaking, to express themselves.

On a behavioral level, sequencing could mean trembling, crying, laughing, stretching, stomping, pounding, undulating, yelling, reaching out, pushing away, grasping, and any other bodily activity. However, doing these things is not necessarily sequencing. If we behave or move our bodies in a manner that is directed by thought alone, the movement behavior does not sequence through the body, but jumps from one area to another in a nonsequential manner. Often, if thoughts are guiding our behavior, the movement jumps from the head area to the location of the movement. When movement does not sequence out fully through the body, it often spirals in on itself and pools in a particular part of the body. Uncoordinated streams of movement may collide with each other and create turbulence. Other times, a movement or gesture may begin and then just fizzle out before it is complete, collapsing into itself. In contrast, sequenced movement flows sequentially from one location through to the next without skipping anything. This creates a cohesive, integrated movement and means that each part of the self is involved and informed regarding the behavior. Anytime we allow our internal sensations to develop into external actions, that is sequencing. When we allow our internal process to do what it wants to do, that is sequencing. This might look big and dramatic, say when we feel pressure building in our chests and we allow it to sequence and it elongates our throats and opens our mouths and big sounds push out. Or it might look minute, as when we feel a numbness in our bellies and, in feeling, the numbness, it wakes up, and in waking up, it expands and shifts our center of gravity half an inch.

In both examples of sequencing, the big, such as taking an action, and the minute, completing a breath, there is an overlap between feeling and sequencing. As we feel with an attitude of permissiveness, sequencing naturally occurs. This can be a cyclical relationship as well. We might begin by feeling and allow our feelings to sequence through, and as we feel ourselves sequencing, some new feelings might develop.

These new feelings will also need and respond to further permission to move or sequence through the body.

It might be helpful to take a moment off from reading now to allow your body to do some sequencing. Let your body decide where it wants to do this and what position it wants to begin in. Take a few moments to breathe and feel your body. Give your whole body permission to move and breathe and sound, however it wants to. Depending on how permissive you are with your body, and how willing your body is to allow its spontaneous process, this whole body permission could result in a great deal of sequencing. If so, give yourself plenty of time.

When you are ready, scan your body for any area that you intuitively sense needs permission to move. Perhaps it feels full of life and is raring to go; perhaps it feels bound; perhaps it feels weak and neglected. Whatever the case, attend closely to this area. Feel the specific sensations in this part of your body. Notice what those sensations are doing. Sensations are physiological activities so there is always some moving aspect to every sensation, even one that is tightly gripping.

As you are feeling these sensations, consciously give them permission to move and breathe and sound however they want to. If they have some difficulty in doing so imagine how those sensations might want to move or breathe or sound. Try on some of these possible movements and breaths and sounds. Let the sensations feel each option, tailor it, and continue as they want to.

This might result in lying quietly on the floor, or jumping wildly around a large space, or anything in between. Sequencing should reflect your internal state at that particular moment. If it always looks one particular way, then chances are you might need to expand your sense of permission. One can do this by attending move closely to the sensations involved and giving them more permission to move in their own way, even if it is unfamiliar.

Endpoints

While sequencing is an ongoing event in the lives of most other living creatures, as adult humans we frequently inhibit our sequencing through cognitive beliefs, intentions, and control. Sometimes we have a cognitive belief that our mental processes are more important than our bodily processes. We repress our bodies in order to focus on our minds. Often, we are afraid that we may appear crazy, sexual, immature, or confused if we allow our bodies to sequence. So much of not sequencing has to do with keeping our internal processes hidden away from others. However, after doing this for long enough, we get stuck in habits of inexpressiveness. We lament our inability to reveal our true creative natures to the world. For this reason, the endpoints of the body are important in sequencing.

The endpoints of the body refer to the face, hands, feet, and pelvic floor. These are the free ends of our skeleton, which are endowed with an increased concentration of sensory nerve endings and fine muscular articulation. In order to hide our process from others, we must stop our sequencing before it arrives at our endpoints. Most adults in this culture have habituated to limiting much of their sequencing at the endpoints. For this reason, special attention must often be paid to the endpoints to allow them to reopen.

□   □   □   □

Take a deep breath and a relaxed position. Contemplate the question, "How much of my inner nature do I allow out into the world?" Feel this question in your body. Feel the insides of your head, throat, chest, waist, and pelvis. Adopt an attitude of inviting this internal energy to sequence out of your endpoints—your face, your pelvic floor, your hands, and your feet. Pay special attention to the sensations of your endpoints. Give them permission to breath, touch, move, and gently open themselves so that your internal energy is allowed to move out into the space around you. At times, allow yourself to focus specifically on each endpoint. At other times, open up to a general sense of all of them.

□   □   □   □

For many of us, as little as two weeks of daily practice for a few minutes each day, can begin to reestablish flow through the endpoints. However, if there are strong habits and beliefs that contradict that, more work may be required. Many psychotherapists regard the face as the ultimate tool. The face is seen as the primary contact point, and the expressiveness of the face is the vehicle for the communication of deep reflection, understanding, and love. Culturally, we are taught to practice using our faces as masks to convey only the information that we wish to convey and to hide much of our inner truths. This is true of all of our endpoints in more subtle ways. In Chapter 10, which covers the basic neurological actions, we will examine the endpoints in greater depth. In working with this step of the interaction cycle, the endpoints can be used as encouragement to complete the sequencing of a process. The following case study illustrates this.

In relationships with women, Jack felt himself flip back and forth between behaving as an aggressive victimizer or a sensitive, loving friend. He said that neither felt authentic. The stress of this confusion led him to avoid sexual relationships for the most part. When he did engage with a woman, he generally found that the closer they became, the more his internal tension would mount and he would prematurely abort the relationship.

I asked Jack to embody the aggressive victimizer, and suggested that there must be some basic health in this character. "What aspects of this energy do you want to keep? What feels authentic in this?" As Jack stood sensing his body, a subtle shifting began in his waist. His upper trunk elongated; he took a full breath into his chest. His mouth opened slightly. There was movement and sequencing from the top of the pelvis all the way through his head, but his pelvis remained relatively immobile and slightly tucked. "Let it go through your whole trunk." He took a breath into his belly. "Yes, through your pelvis."

Jack opened his eyes and looked at me with a soft, but strong gaze. He nodded his head. "I forget this," he said. "I forget all the work I've done to feel good about being strong."

With a little encouragement, Jack allowed movement to sequence out his head, through his mouth and eyes, and also through his pelvis to a certain degree.

The Therapist's Role in Supporting Sequencing

As with Jack, the therapist might support sequencing through suggesting a direction, "Let it go through your whole trunk." Jack took this suggestion easily and included his pelvis. I articulated this shift in order to make it conscious, "Yes, through your pelvis." Let us suppose he had not responded so easily. Instead let us imagine that Jack had continued to breathe into his chest, elongate his upper spine, and release his jaw and his head. In that case, the therapist should generally assume that he has misjudged the client's developmental edge. Perhaps it was so new and engaging to allow these feelings to sequence up through his chest and head that Jack was completely captivated by this developmental edge and not yet ready to venture into his pelvis with this energy.

In recognizing the organicity of the developmental process, the BMP approach is to wait to include the next part of the body until some sequencing begins to move in that direction. This follows the principles of development and nonaggression. Our task is to support development as it is occurring, not force its hand. Several assumptions underlie this decision. In order to move successfully from one developmental stage to the next, one must be thoroughly grounded in the first stage. The nature of body-mind development is such that it literally cannot be rushed. On a purely body level, there might be something physical that needs to shift in Jack's upper body as a prerequisite to his awakening his pelvis. It is this sort of organic developmental process that truly changes one's life. For Jack to develop a more mechanical, forced sequencing in his pelvis would not be as life changing as a spontaneous shift in that direction.

On the other hand, in order to resolve these issues revolving around his sexuality, Jack will eventually need to allow this shift to sequence into his pelvis. Let us continue the imaginary scenario with Jack. After becoming comfortable with allowing this newly discovered state, Jack still does not respond to the therapist's suggestion to "Let it go through your whole trunk," by including his pelvis. In this case, the therapist would observe his body and try to discern why the energy isn't yet ready to sequence into his pelvis. Where are the next developmental edges in his body?

The Developmental Edge in Sequencing

On a body level, the developmental edge could be regarded as a boundary in the body. On one side of the developmental edge, energy is freely circulating and moving toward the edge. At the edge the energy does not move through. Either it gets dissipated, diverted, convoluted, or builds up pressure in the area. Seeing the bodily manifestation of the developmental edge is quite subjective, as usually there is a large area or zone involved. One might see the beginning of the developmental edge, the point at which the energy begins to get confused. Or one might see the end, the last point through which any energy sequences as noted in Figure 5.1.

Returning to Jack, using Figure 5.1, we see that there is an incomplete sequencing of energy through the left pelvic half. This twisting sequence ensnares the energy of the right pelvic half and only a tiny portion of pelvic energy can move through the diaphragm. The area below Jack's diaphragm is relatively disinhabited. Another developmental process must occur to connect with the pathway from Jack's legs up through his pelvis. After that is complete then perhaps the upper trunk energy will have something to connect with.

FIGURE 5.1 DEVELOPMENTAL EDGE

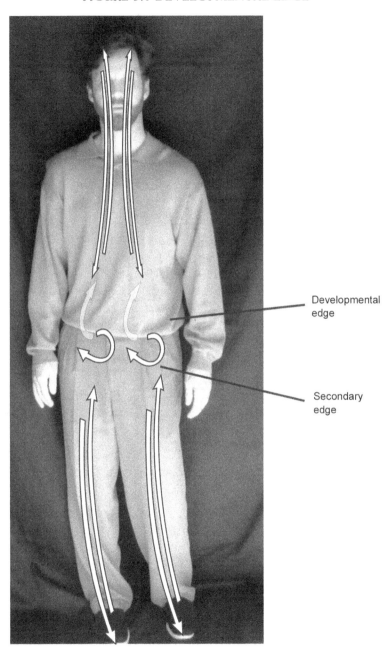

Jack's primary and secondary developmental edges are shown. The rotation of the right pelvic half allows only a small portion of movement to sequence through the pelvis.

Observing the physical developmental edge is an ongoing process for the body-mind psychotherapist. However, that information is only necessary to share with the client when it will further the client's developmental process.

Jack began the session communicating about his frustration with his process of sexual empowerment. He stood with weight on both legs, but a bit less on his left leg. He jiggled his left knee and leg as he spoke. "I don't know. I don't get it. All this stuff we've been talking about makes sense, and I can open my heart now. I can talk. I told Phyllis that I thought I was in love with her, and I think I really am. And that's good. She's a good person, and she's beautiful. But, I miss the excitement of going out and picking up somebody and just going for it."

Therapist: So this is the energy that can lead you to become an aggressive victimizer, which you've said you don't want to be, but this energy is real. It's jiggling up your leg, I think. Breathe into that. Give it permission to move through your body. Pay attention to it. Find out more about it."

Once again Jack's breath bypassed his left pelvic half. However, this time I felt that enough of his attention was with this process that I could encourage it further with specific feedback. "So Jack, try standing evenly on both feet as you breathe. What I see it is that you're really breathing into the right side of your pelvis, but not so much the left. What do you feel?"

Jack: Yeah, I guess that's right.

Therapist: So intentionally breathe into that left half of your pelvis. Yes, put your hand there. You're just waking up a part of you that's been asleep for some time. Just pay attention to any thoughts or images that come up as you keep breathing into it.

Jack visibly struggled to keep his attention on his left pelvic half. He fidgeted a bit, but kept coming back. As I sensed he was getting to the end of his attention, but right before his attention shifted, I engaged him.

I asked Jack what he thought about this pattern he had of only breathing into his left side. He shrugged. I showed him his earlier stance with the jiggling leg and reminded him he had been talking about wanting to express more of the aggressive side of his sexuality. He nodded. I reminded him of this feeling of wanting to express this particular energy. I suggested he close his eyes and breathe into his pelvis again. I suggested there were other, healthier, more satisfying ways to express his sexual power, ways that would feel really good to him and allow him to feel good about himself, ways that wouldn't hurt anybody. He nodded in recognition of a concept that we had been discussing. I suggested he breathe this idea into his pelvis. There was a bit more sequencing, but not a huge shift. I took this as the appropriate developmental shift for that moment. The fact that his face continued to be clear and open signified to me that on a conscious level he was open to this concept. The fact that there was not full sequencing through his left pelvic half signified to me that there were unconscious, conflicting feelings about this. Knowing Jack's history, I suspected that these might be in relation to his father. I put this issue on hold to explore later and supported the current shift, asking him how it felt to have more breath and movement in his pelvis.

Creative Insights and Dialogue

Sequencing can be approached in an open-ended manner, as in the exercises at the beginning of this section. Or, as in the session with Jack, the therapist can add an imagined desire or intention as the starting place. In that case, sequencing becomes more focused. For many clients, just the opportunity to focus on what they want, and to feel that on a bodily level, begins a process of discovery and creativity.

One such creative process might be the realization of internal conflict around the desire. As Jack explored his issues with his father, he realized that he was afraid that if he fully embodied his sexuality, he would be a threat to his father's fragile masculinity. "I remember strutting in the house. I can see him scowl. I feel my pelvis cringe up on the left."

Internal conflict is generally present around a developmental edge. When there is no such internal conflict around our desires, then we are generally in the process of actively moving toward them. There is not a sense of confusion about them.

When there is an awareness of the internal conflict, one can feel the contrast in the body between the two states. There are many possibilities regarding the choice of which two states to contrast here. Choose whichever is most pertinent: either the feeling of wanting and the feeling of lacking; or the feeling of wanting and the feeling of rejecting what the client wants; or the feeling of the problem and the feeling of the solution; or the feeling of the old pattern and the feeling of the new possibility.

When the client is not aware of the conflict, but the therapist perceives that there might be an important conflict that needs attention, the therapist could invite awareness of the conflict. "Feel the part of you that is really saying yes to this. Now check and see whether there are any parts of you that are saying no. Take the time to feel both states in the body. First feel one then feel the other." Articulate the specific sensations and body parts involved in both responses.

Sometimes people make this transition spontaneously and at once notice the contrast. At other times they may need help with either or both of these steps. The therapist can ask: "What happens inside you when you think about this? How do you feel inside when you think about this? How do you feel this desire in your body? When you imagine this, what do you feel in your body? What opens up or relaxes to this idea? When you think about your fear or reluctance or concerns, what do you feel in your body? What parts of you constrict or retreat around this possibility?"

Then in the manner of creating a dialogue between two parts of the body, allow those two parts to have a verbal or an energetic conversation. When the client seems close to verbalizing, allow them to speak for each part, shifting back and forth in conversation. "How can you marry Joan? What would mom think?" "I don't care what mom thinks; I love her." "I care what mom thinks. We'll be miserable for the rest of our lives if mom hates her." "Okay, you're right maybe I do care what mom thinks, but couldn't we work with that?" Couldn't we move slowly and communicate with mom and dad about Joan? We can't just give up on love because mom wouldn't approve." At this point the dialogue is actually moving into a deeper understanding between the two parts, so that neither part holds the other hostage. Somatic dialogue is the communication between two parts of the body and can be verbal as illustrated above or nonverbal.

In the nonverbal aspects of a somatic dialogue, initially one can merely shuttle one's awareness back and forth between two parts until the sensations start to move and create a flow between the two areas. Both flow and blending of sensations are signs that integration is taking place between the two sides of the conflict. Once there is a sense of complete sequencing that goes all the way out to the endpoints of the body, then the dialogue is complete and a full understanding has been achieved for that moment.

Somatic dialogue of this sort can be used in any problem-solving or decision-making process. In *Descartes' Error* (1994), Damasio discussed his work with patients suffering from injuries to the prefrontal lobe of the cerebral cortex. While such damage leaves all analytical functions intact, there is an inability to coordinate rationality with feeling tone. Damasio observed that these patients consistently made bad decisions resulting in such life circumstances as failed marriages, unemployment, and bankruptcy. Damasio postulated a **somatic marker** hypothesis by which a particular response option is marked by a particular gut feeling (1994, p. 173). Somatic markers are a biasing device that can help us to weigh future benefits with current costs. Our bodies nonverbally remind us of past experiences. For example, in meeting a new person, we might consciously remember similar people from our past and think that interacting with so and so was great (or terrible). Maybe this will be similar. In addition, even if we do not consciously remember, our bodies will generate a state that reminds us, warm and expansive if it was great, or perhaps tense and withdrawn if it was terrible. When there is proper communication occurring between the brain and the body, somatic markers influence our decision-making process. Damasio acknowledged that somatic markers may be established without coming to consciousness. Within a somatic dialogue process, we can enhance the utilization of information coming from our bodies by consciously feeling our sensations in regard to a particular decision or problem.

Integration

The final phase of the interaction cycle involves allowing the information gathered in the previous steps to be integrated within the client's being. This is the phase in which the awareness gathered might be allowed to introduce change with the client's system. Creating space for this integration process may range from an extremely quiet, almost meditative state to more dynamic moving, talking, or interacting. How does this awareness of the feeling in our bodies relate to the tasks of psychotherapy? Attending to our bodily process can allow us to:

- Restore flow
- Support physiological functioning
- Complete actions
- Resolve internal conflicts
- Complete the past

Within this phase of the interaction cycle, the therapist may support the client to breathe and stay aware of the various sensations, thoughts, and emotions that have been unearthed during the previous phases. Attention to any bodily process increases blood flow and therefore aids any physiological activity that has begun. Increased circulation might allow a variety of changes to occur. A part of the client's being that has been inactive, slumbering, withdrawn, might be allowed to come forward and participate more fully.

Carole had a history of having very passionate sex with men she didn't love and very boring sex with men she loved. She sat with her legs splayed open and her pelvis leaning back. She had become aware that she didn't feel very much in her pelvis, which generally felt unengaged in her life. She described the sensations there as "Blah." When she discussed certain aspects of her sexual history, she felt shame. Her brow and shoulders pulled together, and her pelvis became even more shut down, even more flaccid, saying in effect, "I feel so disgusting." I encouraged her to breathe and feel the shame and the "blah." The energy in her head and shoulders released, and there was more movement in her pelvis. She seemed a bit bewildered. We stayed with this for just a couple of minutes.

To bring the energy of her pelvis even more alive, I asked how she felt there. She didn't have much to say, "Okay, a little more energy," but the attention took her a bit further into contact with her pelvis. To go even further, I asked, "So from this place, what do you want?" Carole burst into tears, "I feel so bad. I feel so creepy. I didn't even care about those guys." "Yes, good, breathe into that. Let these feelings come out." She cried more, and after a while I said, "So I guess there has been shame hiding in your pelvis as well. Keep breathing and see how it feels to allow these feelings to come out. She cried, pushed through her pelvis so that she was sitting up. Her head was down, so I encouraged her to look out. We talked about the shame and hiding. I said, "You were a young girl. You weren't getting the love and guidance you needed. Can you forgive yourself for trying to get attention sexually? Can you feel proud of who you are, of the energy in your pelvis?" She kept breathing and looked around a bit. I suggested she stand up and notice how her pelvis felt standing, and then walking. "It feels good," she said, "I feel more powerful." I shared my perspective, "This is you reclaiming your sexuality. This is how it feels when you include your pelvis and your sexual energy in your life."

Integration allows our cognitive awareness to recognize, name, and share the new experience. Carole's work involved allowing energy to flow into a part that had shut down and become flaccid due to shame. In the following case, the opposite is true. The client had to open up what was constricted. Nevertheless, the moments of integration are very similar.

Joel was always angry. His normal facial expression was a scowl. His mother had shared that even as a child he had had quite a temper. Now at 19, he was struggling with becoming aware of his anger toward his parents for their divorce, toward his father for having affairs with beautiful women whom Joel hated, toward the world for being so insensitive and cruel. He had become aware of his anger as a cramping in his diaphragm. He lay down to breathe into it, I encouraged him to let this part move. He began to writhe, arching and flexing his trunk from the diaphragm. "Let the movement come all the way out your face," his face contorted, "and your teeth." He began to snarl: "Hate. I hate. I hate my parents." I urged him to let this energy move out. "Keep feeling the part that was locked up and give it permission to come out. This is just energy moving. It is you coming out." When his movement died down a bit, I encouraged him to breathe and feel his energy moving. He reported feeling good, strong, "really awake." I suggested he try standing up and feeling this energy in the world. "Who are you from this place?" He nodded his head without answering, looking very grown up and masterful. "I feel good." "Do you feel like a boy or a man right now?" He grinned and nodded, seemingly implying that he felt like a man. "Really notice how your breath feels right here," I said pointing to his diaphragm, "you released a lot of energy there, all the anger. That's how you were controlling it." He said, "It's better this way."

Joel's work involved reorganizing his relationship to himself. His integration phase consisted of just enjoying that reorganization. However, sometimes the work in this last phase of the interaction cycle is more relational.

Laura had come into therapy to work with her grief over yet another breakup with a boyfriend. Her heart was broken, and she wondered, "Why me? Why does everyone leave me?" As she explored her state, she became very aware of her heart reaching forward with great longing. In this gesture, her head would fall back somewhat and her arms would hang limp by her side. She was very aware of what she wanted—to be loved—but felt hopeless about that possibility. When she thought about being loved, she felt some energy from her heart move upward, but then she collapsed immediately.

I observed, that she seemed able to sustain that feeling for a couple of seconds and then she gave up again. I suggested she try forgetting about men and focusing on her ability to feel love. "Breathe into your heart and think about love. What about the idea that love and creativity permeate the whole world? How does that feel in your body?" Eventually, she began to play with the feeling of love. It appeared that all the feelings that had been pouring out of her chest began to be channeled primarily from her heart through her throat and head. Some of the energy also appeared to move down from her heart into her lower trunk. She shifted from embodying the phrase, "bleeding heart," to looking like a goddess of love.

She began to play with walking around the room touching things as if her touch were magic. She giggled and laughed. I remarked that this was very different. More giggling. "So what happens if you think about a relationship from this place?" She collapsed momentarily. "Come on," I chided. She giggled again and began playing a princess character, somewhat haughty, "Oh, you want a date with me? You must get down on your knees." "What if you actually want to go out with this person?" She looked confused. I coached her, "Feel the energy in your heart. Can you feel how it's moving up and down through you?" She nodded. "And when you were in your 'Nobody loves me' place, how was your heart energy moving?" She collapsed again to observe herself and gestured with her hands to from her heart out the front of her chest. "So feel this heart energy when it moves through you and empowers you." She shifted back to her fairy princess character. "Yeah, keep feeling it and be yourself." I stepped in front of her; we looked at each other. She smiled a radiant smile. She was herself, a beautiful young woman again. I put out my hand, "Can you keep feeling it and be in contact?" She took my hand and silently smiled. There was a sense of completion.

We talked about noticing her heart and owning her feelings rather than always feeling at the mercy of her latest crush. We connected these states to the different feelings and postures she had experienced in the session.

The last phase of the interaction cycle is about supporting energetic movement and internal development. Out of internal development and reorganization, our outer behavior can begin to change both spontaneously and intentionally.

Bringing it All Together

The interaction cycle can be repeated endlessly. Each step can be brief or develop over a period of time. Interaction and education can support each of the various steps. At any stage, one can regroup and start the cycle again, "Okay, from this place, now what do you want?" Some cycles can take just a few minutes; some fit nicely into one session, and some can extend over a number of sessions.

What is the point? The point can be defined variously as helping someone get what they want, or helping someone experience how their internal process relates to what they want. Focusing on desire harnesses motivation. We can always relate this desire back to the developmental process that is occurring in the person's life. Linking desire to development brings motivation to the developmental process. Feeling this whole process in our bodies provides us with tangible leverage to move toward change. The interaction cycle empowers clients to move actively toward their desires.

Chapter 6

Cultivating Bodily Awareness

Synchronizing Body and Mind

All problems are psychological and all solutions are spiritual.
—Thomas Hora, *Dialogues in Metapsychiatry*

Hora might have added that all experiences are physical. What is psyche? What is spirit? How does the body relate to these? To examine the role of the body in psychotherapy, we must examine the nature of these phenomena. I very much appreciate Thomas Hora's point of view expressed in the quotation above. To me all solutions being spiritual signifies a level of healing which returns us to our rightful place in the universe, to a sense of unity with the world. Psychological problems arise when we are not able to integrate our own process with the flow of life around us, either by ignoring it or trying to direct it unnaturally. The inability to integrate various aspects of our lives relates to the third principle of BMP, acceptance of reality. Our bodies can act as monitors to this process. They tend to let us know when something is off. By tracking the sense of flow within our own experience, we gain a tangible way of interacting with our selves.

Generally, modern psychology concerns itself more with mind than with spirit, which certainly can have overlapping definitions. What is mind? What is body? Suzuki Roshi, an important Zen teacher, has said that, "Our body and mind are not two and not one" (1970, p. 21). How are they the same and how are they different? In our culture, we often equate mind with brain, but if we locate the mind in every cell of the body, our basic paradigm gets turned on its head.

In the worldview in which we equate brain with mind, we also tend to view the brain as having nearly total control of the rest of the body. The body is seen as the machine attached to the brain to keep the brain functioning. Following Descartes, the body and the emotions are relegated to secondary status. Psychotherapy based on these views has been primarily concerned with setting the mind straight. This perspective could take the form of a primarily cognitive process, such as in rational emotive behavioral therapy, the work of Albert Ellis, in which false logic and assumptions are recognized and clarified. Or psychotherapy could be seen as a process of reconciling the unconscious with the conscious, as in many psychoanalytic approaches. A variety of theorists and clinicians have invoked the body as a good representative of the unconscious mind in the same way that dreams are also seen as representing our unconscious mind. The body can be seen as one way of observing the unconscious. If the mind is in every cell of the body, then we might include body as a representative of all levels of mind—conscious, as well as unconscious. This is the stance taken by most approaches to somatic psychotherapy. The body is seen as integral to expressing one's mind, maintaining a state of being, and shifting into a new state.

THINKING, FEELING, AND DOING

One way to understand the role of the body in psychotherapy is to understand how the body functions in the three major divisions of human processing, thinking, feeling, and doing. At any given stage of psychological processing, we might assess what really needs to happen here. Does more thinking need to happen? Is there a lack of understanding about the variety of dynamics at play? Is there a lack of understanding about various relationships within this scenario? Is there a split between communication and intent? In these cases, the client has not given the situation enough thought and may need to be encouraged to keep exploring. On the other hand, our culture is very thinking oriented. Overthinking is an extremely common issue in this culture. Often, people will think their issues to death. "I really want to figure this out," is a common phrase used in this pattern. Often, the client needs reassurance, "I actually think you understand the whole thing really well." Thinking can be used in this way to avoid feeling or action.

On the level of feeling, often we do not want to take the time to allow feelings to blossom and reach completion. Emotions have a function. They change us internally and alter our relationship to the world. If emotions are repressed or short-circuited they might not have an opportunity to do their job completely. Often, out of fear of indulging in emotions, we limit them in a way that does not allow them to develop and change. In this way we can actually get stuck in a particular emotional state. Through working with embodiment, the therapist gains a comfort level with feeling that goes beyond our cultural limitations. The therapist can then help initiate the client into an organic relationship with feeling when that is needed. Feeling is clearly a body-oriented activity. If we are not feeling on a bodily level, then we are stuck in a conceptual relationship to feeling. We are thinking about our feelings or experiencing them indirectly through our thoughts about them. We are not allowing the rhythmic flow of emotion to move through us, transform itself, and leave us in a different place. Often the process of supporting feeling can be nearly synonymous with facilitating body awareness.

Doing is also clearly a body-oriented activity. In order to take action we must use our bodies, even if it is only to face someone and speak. Often, clients need support in envisoning action that might resolve their dilemmas. Beyond this, they may need support in preparing for or practicing actions that they envision. To carry out an action bears fruit. When a client has completed thinking and feeling about a particular situation, the time comes to take action. Culturally, we tend to prefer action to feeling and may rush the transition between the two. In a survey of American adults, the average respondent felt that two weeks was adequate time to mourn the death of a close family member and "get on with life." On the other hand, often in the therapy session, the client may prefer to keep the work on a more abstract level, not wanting to actually do what is being discussed. However, the ability to actually practice a new experience may provide the anchoring that is crucial to translating insight into new behavior. Acknowledging the client's shyness about "doing" within the therapy session, accompanying them in the activity, breaking the activity down into manageable pieces, are all skills that allow the client to experience themselves more fully. The following case illustrates the integration of thinking, feeling, and doing.

At age 19, Don had already given up on his life. He lived in a small apartment in his brother's house. His continual health issues seemed to him to signify that he was not strong enough to work or go to school. Yet, the doctors could find very little that was medically significant, and suggested that his problems were emotional. Don felt offended by this suggestion. His array of symptoms felt very real to him. He felt cold most of the time and had chronic diarrhea and headaches. He tried Chinese medicine, chiropractics, herbology, and massage to address his concerns, but with very little result.

Don's father had died recently and sounded as if he were a similarly reclusive man. Don's mother was an orphan who had adopted a very aggressive strategy in life. Don felt that neither of them had been able to help him with his intensely introverted nature as a child. Don had suffered greatly in school, unable to speak up in class, and tormented by his peers. When he graduated from high school, his physical symptoms began, convincing him that his life was over. His family and family friends made efforts to "get him out and help him practice socializing." Don felt patronized and offended by their efforts and their intimations that he did not want to get better.

Don spent time in the therapy feeling his fear. Like his father, he collapsed into his fear and let it control him. And like his mother, he pushed himself harshly to move forward. Both strategies together left him feeling immobile and crushed. He revealed that he awoke each morning with a belief that his life was over. He experienced this as a stabbing in his chest. Don shared fantasies he had about going back to school to study chiropractics. But when he brought the fantasies closer to reality and imagined going to college to get a degree and take the prerequisites necessary to attend chiropractic school, he experienced intense fear. His body drew in around his heart. His breathing became very shallow. He experienced an overall quality of being frozen. We spent time together talking about how Don experienced his fear. I shared with him my observations and empathy. Don became familiar with the feelings that the fear entailed.

As Don came to know his fear, he recognized the intense effect that it had on his body. We began to explore the possibility that many of his symptoms arose from the fear's constriction of his life force. This gave him a way of reconciling his belief in the reality of his symptoms and the medical view that they were hypochrondriacal. This also gave him an immediate strategy in the moment for working with his symptoms. When he became chilled or a headache began, Don practiced feeling his body, allowing himself to breathe, and moving in a way that allowed his energy to move out instead of constricting around his heart.

As Don began to pursue the idea of attending college, we began to work more directly with the fear. Don discovered that he would employ either his father's strategy of retreating in the face of fear or his mother's strategy of aggressively pushing through the fear. When he employed his mother's strategy, Don realized that he would talk to himself in a berating, critical manner ("Well, I guess if you want to be a total loser."). After identifying a strong longing in his heart to go forward in life, Don and I began to role-play together, one of us playing the longing and one of us playing the fearful part. Don began to develop a healthy dialogue with his fear, finding ways to both respect it and encourage himself to take risks when appropriate. He realized that he had never experienced this with his parents nor been privy to this kind of dialogue anywhere else in his life. He needed this kind of practice in working with himself. The concreteness of the role-playing process allowed Don to develop specific communication skills that he needed to go forward in life. The ability to dialogue was so abstract to Don that he needed to practice it. In this situation it was essential to actually do the role-playing rather than just discuss how it might occur.

INSIGHT, RELATIONSHIP, AND EXPERIENCE

Another way to understand the role of the body in psychotherapy is to take an overview of the development of psychotherapy. From a historical perspective, the function of psychotherapy has developed over time. Initially, psychotherapy relied on insight as its primary mode of healing. Interpretations offered by the therapist were the primary intervention that led to greater insight.

Quickly following the emphasis on insight, there was a general recognition of the paramount importance of the therapeutic relationship. Transference and countertransference, the exchange of symbolic feelings between client and therapist became more important. Creating a holding environment became a primary focus of the therapist.

In the United States in the 1950s and 1960s, with the advent of encounter groups and new experimental approaches to psychological growth, a new movement emphasizing experience developed. For a few decades, the experiential vein of psychological exploration was actively growing, developing such forms as rebirthing, group breathwork sessions, and primal therapy. Much of this work was very body oriented. Many of the basic techniques of somatic psychology developed within this movement.

From the BMP perspective, all three aspects of therapy—insight, relationship, and experience—are important. The therapist and the client work together to understand the fundamental dynamics of the client's life. They work together to create a healthy relationship between themselves and this becomes a template for healthy relationships with others. Finally, they work together to provide the client with the experiences needed to further the client's development. This integration is definitely an advantage, each function (insight, relationship, and experience) enhancing the others. This integration reflects the innate range and possibilities of human exchange, allowing for an organic process to unfold.

BODY-MIND UNITY

If we pursue psychotherapy from the perspective of body-mind unity, then all aspects of bodymind, spiritual and material, as well as conscious and unconscious, and all our human functions, thinking, feeling, and doing, as well as insight, relationship, and experience, have room to arise in their own way, at their own time.

In Chapter 4, we explored the body's involvement in each of the three tasks of psychotherapy: healing developmental deficiencies, resolving trauma, and supporting further development. A developmental deficiency occurs when any fundamental psychological need is not met within a critical period of development. In this case, the bodymind will begin to manifest some ongoing sensorimotor disorganization. On the simplest level, this disorganization may appear to be a constriction or a collapse somewhere in the body. Such a disorganized response may be accompanied by a belief regarding the self or the world that falsely estimates the potential of either the self or the world. Somatic psychotherapeutic treatment of a developmental deficiency would involve not only recognizing the limiting belief, but allowing the body to move beyond the physical pattern that developed along with it; for example, the developmental deficiency might relate to a lack of nurturing. This pattern may involve a restriction along the pathway from the mouth to the belly. Careful work with this area may allow it to shift out of the restriction and begin to literally reach out to the world.

In a traumatic reaction, the bodymind is unable to respond effectively to an experience. This results in a pattern of fragmentation in which there are crudely organized layers of agitation and freezing within the bodymind. In order to cope with this breakdown of the self, often further fragmentation occurs through the construction of partitions between the functional and the traumatized self. These partitions often snowball over time so that less and less of the self can be accessed without triggering a traumatic response. The body is invaluable in helping someone with posttraumatic stress. Through becoming aware of the sensations of well-being, wholeness, and power in the body, we establish resources that allow us to make conscious and gentle contact with the traumatic responses in our bodies. These traumatic responses are generally very physical in nature; for example, rapid heart rate, sweating, shaking, dizziness, pressure in the head, or difficulty breathing. Through very slowly allowing these traumatic physical responses to unwind and sequence out through the body through our breath and our movement, we are transforming them into the healthy, effective responses that could not occur originally.

In working toward further development, our bodyminds need to disorganize and then reorganize into a new sense of self. Our bodies naturally alert us to any disorganization through some sort of response: a sense of cognitive disorientation, feelings of dizziness, sleepiness, nausea, or fear. By anticipating the developmental process, instead of resisting disorganization, we can allow it to sequence through and continue toward our new state of being. Furthermore, to embark on a new phase of development requires behavioral change. Both the old behavior and the new behavior manifest in the body through precise awareness of both patterns, so one may begin to shift into the new possibilities in a concrete way that is supported by the body. The interaction cycle can support all of these processes.

BODY AWARENESS

Most of us have undergone rigorous training in ignoring our bodies. The effects of this training vary widely. Some people have a great difficulty in feeling any but the most concrete sensations. Others seem to have such an innately strong connection to their bodies that they never stray too far from their bodily awareness. And others have just a thin veneer of bodily ignorance that is easily penetrated.

Knocking on the Door: The Earliest Steps Toward Bodily Awareness

In facilitating bodily awareness, it is helpful to be clear about its importance. Bodily awareness is not some peripheral function, but the foundation of our sense of ourselves and our ability to respond to the world. Damasio (1994) speculated that our neurological self-image is based on a combination of bodily sensation, both immediate and past, along with our personal biographies. With this in mind, the questions, "How do you feel about this?" and "How does this feel in your body?" are potentially the same question. However, functionally, there seems to be a fair amount of extrapolation between the two. As we lose touch with our bodily responses, we confuse our feelings with our thoughts so that the two levels cease to work together in a complementary way.

Introducing someone to bodily awareness is a sacred task, one that might involve initiating them into a deeper level of self-knowledge. Through therapists' embodiment, stressed in BMP, therapists can use their own bodies as well as their observational skills to track clients' responses at each step.

In BMP, we are primarily tracking sequencing in the body. Through observing minute shifts in breathing, posture, and voice tone, one can assess whether sequencing has been enhanced or inhibited. With increased sequencing, more areas of the body are communicating with each other. Is the breath easier, fuller, deeper, or longer? As posture shifts, does the shift allow for more subtle, communicative movements between parts of the body? As the voice tone shifts, is more of the body's resonant chamber being used for vocal production?

In tracking sequencing, there are times to encourage increased sequencing and conversely to acknowledge decreased sequencing. With increased sequencing, if the client needs encouragement or support to recognize the shift, a quiet "Yes," might suffice or even a mirroring breath. With decreased sequencing, it might be important to acknowledge, "Is this too much all at once?" or "Let's take this slowly."

Be creative about how you begin. You might carefully prepare the ground through discussing with clients their relationship with their bodies, and then encouraging them to get comfortable and take a deep breath. On the other hand, with some people it might be easier to slip in the back door. In the middle of a discussion of how the client feels about something, the therapist might observe a distinct bodily reaction and ask, "And how do you feel in your body right now?" If the client is able to respond easily, then that is great. If not, then it may be important to set up an opportunity for enhanced awareness as described in the step 3 of the interaction cycle (see Chapter 5). The following scenario illustrates an attempt to make direct contact around an issue, followed by a slow and careful introduction.

Marilyn was a bright and active middle-aged woman. She was quite sensitive to her body, but tended to rush into action before really feeling herself fully. As she explored her feelings about her upcoming reunion with her family, she noticed her anxiety. I encouraged her to check in with her body:

"So, how do you feel this anxiety in your body?" She paused, looked upward and slightly to the right, and said, "I just feel worried (she made a gesture of

constricting her shoulders and chest), but I know the reunion's really going to be fine. It's so silly of me to be worried."

Therapist: So intellectually, you know it's going to be fine, but on a more primitive level there's some anxiety there?

Marilyn: Yeah, I guess so.

Therapist: Sometimes it can be helpful to listen to the anxiety, rather than just overlook it. Perhaps you can work through some of it now, and that will allow the reunion to be even more fun.

Marilyn: Oh.

Therapist: Do you want to try that?

Marilyn: Sure.

Therapist: So, get comfortable, notice your arms and back resting against the chair. Feel your feet on the floor. Just scan through your body to feel the sensations. Take some time with your head and face. Yeah, breathing, and massaging is good, feel your neck, and your shoulders and arms, too. Good, move them around a bit, and your chest. Yes, you might want to open your mouth and yawn and let yourself sigh. Yes, just give your body a chance to relax. Your belly, how are you feeling in your belly? Give it space. Loosen your belt it you like. Yes, squirm around in your chair, or you could stand up or lie down if you want. Yes, and let your legs move too if they want, stretching and wiggling your toes. Good, just feel your body like this and keep giving it permission to move and breathe and make some sounds as it wants to and as you do this, when you are ready, imagine yourself at the reunion and just feel how your body responds.

Oftentimes, therapists with less experience of working with their own bodies are more hesitant about taking this kind of time and being this directive in helping a client settle into their bodies. Furthermore, accuracy of timing and vocal tone of these directions depend on the therapist's own embodiment and subsequent attunement to the client. The more precise the timing and tone, the more likely the client will be able to settle into an experience.

Moving through Numbness

Spending time just feeling bodily sensation can allow sensation to develop. Unless there has been some neurological injury, generally numbness or lack of sensation is the result of habit. We have practiced ignoring the neurological signals coming from certain sensory nerve endings. There are sensory nerve endings coming from every group of tissues in the body, except the brain. This rich source of sensory data is not diminished with disuse. We develop habits of ignoring sensation in a particular area, but generally two weeks of daily attention to this part will easily reawaken it.

If there is a strong neurological injunction against feeling a certain part of the body, then that injunction must become conscious and reversed for sensation to become conscious again. If there is a strong emotional motivation from the past, then this also must become conscious and transformed. If there is a current emotional motivation, this must be resolved.

Patience, kindness, openness, and persistence in **self-talk** are of the utmost necessity in reawakening sensation. The use of self-touch, breath, and imagery can be very helpful. Awareness regarding any form of self-aggression is essential. Even the statement, "I can't feel anything here," is a form of aggression that can delay the process. When the brain hears "I can't feel anything here," it goes forward with this as if it is a command—"Maintain a state of no sensation in the area." Instead, state, "I feel numb here. It has a very subtle sensation. if I listen to it." This opens the door neurologically. In this case, the command is: "Monitor this area carefully for subtle sensation." By reaching with our attention, we may be encouraging new synaptic connections in the brain or reinforcing some connections that have been infrequently traveled of late. Teaching the client how powerfully this sort of self-talk affects the brain may be important.

Dwelling in the Body

Initially, we must cultivate our attention span for sensation. This can be a self-reinforcing activity, as we feel increased comfort and pleasure, as well as a greater level of self-awareness and insight. The therapist can support the client to develop a greater attention span by gentle facilitation while the client is engaged in bodily awareness. The therapist's own embodiment is the foundation and strongest tool here. The therapist's embodiment creates a supportive environment for the client. Second, quiet verbal cues based on tracking the client's sequencing, as described above, can help. Third, watching the client's breathing and head movements can alert the therapist to the client's preparation to shift focus away from the body. If this shift seems premature, quiet comments encouraging or deepening the focus may allow the client to continue for another period of time. To illustrate this, let us continue where we left off with Marilyn.

As I suggested that Marilyn begin to imagine herself at the reunion, she was in the middle of an inhalation, which she froze midway. Immediately I encouraged her to notice what had just happened in her body. She took another breath. I watched carefully to see where she would go. Her brow slightly furrowed. She cocked her head to the side, appearing to be struggling a bit in her thoughts. "Keep noticing how you feel as you think. Let your body respond to your thoughts." The furrow in her brow seemed to sequence down into a slight pursing of her lips and a contraction in her abdomen. "Yes, really feel your body here." Her attention seemed focused in her abdomen. Her facial muscles lost some of their contraction and her abdominal contractions increased subtly. There seemed to be a sequencing dialogue between her face and her abdomen as, over the next couple of minutes, they decreased and increased their muscular contractions slightly. I continued to breathe and allow my own energy to circulate in my body as I observed Marilyn.

Following this, there were a few seconds of relative inactivity. I encouraged her to really listen to this part of herself. What was it feeling? What did it want? Another pause ensued. In this one, however, her face looked a bit less slack and a bit more attentive.

In the final part of this exchange, the few seconds in which Marilyn shifted into a period of inactivity may have been a prelude to her shifting her focus out of her body. I noticed this and encouraged her just a moment before she shifted out of her body. **Prolonging attention** is an important technique for cultivating both increased attention span and greater depth of relationship either to particular feelings and sensations or to the body in general.

Listening and Allowing

As the client is beginning to establish the ability to attend to bodily feelings and sensations, there is often a temptation to treat the body with some mild form of aggression. Our culture has taught us to attend to the body only when it is in an extreme state and then do so only long enough to "fix" the problem. This generally means stopping the sensation, which might occur by repressing it or medicating it. Whenever we are trying to get rid of a sensation, at least a subtle level of aggression is involved. Trying to eliminate a sensation is contrary to the basic principle of respect in body-mind integration. When we recognize that sensations reflect emergent physiological events, we might shift into a greater trust for our bodies' natural intelligence, and instead listen to the sensation and allow it permission to complete its physiological function. An attitude of listening and allowing is perhaps the most fundamental and important aspect of the entire BMP approach. Developing it takes time. Our bodies do not necessarily respond the moment we give them permission. Often, trust has to be built slowly over a period of time as the attitudinal change deepens. Therapists' experiences with the subtleties of this process can allow them to educate and support clients in developing the patience and perseverance to persist.

Coming to Fruition

When clients have stabilized the ability to allow their attention to hover in their body without too much impatience or aggression, then awareness starts to blossom into greater communication. This can come in the form of greater insight, words, images, or movement. Therapists can encourage this process by inviting clients' curiosity and awareness of these communications. Let us return to Marilyn again to illustrate this.

> *As Marilyn attended to her body, there was still some contraction in her abdomen. I asked, what she was feeling in her body. Without speaking, she gestured toward her abdomen with her hand.*
>
> *Therapist: What do you feel in there?*
> *Marilyn: It's tight.*
> *Therapist: Is there an emotional quality to the tightness?*
> *Marliyn: Fear. I'm afraid.*
> *Therapist: Yeah, take a breath and just acknowledge that fear, listen to it, find out more about it. Do you know what you're afraid of?*
> *Marilyn: My mother. She's so domineering.*
> *Therapist: Good, it's good to know about this. Keep attending to your belly, and give it permission. What does it want to do? How does it want to breathe and move? Are there any sounds that it wants to make?*

In a situation in which the client is not able to make contact with the emotional quality, we might explore the sensation even further. What is its shape? How is it moving? Is there a pulsation there? Are there any images or words connected to this sensation? Again, asking these questions requires a timing that is sensitive to the subtle shifts and nuances of sequencing, which the therapist tracks in the client's body. Simple conceptual skills are required to support bodily awareness, but they require the therapist's embodiment. In order to support others to ease into their bodies, we must work with ourselves to do so.

MOVEMENT

As bodily awareness develops and permission toward the body grows, awareness will naturally blossom into movement. Just as sensations are physiological events, physiology is naturally moving. Every physiological event occurs as some sort of movement in space. Internal movement allows these physiological processes to develop freely. External movement can arise as a natural sequence of internal movement. In following the progression of body awareness above, the reader can perhaps discern that movement can arise spontaneously out of bodily awareness and permission. In the example above, with Marilyn, there was already some movement occurring in her trunk between her head and her abdomen. As she attended to her abdomen further, she was encouraged to explore how her abdomen wanted to move. Continuing with Marilyn, we find even further movement.

As Marilyn attended to her abdomen with the question of how this part of her wanted to move, breathe, and sound, she contracted her belly even further. As she did this her face, and particularly her mouth, drew into a tight grimace. I encouraged this: "Good. Give these feelings lots of permission. How do you want to breathe from this place?" She made a forced, aspirated exhalation. I acknowledged, "That sounds almost like a growl. Keep going. Are there sounds, are there words?" Her fist begins to clench. "Yes, let your hands get involved and every other part of you that wants to get involved." At this point she popped quickly out of her focused state, "Wow, I had no idea I was so angry at my mother. This is really weird."

Therapist: There are strong feelings there, but that's not unusual. This culture doesn't teach us to work with feelings like this very constructively. Often, we just rationalize them away and tell ourselves that there's no reason to feel these things.

Marilyn: [nodding] Yes, I guess I felt that now that I'm adult and hardly see my mother I can just put up with her bossiness.

Therapist: And you can, and feeling these feelings can help you do that.

Marilyn: But, they were so strong!

Therapist: Yes, and we are not taught to allow strong feelings to move through us, but you were doing really well with it. How do you feel now? [Marilyn lowered her gaze.]

Therapist: Yes, check back in with your body. Take a breath. Let's go back into your body and check it out, how did it affect you to really feel your body that intensely and allow it to express itself the way you did? Yes, give yourself permission to recuperate and adjust.

Marilyn: [taking a deep breath] I kind of feel like I was possessed or something.

Therapist: Well, I think we are kind of possessed by feelings that we've been unaware of. But allowing your body to feel and move the way you did can allow you to be more empowered at the reunion and in your relationship with your mother and wherever else these feelings affect you. It's a different model from our normal cultural attitude toward emotions.

Marilyn shifted gears quickly out of movement and into her concern about the movement she had just done. She appeared to have a genuine need to explore her feelings about this new activity. It is the therapist's judgment call when to encourage clients to continue exploring the body and when to support their need to understand what they have done. This is related to the distinction between thinking, feeling, and doing discussed above. The brain or cognitive self must feel comfortable with the safety and rationale for listening to the body and allowing it to express itself. It is always relevant to explore concerns and deepen an understanding of how *allowing the body* might further their development and help them reach goals.

As comfort level with the body increases, some clients might naturally gravitate toward more in-depth movement explorations. This depends on their level of acceptance of their movement impulses, the degree to which they innately need to process through movement, and the nature of the work they are exploring.

More in-depth movement explorations might take many different forms. Consider that every type of movement developed by human beings—dance, improvisation, martial arts, yoga—begins as an individual's expression of the life force moving through them. From that perspective, movement might spontaneously arise that resembles any of these forms, or none of them. Some practitioners of somatic psychology prime the possibilities by utilizing a particular movement form with clients, such as dance, **authentic movement**, yoga, or tai chi, even introducing postures, as in bioenergetic work, or spatial relationships as in family sculpting or role-playing. These particular forms can also grow out of the more personalized embodied movement as presented above. Most approaches working with movement recognize the integral relationship between movement and emotional expression.

EMOTIONAL EXPRESSION

What is the healthy balance between expression and containment of emotions? In animals, emotions are embedded in functional behaviors. The functionality of an emotion provides a cue to the healthy balance of its expression. Does the emotional expression have its desired effect? By looking at the animal function of an emotion, we learn a great deal about human emotional expression. Anger is about territorial defense. Grief allows a readjustment to new kinship configurations. Nurturing supports immature offspring. Fear avoids danger. Play educates about proper behavior and relationship. These responses each involve their own particular brain states that create overall behavioral patterns in the animal.

Finding Balance

All of the basic biological responses in animals mentioned above are present in the human brain in a more complex form. The increased complexity of our neocortex and speech mechanisms has created the possibility of exaggerating or repressing emotional expression. In exaggeration, our fascination with an emotion takes it beyond its functional duration or intensity. Repression begins initially by stopping the movement of the emotion. We become still, hold our breath, our limbs go flaccid or recoil. Second, conscious awareness of the emotion may be inhibited as well. On the positive side, the repression of emotional expression is linked to the possibility of reflection and a creative range of response. On the other hand, unconscious or habitualized emotional repression limits vitality, creativity, communication, and growth. The ability to contain our emotions, to contemplate our responses, to choose when, where, and how we express ourselves is the very hallmark of being human and has allowed the possibility of intricate cultural development. What is the balance between expression and constraint? When there is difficulty in finding the balance, how do we cultivate it?

Particular psychological approaches tend to emphasize one half of the equation or the other. Many of the somatic approaches have emphasized expression over containment. Many of the cognitive approaches have emphasized self-control over expression. How do we define this balance between expression and containment? Socially, we define it through a behavioral norm. Every culture and context has a sense of what is too much emotionality or what is too little, overly rational, mechanical, or cold-hearted.

On an organismic level, we could define the balance in terms of energy flow. If the energy of an emotion is repressed, it is not allowed to be felt, to sequence, to be in dialogue with the rest of the organism. This could be seen as too little expression. But from an energetic point of view, there is a seemingly infinite number of ways to express an emotion. Just because there is anger does not mean we need to throw a temper tantrum to express that feeling. If I experience anger as a surge of warmth and pressure in my solar plexus, I might allow that energy to sequence up the front of my spine and into my eyes, forehead, and brain. My breath deepens along with that. I feel energized and fiercely upright, but no word has been spoken, and no movement has been made in my limbs. The energy has been felt, sequenced, and acknowledged consciously. In essence, it has been expressed quite fully.

Conversely, if emotions are not contained properly, the energy of that emotion will be expressed in a draining or disintegrating fashion. Have you ever witnessed someone crying in a way in which the crying did not seem to be cleansing or rejuvenating, but rather it felt as if they were getting lost in the very process of crying? The crying itself becomes more important than the person who is crying. When an emotion takes over our being and there is no room for other aspects of ourselves, it might be expressing itself in an isolated fashion. In this case, it is not sequencing through and dialoging with other important parts of the body. Rather it is flooding the whole self. Generally when this happens, major parts of the body are being ignored. Imagine a rage that is cut off from the heart and denying any feelings of care or compassion for the people involved. A fear that is cut off from the limbs could leave one feeling trapped and unable to get away. A sadness that is cut off from the pelvis might feel inconsolable and unable to support itself. These are merely examples, and not meant to be formulaic in any way. Any emotion that is cut off from the head might be in danger of acting impulsively or irrationally.

A major task of psychotherapy today is to support people in developing a healthy relationship to their emotions. BMP utilizes the basic tools of sequencing and dialoguing to create a baseline for healthy emotional expression. To reiterate, the hallmarks are (1) feeling the whole body, as much as possible, and (2) allowing key feelings and parts of the body to stay in dialogue (as in dialoguing between the *yes* and the *no* in the interaction cycle). Specific functions that might need to coexist are the ability to think and feel at the same time, the ability to feel oneself and to stay aware of the environment or the other people present. This may be done through eye contact or through speaking. However, either eye contact or speech may bring the person entirely out of the emotional process. In this case, gently shifting back and forth between feeling and looking or feeling and speaking may help to integrate those functions.

Within the body, attention might need to be paid to any parts that feel or appear to be left out, while remaining grounded and centered during emotional expression. As always in BMP, the therapist's own embodiment is the platform for observing the client's behavior and therefore the primary tool in gauging this balance.

Vocal Expression

Innate to all mammals is the natural tendency to express our states and intentions vocally. As human beings have worked to hide their internal process from others, we have habituated a tendency to repress our vocal expression. Rather than naturally sighing, groaning, grunting, yelling, crying, or laughing, we run all our vocal impulses through a neurological mechanism to censor these for social acceptability. Unfortunately, this mechanism often goes too far, and as the process of nonexpression becomes more deeply habituated, it often becomes difficult for adults to express through their voices. As we have explored previously, blocking one area of expression often affects us in other related areas. This repression can lead to all the issues explored earlier—from physiological problems to lack of self-awareness.

Facilitating the use of vocal expression is often a last frontier for many adults. One middle-aged man told me not to "even try to get me to cry out loud. It's been beaten out of me. I learned never to make a sound, even if he was about to kill me." Another client said, "I learned not to cry out loud. It was more painful to be heard and ignored, then not to be heard." Even without this conscious memory of repressing sound, many adults will say, "I think that making sounds is really hard for me, harder than moving is." In general, slow encouragement is helpful. Beginning with an aspirated exhalation, moving toward sighing, adding just a touch of a tone, the therapist can support the client by following the client's breathing and quietly making parallel sounds with them. The following is a case vignette that illustrates several of the basic strategies of facilitating sound.

Britney was nearing the end of a two-year therapeutic process. Severe depression had instigated the beginning of therapy. Immediately, we discovered that she had very harsh internal judgments about negative emotions. These judgments were so debilitating that nearly any negative emotion could land her in a severe depression with extensive suicidal ideation and minimal ability to function. Britney had struggled with this for 10 years and was extremely resistant to medication. While Britney "felt" intensely, she expressed nothing save disdain for her own pathetic emotionality. She was very actively engaged in her jaw, diaphragm, and visceral organs to repress any emotional expression. We worked extensively to cognitively reframe her attitude toward emotions, to gently feel her emotions, to begin to let them sequence through her, rather than panicking when they arose. After two years, Britney had fairly healthy ideas about emotions and was able to weather intense situations, like the breakup of a love affair, without getting stuck in depression. As we prepared to end our work together, Britney was aware of experiencing some anxiety in the area of her stomach.

Britney placed her hand on her stomach. She was at this point able to feel it, listen to it, and allow it to breathe as it wanted to. I asked if there was a particular emotional tone that she felt in those sensations. She smiled and mimed panic, making a mock panic sound, "aeahhhhh," a short "a" sound. I suggested that she try to allow her stomach to speak for itself, to let those sounds out directly rather than having her brain interpret them. She acknowledged that this was difficult. I suggested she just open her mouth and start with a sigh from her stomach area. She sighed. We sighed together. As the sigh began to have a more emotional quality, she cut it off with a purse of her lips and a raspy disgusted sound. I acknowledged this surfacing of the old quality of judging her emotions, and suggested she keep going, letting the sound continue until there was no more breath. She made a sound that continued longer, but not all the way. I had been sounding quietly with her and continued after she stopped, pushing the last sound out with the very tail end of my breath. She heard this, understood, and continued. As she did this, she was able to deeply feel her fear about ending our work together.

Often the tail end of the breath holds the pith of emotional intensity. Encouraging clients to complete their vocal expressions can allow the emotional content to emerge. Without this, it is often possible to miss the emotionality of the sound. In general, sound is a fundamental part of our organismic expression. Reclaiming the ability to make sounds can have far-reaching effects.

Finally, the most important form of vocal expression is speech. Through internal clarity, we can state our simple emotional realities: "I am really angry"; "I am so sad"; "I miss her"; "I truly want this." When we can speak this simply and this directly, with the full presence of our whole selves, we have come into a full relationship with that emotional truth.

Jack was telling yet another charming story about his mother. As always it was entertaining and had me laughing. Out of this, he switched back to his dilemma with his girl friend. I encouraged him to practice setting a boundary with her. He began with the boundary and completed with, "and if you don't, I'll kill you." As he said this he twisted his face and head over to his right. "Wow, you are really angry," I said.

Jack: You think so?

Therapist: Well, that last line about killing her was kind of a clue.

Jack: Yeah, I guess so. I guess I am. [As we explored this, Jack's anger toward her remained nebulous.]

Therapist: Maybe it's someone else that you are angry with?

Jack: What? I hate it when she ignores me like that.

Therapist: Who?

Jack: Who? Brenda. I mean, my mother did it too, but.
Therapist: But, what?
Jack: But what's the point of being mad at a dead old lady?

This was the beginning of Jack's dawning realization that he might be furious at his mother. Over the next couple of months he explored his relationships to women more deeply. Finally, it became clear to him that he was in fact most furious at his mother and that his girl friend was getting the brunt of it. Recently, however, his daughter had confronted him on an issue in their relationship and he relayed proudly that she "just got right in my face. She didn't back down at all until she had made her point."

I pointed out that it was possible for him to be angry at his mother and love her at the same time. He looked bewildered. I suggested he might like to have a fight with his mother as he had with his daughter. "But she's dead," said Jack. I said that he could still talk to her. That maybe she could understand him now more than ever. Jack looked me as if I were crazy. I said, "It can't hurt. You're spending your whole life living for her. You might as well talk to her."

He looked at me, slightly confused, slightly defiant, and began to cry. Then he spoke directly to his mother and experienced great relief.

The next week he reported feeling much lighter, much less angry at women, and clear that, while he loved his mother and understood her, he had been really angry at her all his life, and hadn't known it.

It is often important to say things clearly, simply, and directly to begin to resolve our feelings. Talking directly to people who are not present, alive, or interested in our feelings, can be surprisingly satisfying. On the other hand, of course, talking directly to people who are present, alive, and interested in our feelings has its own benefits.

Grounding

Grounding is a term that was borrowed from electrical physics for use in the somatic field in the 1960s. As in electricity, in somatics, *grounding* refers to channeling an energetic charge toward the ground so as to dissipate it. In emotional expression, there is often a tendency to allow the emotion to move upward through the body without any tether to the situation at hand, the earth, or reality. *Grounding emotional expression* may involve breathing into the belly, feeling the pelvic floor, legs, or feet, or standing or squatting on the feet to give them more involvement. Sometimes even when standing, we might lose connection to our lower bodies as we get "carried away" by our emotions. In this case, shifting our weight evenly onto both feet, bending our knees, taking a big breath, and letting our weight release downward as we breathe out, might all be helpful in grounding the emotions.

Grounding emotional expression means that the emotion stands a better chance of being appropriate to the situation. Grounding brings one's attention back to the body and back into awareness of parts of the body that are not necessarily involved in the emotional experience. This creates some sense of perspective about the emotion. There is, therefore, less sense of identifying fully with the emotion, and more ability to see a larger picture.

Embodiment practices in general are grounding in the sense that they bring the mind back to the body. More specifically, any focus in the lower body can further connect us to the literal ground we stand on. Therefore awareness of the feet, legs, pelvic floor, pelvis, and viscera generally provide a grounding influence.

THE CORE SELF

One of the most important reminders that we can offer each other is to remember ourselves. Often in the flurry of the overstimulating world around us, we focus our attention outside ourselves and become lost in behavior that seeks to cope with the outside world. When our behavior or thought process becomes overly focused outside ourselves, a gentle reminder to come back may be helpful. In psychotherapy, I often encourage my clients, "Now come back to you. Feel yourself. Take a breath."

Centering

Centering is a 1960s term that has become somewhat dated. Yet it remains functional and even indispensable in somatic work. In BMP, we see centering as the somatic correlate of self-awareness, keeping our awareness literally centered in the body. In that sense, centering may be a key component in any process of developing a fuller sense of self. Since so much of psychological development can be related to the sense of self, centering may be an important contribution that somatic work has to offer the psychotherapeutic world. In a healthy process, our bodies are clearly the center of our experience.

This can be true in emotional expression as well. Emotion can take over to the point where it seems to have a mind of its own and be running beyond the client's awareness. Can clients be encouraged to stay in touch with their sense of self and feel the emotion at the same time? All of these shifts are movements away from **dissociation**, the state of being cut off from some aspect of one's process, back into an association with oneself.

Each time one learns to make this shift, each time the sense of self becomes stronger and more rooted, there is a subtle but core growth that is at once psychological and spiritual. Psychologically, we are more able to tolerate the challenges and seductions of the outside world without getting lost, losing our judgment, or dissolving into untethered emotionality. We are strengthening a self that can ultimately become our connection to the larger world around us. In many spiritual disciplines, dissipation of the ego is pursued as a path to enlightenment, this is not the same as dissociation. Loss of ego and a sense of self can, in a subtle way, be mutually supportive. As we develop a strong sense of our own core, we have less need for extraneous promotion of ourselves or defense of our own territory. We are better able to see the world from a variety of perspectives, our own as well as that of others. We are more able to make decisions that respond to this broader perspective, rather than knee-jerk reactions that are often more narrow-minded.

In the body, our core can be seen as an axis or a nexus. In the martial arts, and through association with the martial arts, some dance forms and somatic approaches, the center is seen as the center of gravity. In Japanese, this is the *hara*. In Chinese, the *dantian*. The center of gravity is a spot in the center of the pelvis, approximately four finger widths below the navel. This is a nexus through which many of the major pathways in the body pass. However in BMP, we tend to view the entire central core of the body as equally important, with the focus of our energy moving up and down fluidly through the core with different activities. Physically, the core includes the brain and spinal cord, the face and viscera, including the endocrine glands, extending all the way down to the pelvic floor. In BMP, we encourage a sense of flow through the core and a fluid awareness of the core as center of the self. A fixation of breath, posture, or movement through the core correlates with a limited sense of self at that moment. Reestablishing flow through the core correlates with a renewed awareness of oneself, one's center, and a reengagement with one's environment (Figure 3.1). This core flow includes a sense of awareness that radiates from the core out through the periphery of the body and into the environment. Initially, the work may be to become aware of the core, but ultimately that transforms from an awareness of the core to an awareness *with* the core. In this case, the core is the center of our awareness; our attention can radiate effortlessly from this center.

Establishing this core flow, an identification with it, and finally allowing the core to become the center of our awareness, is foundational to the process of BMP. This strongly resembles the basic theory of Wilhelm Reich. However, the interventions used to develop this differ greatly from Reich's methodology. In BMP, clients are encouraged to strengthen their core gently over time, through education and subtle awareness of breath, sensations, and state shifts. Furthermore, the BMP approach differs greatly from the Reichian in that much emphasis is placed on integrating core flow into a variety of life situations. Clients are supported to observe their shifting sense of self and to use awareness, breathing, and posture to return to their core experience. Naomi's experience outlined below shows the benefits.

Naomi entered the office with a sense of exhilaration and triumph, this place that she had struggled in for several years, first to liberate herself from a physically abusive relationship, then to learn to trust herself and express herself more in the world. Now as the director of a nonprofit service organization, she had been out of therapy for a number of years and was returning for a visit. She reported the details of her life with strength and excitement. She talked of struggles she faced and how she handled them. "And mostly I just use the simple tools I learned with you. Breathing, feeling my core, letting the emotions move through, while staying centered. I really don't feel like I need to be in therapy. I can pretty much work my issues out on my own." Her bright eyes and successful life supported the truth of that statement.

Working with flow through the core can also be a basic tool in relationship as well. By allowing our perceptions of the world to flow into us and through our core, we change our relationship to the world. As this sequences through our core, we will literally, though perhaps subtly, shift our position. With this shift, we perceive the world from a new perspective, and the cycle begins anew. With this flow through the core, it is possible to attend to ourselves and the world in a continuous manner. This is similar in dynamic to the circular breathing that skilled horn players use, in which they are inhaling and exhaling simultaneously and continually. Allowing the world to circulate through our cores is like being a complex fountain, water coming in, going through, and going out, continuously, all the time (Figure 3.1). This core flow allows us to balance our internal perceptions and needs with the external world. They are mixing and informing each other continually. In BMP we call this process **circular attunement**: the sequencing through the core may be moving up or down. Likewise, the sequencing may be moving in or out through any of the endpoints. The following vignette illustrates this point:

Tracey felt overwhelmed by the enormous attention her uncommon beauty drew from men, and she was constantly surrounded by them.

Unfortunately, she found dating really frustrating and unsatisfying. She felt that she always worked hard to keep the conversation going, and she never felt the men were really interested in her. In order to understand better what she was doing in the interactions, I asked her to role-play them with me. I played a man. What Tracey did in the role-play was very revealing. She leaned toward me at a drastic angle. She face sparkled with a brilliant smile. Her eyes twinkled. She was literally "pouring on the charm." Energetically, it was as if she had pulled all her energy up and out of her lower body and into her face. I felt overwhelmed by the volume and intensity of her attention, and felt that I must shrink in response. There was no perceptible opening for me to move toward her in any way. I shared all this with Tracey and showed her what I had seen her doing. She understood the dilemma immediately. In response to the dilemma, I talked to her about circular attunement:

We sat across from each and went slowly through the process. "I see you, and my perception of you enters my eyes and is communicated downward through my whole body. I feel myself and I feel myself adjusting to my awareness of you. Whatever happens inside me, I feel. When you make a shift, I perceive it and that perception mixes with my experience of myself. Together we make a loop of communication. I see you seeing me. I feel myself seeing you. I see you seeing me, see you." We practiced this together. "Wow," Tracey said, "That's really different. It's like the workday at the office." When she and her team at work moved the offices around she had really enjoyed coming into the office in jeans as everybody worked together to move desks and filing cabinets. She said that she felt really comfortable with the guys in her office that day. "I wasn't trying so hard." She had allowed herself to stay with herself and be in relationship. Tracey began to practice this in her life. She realized that she had been lying to people about what she enjoyed and wanted. She realized that she wanted to learn to do what she wanted to do and not what she thought would be good for the others.

This practice of circular attunement can be important in working with couples and can provide a helpful metaphor for sexuality. In addition, psychotherapists working with their own embodiment, can use circular attunement to stay in touch with themselves and their clients. In BMP, as therapists develop their own embodiment, circular attunement is the bridge into embodied relationship.

EMBODIMENT PRACTICE

Breath, sensation, intrinsic movement, emotional expression, and the core self are all means to approach embodiment. If we combine all of these elements within a context of awareness and respect, we have the practice of embodiment. This practice allows the more self-directed individual to work with themselves in a potent, developmental manner. Occasionally, a very astute client, drawing from pieces of work with breath, sensation, and movement will assemble this practice spontaneously within a therapy session. With some mature clients interested in tools for working with themselves and particularly open to somatic approaches, it is appropriate to teach this practice for their use outside of therapy. Embodiment practice, when combined with embodied relationship exercises, can also be used well with groups of high functioning clients.

Beyond those uses, the bulk of psychotherapy is better served by using the individual components that are tailored to the specific needs and interest of the individual. This may mean that the client takes a moment to breathe in their office before important meetings. For someone else, it might mean that they begin going for walks in the evenings. For another it might mean focusing on tension and breathing in a particular part of the body. Most individuals find it difficult to focus directly on their own experience. Breaking embodiment down to small, relevant pieces will help them. Some people are overwhelmed by an open-ended relationship with themselves. For these reasons, particular aspects of embodiment can be used as a means toward problem solving or healing. As the pieces accumulate, the client may grow painlessly into a more direct relationship with themselves. This is true for us all.

However, for helping professionals interested in integrating a BMP approach into their work, embodiment practice is the fundamental tool for cultivating the full depth of embodiment so that it can permeate their work. Read through the following introduction to embodiment practice and then give yourself a period of 15 minutes or so to try it.

□ □ □ □

Find yourself an area with room to move around and a comfortable spot to lie down. Begin to check in with your body. Let yourself do whatever you need to do to begin. Pace, stretch a bit, lie down, yawn. As you do this, let go of your breath. Allow your breath to come and go in its own rhythm and depth. If you are unsure about the natural rhythm of the breath, open your mouth for a few seconds and see how your breath shifts. If necessary, keep opening your mouth for longer periods until your system can allow the whole body to breath at its own pace. Also let go of your voice as you exhale. Allow a sigh to come out with an exhalation. If that feels good, keep experimenting with sighing in different volumes and pitches, whatever feels good. And as you do this, begin to check in with the sensations in your body. Wherever your attention goes in your body, feel the sensations there. Notice what they are doing, whether they are moving slightly or a great deal. Sensations are physiological events that move through our bodies. As you feel a sensation, give it permission to move and breathe and sound, however it wants to. You are allowing your physiology to complete itself. Follow your attention wherever it goes. Wherever your attention goes, feel the sensations there and give them permission to move and breathe and sound. If your attention goes to a thought, feel the sensations that arise out of the thought, and let those sensations move. Coming back again and again to the sensations in your body, always give them permission to move, breathe, sound.

Using your sensations as signs of physiological energy, feel how your energy is circulating in your body. Notice areas that have a lot of sensation, areas that have very little, areas where you can feel the flow, and areas that feel congested. Get a sense of how your energy is circulating through your whole body and along specific pathways. Notice particularly how your energy is circulating through your face and head. Feel all the little sensations in your face, your mouth, your eyes, your ears, your lips, your teeth. Give all these sensations permission to move and breathe and sound in their own way. Let your whole head and face wake up as much as you want to. As you wake up your face, feel how that draws energy up from your throat and chest and the rest of your body. Let your face and head lead all of you. And then once again, give your whole self permission to move and breathe and sound, however it wants to. Be kind enough to yourself to grant yourself this permission.

Spend time in this way, with each of the other endpoints— the hands and feet and pelvic floor. Let each part have permission to feel itself. Allow yourself to feel the emotional tone of sensations, and the emotional tone of allowing them to sequence through the body and out the endpoints. Allow your attention to focus into a particular sensation and then shift out to all of you, allowing this shifting to happen in its own way, all the while, letting go of the breath and the voice and your own sense of position.

□   □   □   □

This is the gist of embodiment practice. If you approach it from the point of view of what feels good, it is self-reinforcing. If you are trying to do it right, it becomes elusive. Give your body permission to be kind to itself and do what makes it feel better. Allow your attention span for sensations to deepen and broaden overtime. If you practice this for a few minutes a day for a period of time, say a couple of weeks, it begins to take hold. After developing a full relationship to it, you can use it for particular psychological and physical needs. The more you do it, the more it reveals itself to you. The more permission you give yourself, the more your repertoire can expand and the more nurturing and revealing the practice is. Always the practice is coming back to the sensations in your body. In the next chapter, exploration of the body systems can be added to embodiment practice, checking in with each system and noticing how it is participating. Practicing it alone allows the benefits of privacy; practicing it with others allows the benefits of shared inspiration; practicing it with a guide allows blind spots to be illuminated. Using this embodiment practice can be a laboratory that allows one to explore embodiment without the impediments of rules and roles and socially appropriate behavior. Out of these experiences, becoming embodied in your clinical practice becomes less abstract and more practical.

All of these basic approaches to including the body in psychotherapy presented in this chapter form the ground of the BMP approach. The interaction cycle provides the container. The next three chapters on the body systems, energetic development, and the cellular level of change comprise the substance of BMP.

PART III

BODY SYSTEMS

Chapter 7

Observing the Body Systems

If you want to know how the wind is blowing, you can look at the sand. Our body moves as our mind moves. The qualities of any movement are a manifestation of how mind is expressing through the body at that moment.

— Bonnie Bainbridge Cohen, *Sensing, Feeling, and Action*

In order to fully utilize the body in psychotherapy, somatic psychotherapists must learn both to observe their clients' bodies and to use their own bodies as observational tools. Without a deep awareness of our own bodies, we cannot deeply observe others. Through this awareness, psychotherapists learn to support both their own and the clients' bodies to express their emotions, desires, and intentions. Clients can learn to reunite fragmented aspects of the self through discovering the bodily pattern that concretizes the fragmentation. Clients can learn to support new behaviors through allowing their natural bodily responses to manifest.

DYNAMIC INTERPLAY OF THE BODY SYSTEMS

Each of the body systems offers its own unique wisdom and style. Exploring each of them offers a wide array of resources to the psychotherapeutic clinician. While these systems are presented here as somewhat independent, we separate them to learn about their specific qualities. However, beyond this initial study with the somewhat artificial overlay of separation, in practice we return to a dynamic view of the whole system, in which all the body systems of the organism are working together in a team effort.

Culturally our preference is too lead with the frontal lobe of the central nervous system. Though our somewhat naïve belief that our culture is based on rationality has been disproved from many quarters—for one, Damasio (1994)—it is still the dominant worldview. This has led to systematic repression of intelligence from other systems, especially those that have the most to offer. Specifically, the viscera, the fluid systems, and the endocrine system are greatly ignored and, in some ways, feared in our cultural view. We are generally suspicious of visceral expression as leading to either physical illness or excessive emotionality and irrationality. Flow and fluidity are seen as potentially leading to sloth and hedonism. The endocrine system represents the threat of potent energy of all sorts, though it enjoys a complex cultural role of being simultaneously exalted and repressed. We avidly pursue it through entertainment thrills, but we simultaneously discount its potential wisdom, guidance, and link to spirituality. While the musculoskeletal system is enjoying a revival of interest through the fitness industry, it is being approached in a mechanistic manner, purely trying to condition for aesthetics and prowess. This is a far cry from actually allowing it to express the myriad impulses that it is carrying from all our emotional and developmental processes. Other systems are of less interest to our culture and are relegated even more completely to the unconscious.

In the field of organizational development, we are recognizing the importance of teamwork and shared leadership. In a healthy system, each team member can step forward to offer his or her unique resources and expertise. This model lends itself readily to the body system. If allowed, each body system can offer resourceful leadership in particular situations. A healthy system resists the fixed control of the nervous system. Rather, the nervous system can act as consultant and organizer, drawing information from all the systems, coordinating efforts, and supporting the leadership abilities of other systems. The body systems are inherently interdependent, always working together. However, by focusing on the individual systems, we can tease apart the complex of interrelated roles that they play. Let us look now at a case vignette that illustrates the systems' basic interdependence.

At 84, Ingrid was more vital than many 60-year olds. She exercised to stay slim, dressed to the "nines," volunteered, and attended lectures and concerts. She had been in therapy much of her adult life, including an aborted attempt at analysis. She had been a social worker as a younger woman. Her desire to communicate and help others was a driving force in her personality. Her insecurity and inadequacy were equal in intensity to her passion for life, flair for the dramatic, and love of the arts.

In the first session, Ingrid talked about her fears and her inadequacy. I asked her to feel this in her body, and she became aware of a posture of cowering and curling into herself. She then felt anger at this constriction. When I encouraged her to breathe into the anger and give it room to move in her body, she was able to do so quite readily and authentically. With only the tiniest bit of encouragement, she stood up and began to strut around the room, with a dominating attitude.

Let us use this brief introduction to get an initial sense of Ingrid's body systems and how they worked together. The accepted leader of the group was her nervous system, which was visible in its freedom to run unfettered with both fantasies and obsessive negativity. She had a fairly lenient connection with her muscles, allowing them a fair amount of room to express emotions, as well as general vitality. On the other hand, because of her age and the number of unresolved conflicts in her psyche, her muscles had a significant amount of tension and distorted her skeleton in a number of uncomfortable ways. Her shoulders were quite elevated and her pelvis was locked in a pretty extreme posterior tilt (flexion, relative to the spine). Her endocrine system was vital and full of energy, but only allowed to express itself within a rebellious, defiant role. Like the muscles, the nervous system gave it some leeway—a fairly long leash—but far from total freedom. Her fundamental belief was that she was powerless, alone, and artistically without talent. She was not free to experience love, artistic expression, and an autonomous power. In contrast, she allowed herself tremendous freedom to express both her fear and her anger. These charged expressions had some quality of fluid support, but the limitations of that expression did not allow for much flow to develop. In most of her communication, she was not totally rigid, but the fluids were not prominent in any way, never really leading an expression, but not totally rigidified either. Her viscera appeared to be ignored and slightly constricted.

The first phase of our work together consisted of challenging Ingrid's view of herself as hopelessly neurotic. Was she sure that she couldn't trust herself? This is one of the ways her conscious, thinking nervous system kept her restricted. Over time, she began to entertain the possibility that she might not be quite the mess she thought she was. At this point, we worked with becoming more aware of her self-denigrating comments, both spoken and subliminal. Her awareness became quite sharp and she was able to drastically change the content of her self-talk. This initial work with her nervous system opened the way for work on other levels. She began to experiment more with having fun and expressing herself in creative, satisfying ways. This brought her into more intimate relationships with her friends and she began to focus more on relationships. Through this she stumbled on the truths of her loneliness and longing for love.

She had been sharing with me her love for white crocuses growing outside her window. She had been unusually tender and vulnerable in sharing her feelings about these crocuses. Then later in the session, she explored an ongoing conflict she had with a friend. She felt the argumentative stance that she had taken had provoked the friend, and pushed her away. She felt the constricted, protected state (muscles) that situation left her in and the confusion she felt mentally (nervous system). Why was she doing this? She saw the confusion of this pattern nakedly for a moment. After she had spent a moment with her confusion, as she was beginning to shift her attention, I asked her how she felt in her heart. I put my hand over my sternum, "What do you feel right here?" "I don't know. Tight, hard." Long pause. I wondered out loud how she felt when she was talking about the crocuses?

The crocuses and then the lilacs that came later provided a safe way to experiment with feeling her heart. She could in fact notice a softening and an open feeling in her heart when she contemplated these flowers. Eventually she could even look at me and feel this softness and openness in her heart. It was very delicate work. She would touch the feeling and then later assert that she had not felt her heart at all.

In terms of the systems, feeling this softening in her heart was the beginning of a new openness to all of her viscera. Her whole relationship to herself began to shift. She began to really believe that perhaps she was okay. She began to lie in bed and sense her body and sometimes breathe into her heart. Other times she dismissed the whole thing. Issues of self-love began to surface. In her relationship to her skin and fat, there was a certain appreciation and sensuality that she expressed indirectly through vaguely caressing movements and gestures, but it was clear from her comments regarding her appearance that this was purely conditional, based on maintaining herself at an exceptional level.

We stayed on this edge with her heart. She became a little more conscious in her interactions with friends. She was able to maintain a certain level of improvement in her appreciation and respect for herself, but not much movement beyond that. At 84, this seemed like a great deal. I congratulated her when she declared that she thought she was done with the "whole therapy thing," and had more important things to do. I agreed, but said I would be here if she wanted contact.

Hypothesizing

Ingrid's relationship with her systems was generally consistent with our cultural biases, with the exception of the freedom that she gave her endocrine system to express passion and intensity. Each person's organization is unique, and the interrelationship between systems is a complex and dynamic system that requires that the right players be addressed in the right way in the right order. We can never know what another person's internal organization is about, but can only hypothesize and then test our hypotheses for their efficacy. Through observing movement, breathing, voice tone, and posture, we develop an initial hypothesis regarding the organization of the body systems. Through interviewing the client regarding behavior, sensations, and health history, we can further develop a working hypothesis. This hypothesis can be refined and amended throughout our work with a client. It is never complete or definitive. Nonetheless, the systems provide both an excellent tool for character analysis as well as a good metaphor for organizational systems. As a client learns about their psychology and their bodies, they may be able to confirm or correct our hypotheses.

THE THERAPIST'S BODY

Communication specialists generally agree that 70% of communication occurs nonverbally. Therefore, the therapist's body is doing 70% of the work of therapy. The more that we become aware of our bodily processes, the more effective we are in both observing and communicating. Unconscious recognition of facial expressions takes place within fractions of seconds. All the facial expressions that flicker across the therapist's face register in the client's unconscious without necessarily entering conscious awareness. Gestures and postural shifts register in the same way. Vocal tone and rhythm are a further dimension of nonverbal communication.

It is important to distinguish between bodily awareness in the moment and the cultivation of an ongoing relationship to one's bodily

process. Any moment in which the therapist becomes either spontaneously or intentionally aware of her own bodily process can be tremendously helpful to the therapeutic process. For example, in listening to
a depressed client, I might become aware of a heaviness in my own
body. This could be a clue to the extent to which the client's depression has begun to affect me. However, it is always important to check
back with the client, either directly or indirectly. When I am having
an experience that seems to be in response to my client's, I first observe the client to see if any clues support the relationship. In the
example of the heaviness, I might look to see if the client appears to
feel heavy. If it is important to bring out this aspect of their experience, I might ask how the client feels in her body at that moment. If
there is no mention of heaviness, and yet I am still convinced that the
heaviness might be an important aspect of their experience, I might
ask directly, "Are you feeling a sort of heaviness in your body?" If so,
we pursue it. At times the client may disaffirm my experience, while I
still suspect that it may be true. In this case, I hold the hypothesis and
wait until it might become pertinent again. More often, if a client
disaffirms the experience, I assume that it is solely my own experience.
I then explore the experience to see if it is in some way countertransferential. Bodily awareness allows us to discern countertransference in
a very concrete way. The usefulness of countertransference has been
illuminated by many of the great psychoanalytic theorists. By becoming aware of our countertransferential experiences, we gain a unique
window into our clients' psyches as well as those of their parental
figures. Thus, momentary awareness of the body can be tremendously
helpful.

The cultivation and deepening of bodily awareness offer a more
profound possibility. Through an ongoing cultivation of embodiment,
therapists can actually tap levels of self-awareness that are normally
difficult to reach. This can further therapists' personal development.
Finally, the depth and continuity of therapists' self-awareness affect
the depth of the exchange between clients and therapists. In BMP,
we train therapists primarily through cultivating a personal sense of
embodiment. Initially this is done through a thorough practice of embodiment. Therapists make a practice of spending time feeling sensations and allowing those sensations to breathe and sound and move
however they want to. As embodiment practice develops, more sensations come into awareness and a thorough exploration of each body
system can be made. In this way, each tissue and fluid of the body
can be scanned for sensation. Taking time to acquaint oneself with
the experience of each body system is fundamental to this process.

Once that acquaintance is made, then the systems can be incorporated into embodiment practice, making sure that each system is present and participating in its own way. Exploration of the body systems is an approach taken from body-mind centering (BMC). However, in BMP this exploration is more personal and psychologically oriented. In BMP, we attend to the emotional tone of each system as well.

OBSERVING THE BODYMIND THROUGH
THE BODY SYSTEMS

In observing the bodymind, one can observe specific behaviors: breathing, posture, movement, speech, voice tone, or larger behaviors such as lifestyle, history, relationship patterns, career choices, activity preferences. As we observe the various tissues and fluids of the body, we find that each part expresses itself somewhat differently through these specific behaviors. From this we can discern different aspects of the self, different parts of ourselves. Studying the body systems is a way to bring a concrete, somatic focus to parts of the personality. The study of the body systems is essentially the study of psychophysical states.

In studying the organization of body systems within a particular person, basic questions arise. Which systems are having a strong influence on the person? Which resources are well utilized? What resources lie dormant? What kinds of sensations are readily perceived and responded to? Which of these perceptions are conscious and which are unconscious? What aspects of the self are overused and fatigued? What strategies are relied on repeatedly or even ineffectively? How do transitions occur? When there are major state shifts in different contexts, which systems support these various states? Are certain systems only allowed to function in certain settings?

These are the kinds of questions that can be answered by observing the body systems. The answers can support an understanding of the organizational structure of each person's character. In combination with the basic neurological actions discussed in Chapter 10, we can form a pretty complete assessment of character structure. Furthermore, with an understanding of the family, education, and cultural background, we can support the client to hypothesize about what aspects of the character are learned and what aspects are the result of conditioning.

The therapist's task is to first experience his or her own bodily systems. Through this one begins to understand this approach directly. Once mastered, it becomes a simple, direct way of observing and hypothesizing about an individual's functioning. The therapist's own embodiment is key to that happening. After therapists have thoroughly explored their own body systems and embodiment has become the foundation of their approach to psychotherapy, they can use their own bodies as tuning forks to attune to clients. By letting visual and auditory perceptions of the client filter down from the brain through the rest of the body, we can feel what we are seeing and hearing.

This happens spontaneously in human beings. Much of the task here is to become conscious of what is unconsciously perceived. We have an innate ability to perceive and empathize on a bodily level. An elementary schoolteacher brought a lemon, a cutting board, and a knife to class. As the class watched, she cut the lemon in half and put a half in her mouth. She looked out at the children whose mouths and faces were contorted in response to the imagined sourness, and said, "What you are experiencing is called *empathy*." This is one example of allowing sensory information to inform our bodily selves. Obviously, there are more subtle and more conscious versions. As mammals, we have millions of years of evolution behind our ability to perceive what is happening in other animals. Each subtle shift of attention and activity is recorded acutely in our unconscious. When we encounter another animal, we need to know within seconds if there is any chance of eating them, being eaten by them, or any need to avoid or attempt a sexual engagement. As human beings, we have not bothered to translate much of our observational abilities into our verbal awareness. The process of BMP observational training is largely about bringing our unconscious awareness of others' bodies into conscious articulation.

Another aspect of observing the body systems is to recognize each part's relationship to the whole. Any time we seek to understand parts of whole systems, we must inquire about a particular part's relationship to the whole. With body systems, it might be helpful to ask the following questions.

- What is the healthy aspect of this part's role?
- Does this role fully express this part's strengths and wisdom?
- Does this part tend to function more supportively or expressively within the whole?
- Does this part have unmet needs?
- Is there a healthy intention behind the neurotic aspect of this part's manifestation?

Attending to the body systems and asking these sorts of systemic questions can be a transformative process in and of itself, a process that brings to light previously hidden aspects of the body-mind relationship.

This sort of observation of all the body systems and their interactions yields a large amount of data. BMP is committed to pursuing the client's goals in the most direct and efficient manner possible. Therefore the bulk of the information gleaned through observation of the body is not shared directly, but rather folded back into the therapist's internal pool of hypotheses and understanding of the client. Only the specific feedback necessary to the client's process is shared, and as discussed previously, only if the client does not discover it independently.

We all receive sensory data from all the tissues and fluids of our bodies. However, each person is unique in his or her patterns of attention to that influx of data. From birth onward, everyone has preferences regarding what sensory data to attend to. In addition, our experience, family preferences, education, and cultural attitudes both positively and negatively reinforce what sensory data we attend to. Each type of tissue and fluid in the body has its own unique resources, including perceptual abilities, rhythms, capabilities, and psychological style. Through attending to particular sensory data coming from a particular body system or combination of body systems, we shape our psychophysical states and our behaviors. By acquainting oneself with the sensory data coming from a particular system and by learning to observe it in others, we tap into a powerful mechanism of expanding the self.

Parts

There are many approaches to working with aspects of the personality in psychotherapy. From Gestalt techniques, to Jungian archetypes, to the Internal Family Systems work of Richard Schwartz, to basic integration techniques with dissociative identity disorder, all of these methods of integrating different parts of the personality can be enhanced through understanding the body systems. And the body systems offer their own approach to working with parts. While each aspect of the personality most likely manifests through more than one body system, often there is a predominant system that is in the leadership role. Even when this is not the case, understanding the systems can allow one to see how that personality aspect is anchored in the person's body. In BMP, we work with respect toward the role of each aspect of the personality, and the potential of each body system involved. We work with the basic principle of inclusivity and shared leadership, so that each body system can emerge as a healthy leader in the appropriate circumstances. Often in working with painful or disruptive parts of the personality, people will have the impulse to annihilate those parts. An awareness of the physical component of the pattern can help support both the necessity and the potential of integration, rather than annihilation. For example, perhaps our endocrine system is often leading rageful fits. We might want to get rid of that part of ourselves, but as we realize that it is the same basic energy that supports our most creative work, this might provide both the motivation and the path for reintegration. As always, actually feeling the physical manifestation of an aspect of the self gives us a sense of direct leverage in working with it.

Chapter 8

Systems of Form

The Muscular, Skeletal, and Nervous Systems

All of the body systems interact constantly, both functionally and structurally. It is often hard to delineate where one ends and another begins. Nonetheless, looking at each system independently allows us to become more intimate with our bodies as a whole. For these purposes, we will examine eight major body systems: the muscles, the skeleton, and the nervous system, in this chapter. In Chapter 9, we will explore the skin, the various fluid systems, the fat, the viscera, and the endocrine systems.

The systems of this chapter all relate to form in some manner. The skeleton creates the basic structure of our bodies. The muscles work with the skeleton to move our bodies through space. Our nervous system directs this process through intention, planning, and coordination. For each system, we will explore its basic function as well as ways to experience it directly and to observe its role and functioning in clients. To introduce you to this process and the body systems, let's begin with the skeletal system, which is one of the easiest to observe in some ways.

THE SKELETAL SYSTEM

Our skeletons provide the basic framework of our bodies. The skeleton fundamentally shapes every posture or movement. Through studying the basic mechanics of gravity acting on the skeleton, we can develop a basic sense of a neutral skeletal alignment for each given position, such as sitting, lying, standing, kneeling, or squatting (Figures 8.1).

We can also develop a sense of a neutral skeletal alignment for each person's structure during movement. By beginning with an awareness of skeletal alignment for static positions, we can expand this to a sense of efficiency and ease in basic movements—walking, gesturing, breathing, and reaching out. By neutral alignment, I mean that the only forces acting on the skeletal alignment would be gravity, and if in an upright position, a simple allegiance to verticality.

However, most human beings are far from neutral. We are constantly engaged: feeling, doing, and digesting (both literally and figuratively). Each bit of our past, present, and future pushes, pulls, and shapes our skeletal alignment. A human being whose skeleton can achieve even momentary neutral alignment is quite rare in our culture.

Alignment

Through observing the client's skeletal alignment, the therapist can glean some notion of where this client is most busy "doing" something on an internal level. Alignment reveals ongoing themes that are often unconscious.

The image of a plumb line is helpful in observing alignment. A plumb line is a line falling perpendicular to gravity. The body is always balancing itself around gravity and can do this with minimal displacement or in a more exaggerated fashion. If there is more than minimal displacement as the body balances in any position, this provides a clue as to how much unresolved activity is taking place internally. The following case example illustrates the possibilities that are opened up by observing skeletal alignment.

Leah and I had not met for several months. When we ended our ongoing therapy, we had planned this meeting as a check-in. After several years of therapeutic work, Leah had resolved a tremendous amount of trauma from her childhood. She had created meaningful work for herself. She had changed a lifelong pattern of sacrificing herself in intimate relationships, and had just begun living with a woman with whom she had a truly loving and mutually supportive relationship. When she arrived she was glowing. We had a joyous time celebrating her recent accomplishments. She was exuberant about how well her life was going. She felt her life was blessed.

FIGURE 8.1 SKELETAL ALIGNMENT

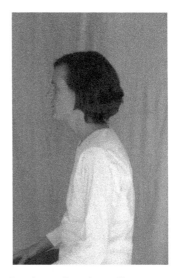

Good alignment of weight-bearing seg-ments. Rotatory effect of gravitational force is minimized.

In this photo, the subject illustrates a spi-nal misalignment common during psy-chotherapeutic processing. Notice that her hand has moved forward.

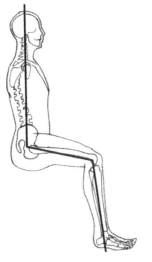

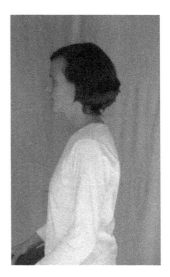

(From Wells & Luttgen. *Kinesiology: Scien-tific Basis of Human Motion*, 6/ed [p. 395], © 1976 Elsevier Inc.)

In this photo the subject has moved her head back in connection to her spine.

As she neared the end of sharing all her news, I invited her to check in with herself for a moment. She closed her eyes, took a deep breath, and broke out in a big grin. I encouraged her to breathe her joy deep into her body. We had, in the past, worked extensively with this process of using the breath to connect various parts of her body with her emotions. She began breathing fully, and her breath moved her whole body. However, I noticed that her clavicles remained elevated throughout her inhalation and exhalation (see Figure 8.3). I suggested that she inhale into her upper lungs. She did this a couple of times and her breath began to pulsate with silent tears. She brought her hands to her chest, pulling her chest back. "Still a lot of grief there?" I asked. She nodded. She breathed and stayed with her feelings for a while. Her crying softened. She looked at me through her tears. "I need to remember that the grief is still there." We worked for a while on allowing the joy and the grief to coexist and, then we parted warmly. We would meet in another six months and Leah would work to stay in touch with her grief on a regular basis. I was grateful for the clue provided by her clavicles.

Movement

In observing the skeleton's movement, we are looking for two qualities: sequencing and release. The endpoints of a neutral skeleton rise and fall in easy arcs. When the skeleton is engaged in conflicting impulses, the joint involved is pulled in two opposing directions and these arcs tend to flatten out (Figure 8.2). A neutral skeleton releases each movement and rests back into a supportive relationship to gravity when the function of the movement has passed. Thus, our skeletal self can guide us with substance and clarity, while using minimal effort. It can offer us a deep and easy sense of self-support. Through that we are most connected to the support we receive from the earth beneath us.

Acceptance

Within this quality of release of the skeleton lies the psychological resource of acceptance, a willingness to go along with things as they are, to release into the basic reality of the moment. The polar opposite of this kind of acceptance is ineffective struggle, overworking to force a change. While there may be a fear of this kind of letting go, release into reality may provide us with excellent leverage for taking the next step at the right moment.

Marrow

A deeper level of psychological and spiritual resource comes from the marrow within each of the long bones, as well as the sternum, ribs,

FIGURE 8.2 TWO ARMS ADDUCTING

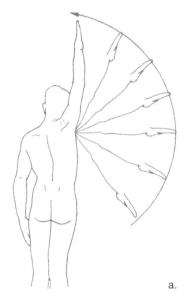
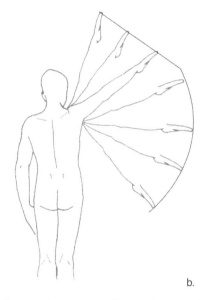

a.   b.

Neutral movement produces an even arc.   Restricted movement flattens the arc of
                                          the movement.

and a few others. At the beginning of life, the marrow is entirely
devoted to blood and lymph cell production. As cell production slows
down, much of the marrow converts to yellow marrow which is primarily fat. Cell production is primarily confined to the proximal ends
of the humerus and the femur, as well as the sternum and the iliac
crest. In theory, the yellow marrow could convert back to red marrow
if an extreme need for cell production arose. Thus, the marrow represents a very deep inner resource, with the quality of infusing life. My
sense is that when people speak of knowing something in their bones,
there is generally some sensory connection to the marrow. For most
people, this is not a conscious awareness, because the sensations are
so subtle.

Basic Skeletal Misalignments

Among the most common basic skeletal misalignments are carrying
the head in a forward position (Figure 8.1). Many chests are collapsed
(Figure 8.1), other chests are pushed forward. Many shoulders are ele-
vated (Figure 8.3). Most pelvises are tilted either forward or back.
Some knees are hyperextended (Figure 8.4). Many ankles are everted.
Consciously correcting our posture can be an irritating and fruitless

FIGURE 8.3 THE SHOULDER GIRDLE

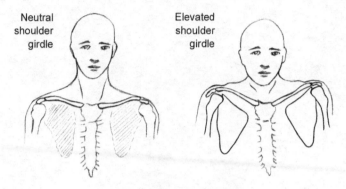

Neutral
shoulder
girdle

Elevated
shoulder
girdle

Shoulder girdle.

In this photo, the subject has elevated her shoulder girdle.

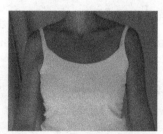

In this photo, the subject has relaxed her shoulders as much as possible at that time.

process. Our skeletons take their habitual postures for many complex reasons. Until those reasons and their accompanying neurological commands shift, we will continue to gravitate toward our habitual posture. However, after an emotional pattern has been released, the nervous system is open to possibilities. Some postures shift unconsciously on their own. Acknowledgement of that shift can help anchor the change. The therapist might point out simply that "You look really different right now." If there is a mirror in the office, the client might want to see this shift. It might be helpful to be more specific: "See

FIGURE 8.4 KNEES

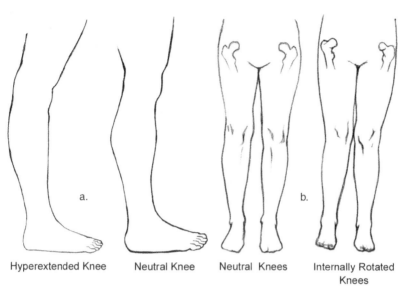

Hyperextended Knee   Neutral Knee   Neutral Knees   Internally Rotated
                                                                                                Knees

how open your chest is," or "Wow, your spine is really erect." At other times, there might be a skeletal shift just waiting to happen. A slight nudge at those moments might make all the difference. The most basic BMP intervention for such a situation in which there is a great deal of shifting within the client, but it is not sequencing fully, is to say, "Let it go all the way through." This directive seems to speak directly to the client's subconscious without overly engaging the conscious. Releasing the breath can help at that moment as well.

Beyond these levels of intervention, some postural shifts are accessible through simple awareness. By simply pointing to the area that is not sequencing, a movement can happen spontaneously. At this level, the therapist might say, "Let it go through your neck and head too." Finally, there are times, though less frequently and as a last resort, that it may be helpful to show the client the postural shift. Again this is only appropriate after some emotional shift has occurred that seems to be trying to sequence through the joint in question. It should be relatively easy for the client to make the skeletal shift without much muscular or cognitive effort. For example, most people are able to become aware of a hyperextension in the knees and release it or an elevation of the shoulder girdle. However, some people may need to be shown the new option. This can be done by illustrating it with your own body. If that is difficult, give them a little movement that will help them find the adjustment. For example, with a tucked chin, encourage them to lift their chin and lower it, while looking for a neutral head position. Give them feedback when they find the correct position. If that doesn't work, and it is appropriate to touch the client, ask if you may do so, and then make the adjustment yourself. First, they must release that body part and then you can gently shift it into position. Many people are able to become aware of the old pattern and self-correct it with a little education. If not, they may need more extensive bodywork. The alignment of the entire skeleton is important. These are but a few patterns that are relatively easy to spot and adjust.

Experiencing the Skeletal System

We began with the skeletal system because it is, in some ways, the easiest system to observe. However, because bone does not generate much sensation, it is more difficult to experience directly. We experience bones primarily through their weight and density. When the muscles surrounding a bone are only minimally engaged and we allow the bone to fall toward gravity, we can experience the weight of the bone. When our skeletons are aligned with gravity, we can experience the support of the bones. When our bones impact a hard surface, we experience vibration through the bone. Cultivating a relationship to our skeletons can provide a sense of ease and support. This may be more crucial in areas in which there is a great deal of muscular activity and misalignment. The bones can provide a weighted sense of simple presence. We only experience overt sensation in the bones during times of bone growth or tissue trauma. However, we can experience their footprint through weight, support, and ease.

MUSCULAR SYSTEM

In contrast to the bones, our muscles are the most active tissues in our body. Muscle tissue is the only tissue that can change its length. This occurs through the sliding of parallel tracks of filaments within the muscle fiber. As muscle fibers shorten and lengthen throughout the body, we speak of this as changes in muscle tone. If muscle tone is too high, an overall shortness of muscle fiber constricts us. Muscle tone that is too low leaves us flaccid and unprepared for action. Balanced muscle tone is accompanied by constant, minute readjustments of length within the fibers, leaving us relaxed, active, and ready for action, but not overly wound up.

□ □ □ □

Take a moment to check in with the overall state of your muscles. If they are feeling bound, give them the opportunity to stretch, breathe, and release. Begin to visualize the sliding of filaments in your muscle fibers and the constant, minute shifting through the muscles. Can you remember seeing a horse or a cat in this state of readiness? The whole muscular layer of the body, right underneath the skin, is rippling in readiness. Allow your muscles to experience this: active, but not yet moving through space; ready, but relaxed.

□   □   □   □

In observing clients, you can see the overall state of their muscle tone through their posture and gestures. High tone will appear rigid, bound, overly still, and controlled. Low tone may appear lethargic, passively propped up. In addition to overall tone, you can observe pockets of extreme tone in the body, areas where the muscles are more or less active than their neighbors. This affects the sequencing of movement in those areas. Movement becomes stopped or diminished in certain segments of the body or it may become exaggerated. The following case vignettes illustrate the varying roles that muscles can take:

Lenore had a long history of posttraumatic stress disorder. She had spent her entire adulthood guarding against the possibility of repeating the dangers she felt as a child growing up in a violent area in South Africa. At the same time, she was by nature an extremely active, energetic person whose anxiety had left her feeling very frustrated and longing for adventure. Fear and frustration waged a war in her muscles. The frustration would charge them with impulses to move, and the fear would hold them still to avoid danger. She complained constantly of muscular tension, headaches and neck and shoulder pain. She had a strong desire to burst out in rage, and at the beginning of our work, a sincere belief that this was the only way she would heal. When she would go toward rageful expression, I could see her muscular tone and movement increase dramatically in her face and limbs, but the muscles of her trunk became more rigid. She dissociated from the fear that her rage provoked, which led her to hold her breath and not move her trunk. She wanted so badly to heal that she was willing to terrify herself in the process. Slowly over time, she was able to recognize the destructive aspect of her rage.

We shifted our attention back and forth between the rage and the fear, and also a deeper level of sadness underneath them both. She had a dream about a bottle with a cork in it. She felt, in analyzing the dream, that it was her soul that was bottled up inside her. As she was able to accept all of her feelings, not just favoring the rage, she began to find ways to uncork the bottle, and allow her muscles to release gently rather than explode. This could include moments of expressing anger, sometimes through pounding a futon as she lay on it, but there was not the imbalanced intensity through her face and limbs and rigidity in her trunk. Instead, there was a gentler shifting of activity throughout her muscles as they moved by pounding, shaking, crying, breathing, and reaching out.

In contrast to Lenore, Anna had extremely low muscle tone.

Anna's face was so slack that it looked as if it might slide right off. She would sit in a collapsed position with her mouth open. She was extremely intelligent, observant, and sensitive, but not particularly active. It appeared that she was not particularly muscular by nature, and she could see how as a child she had become even less so to please her mother and avoid her father. The part of her body that was most still was her pelvis. As she breathed into her pelvis and began to rock gently, she felt a wave of energy rise into her chest. She found this energy uncomfortable and stilled her pelvis. Over time, she was able to recognize how uncomfortable the sexual environment in her family had been. Her parents were not sexual with each other. Her father was having secret affairs that no one discovered until she was an adult. Furthermore, her father's attention to her was subtly colored with inappropriate sexuality. Anna could feel that she had unconsciously stopped feeling her pelvis. She could also remember that as an adolescent she had felt embarrassed of her developing hips and had intentionally learned to walk without moving that part of her body. These patterns of immobility in her pelvis were the template for the larger pattern of invisibility that she struggled against as an adult.

A third perspective is provided by John.

Upon first meeting John, I assumed that he must have a weekly athletic regimen. His muscles were noticeably well developed and well defined. I was surprised to learn that he had always "hated" sports and athletics of any type. He was not active in any way, but appeared naturally alert and active in his muscles. His muscular development was entirely due to genetics and the level of stimulation that his muscles received within a rather sedentary life.

The subtle, but important role his muscles played in his psychological issues emerged over a couple of sessions. John's muscularly active and expressive nature was not acceptable within his family system, so he repressed it. Simultaneously, he did not receive the protection, support, and nurturance he needed. He compensated for these deficits by becoming excessively competent, not only self-sufficient, but actively taking care of others. His muscles served him in this role by both supporting his capability and repressing his core feelings, which constellated around a longing for love and safety and the subsequent fear and anxiety that arose in their absence. Muscles often take the role of literally holding an area still, avoiding breath and movement, in order to avoid stimulating feelings in that area.

John came to therapy due to an ulcer which he thought was related to his child's beginning kindergarten, As a single father, deserted by his wife during their child's infancy, he had struggled for six years to support his child and he felt tremendous anxiety about her beginning school. Through learning to listen to his sensations and feelings in his GI tract, he was symptom-free within three months. He also began to learn to shift out of his anxiety and into a deep, loving attention for himself as a way to soothe himself around the anxiety caused by his separation issues. When he practiced this attention toward himself, he noticed that his child also seemed to vicariously feel more secure.

A key to learning to attend to his GI tract was his need to release the muscles in his jaw and at the base of his neck. Not only did he hold the muscles of his trunk, but the muscles of his jaw and occiput served as sentinels against his attending to himself inside. As he began to attend to his belly, I noticed his jaw and head rigidifying and pulling up and back. John found a little sigh very effective in dismissing these sentinels. Subsequent to our few sessions together, John called to say that he was continuing to be symptom-free, that his daughter was adjusting well to school, and that he had begun ballroom dancing, which, not only was the first enjoyable physical outlet that he had found, but was also a good way to meet single women.

These three people illustrate the diverse roles that our muscles can play within our psychologies. Our muscles can rigidify or disperse our physical energy. Deane Juhan points out that muscles can act as either pumps or tourniquets upon our fluid circulation (1987). Healthy muscles need some degree of movement, release, and activity. If this is psychologically acceptable, a person may naturally gravitate toward this, or may need some encouragement as in the case of Anna (whose work was described above). Anna started using her body gently by studying tai chi.

Mirroring, Polarizing, or Sequencing

In observing the muscles of another person it is often the observer's own muscles that provide the most information. This empathic response is due to the functioning of mirror neurons in the brain. Our brains are designed to read the movement of others by activating the neurons in our motor cortices that would be engaged in the movement (were we to make it) that we are watching in another person. When observing another person, do your muscles feel unusually bound, playful, weak, or restless? Are you picking this up from your client? There is a natural propensity for our bodies to respond to the bodies of others, and this is particularly true for the muscles. We might respond by mirroring our clients, not just neurologically, but actually enacting their activity in minute or bigger ways. Or we might respond by polarizing from their state. Or we might briefly touch their state through mirroring or polarizing and then allow that to sequence in a way that might lead to yet another state. Finally, we might neither mirror nor polarize, but have a more independent response. In either case, it is important to continue to allow our own breathing and movement to sequence through our bodies as we perceive others. These three possibilities—mirroring, polarizing, or sequencing—are generally true within any energetic exchange, regardless of systems. But, it may be more pronounced with the muscles. For example, if a client is using the muscles of his stomach in an extremely tense way, you might unconsciously find yourself imitating this. Suddenly, you discover an unusual amount of tension in your abdominal muscles: This is **mirroring**.

However, with the same client you might find yourself rocking forward with your belly as you breathe deeply into it: This is **polarizing**. Or, you might briefly mirror the tightening in his belly, but allow that to move through you. This might result in a subtle mobility in your pelvis, more aliveness in your abdominal organs, and a slight increase in energy and breath from your belly, through your chest, and into your face and head: This is **sequencing**. Thus, mirroring is a conscious or unconscious replication of the client's physical state on the part of the therapist. Polarizing and sequencing may also be either conscious or unconscious. Polarizing is the movement of the therapist into a state that markedly contrasts or opposes that of the client. And sequencing is the therapist's initial perception of the client's state (which may include momentary mirroring or polarizing) and subsequent allowance of that state to evolve and develop in the therapist's body to a new, more comfortable, self-regulating state.

Muscular Facilitation

As with the skeleton, many muscular patterns will shift as the psychological issue is resolved. However, when there is a lingering pattern in the muscles, first try a light touch of awareness. For example, "You're still gripping in your hand." If that is easily released, no more need be done. However, the client may need to develop greater awareness around the pattern, in order to monitor it in his or her life. With more persistent patterns of constriction, the muscles respond well to an intensification of the constriction to facilitate release: "Really grip. Grip, grip, as hard as you can. And then let go." Be sensitive to the possibility of lingering emotional energy as well.

With long term patterns of flaccidity, some program of muscular toning may be necessary. If the flaccidity is not too extreme, the therapist could draw a movement or gesture out of the client's emotional process. The client could use this as a daily exercise. For example, in the work with Anna described above, she had been lying on her back with her feet on the floor and had lifted her pelvis up into the air as she said, "I don't want to hide any more." Anna worked with this movement each day for a period of about a month. This strengthened her weak psoas muscles in a way that felt more psychologically relevant to her than other exercises might have done.

In clients with an overall muscular rigidity, a simple awareness of when they shift into that pattern might be helpful. First, the awareness arises, which might lead spontaneously to a release of the muscle, and then further into a shift of awareness into the aspect of themselves that they were avoiding. For John, whose case is described above, when his muscles began rigidifying, he took that as a cue that he was having some feelings in his GI tract. By attending directly to those feelings, he disarmed his need to rigidify around them.

NERVOUS SYSTEM

The nervous system is a vast net of neural interconnections that comprises a self-organizing system. Observing the nervous system is a more subtle process than observing the muscles or the skeleton whose function is movement. Rather than observing gross movement and posture primarily, to observe the functioning of the nervous system one must focus on the overall integration of many functions. The nervous system functions are vast in scope: cognition, motor coordination, vision, hearing, speech, sleep patterns, internal and external perception, and coordination of visceral functioning. Within cognition we find many specific functions including memory, analysis, intention, planning, and imagination. In addition there are the overall emotional functions that organize our basic mode of relating to the world at any given moment.

The nervous system is vast structurally as well, and its definition is currently expanding. Traditionally, we have always included the brain and the spinal cord, which together comprise the central nervous system, and the peripheral nervous system, comprised of both afferent and efferent nerves of the somatic and autonomic branches of the nervous system. In addition, modern neurological research has discovered a plethora of neurological tissue in the gastrointestinal tract: 100 million nerve cells, as well as supporting cells, and a complex circuitry of connections. This system is now dubbed the enteric brain or the "gut brain." The gut brain can send and receive impulses, record experiences, and respond to emotions in a similar fashion to the cranial brain. The gut brain and the cranial brain mutually affect each other. However, the gut brain generally acts somewhat independently. The gut brain is primarily involved in gut feelings and digestive processes.

Another less concrete area of neurological activity is the "mobile brain," the network of chemical communication between all the cells of our body. This cellular communication can change both our physiological processes and our psychological processes and often does so simultaneously. For example, the hormone oxytocin (also a neuropeptide) stimulates uterine contractions as well as playing a role in maternal behavior and long-term monogamy. To give the reader a better sense of the functioning of specific neuropeptides and their body-mind interface, the following information derived from Jaak Panksepp's *Affective Neuroscience* lists primary neuropeptides and some of their basic behavioral functions. While this list tends to emphasize the behavioral functions and to a lesser degree the emotional functions, it only minimally acknowledges a few of the more basic physiological functions. Nonetheless, it can aid in a basic understanding of the range of peptide functioning.

Substance P (Pain and Anger)

Angiotensin (Thirst)

Oxytocin (Social Processes, Female Sex, Orgasm, Maternal Behavior, Social Memory)

ACTH (Stress, Attention)

Insulin (Feeding, Energy Balance Regulation)

Vasopressin (Male Sexual Arousal, Dominance, Social Memory)

a-MSH (Attention/Camouflage)

Bradykinin (Pain)

B-Lipotropin (Opoid Precurser)

CCK (Satiety, Panic, Sex)

Prolactin (Maternal Motivation, Social Feelings)

TRH (Arousal, Playfulness)

VIP (Circadian Rhythm)

LH-RH (Female Sexual Arousal)

Bombesin (Satiety, Memory)

Neurotension (Arousal, Seeking)

Met- & Leu Enkephalin (Pain & Pleasure)

B-Endorphin (Pain, Pleasure, Social Feelings)

DSIP (Sleep, Stress)

Dynorphin (Hunger)

CRF (Stress, Panic, Anxiety)

NPY (Feeding, Hunger)

Galanine (Memory) (Panksepp, 1998, p. 101)

Peptide a-MSH disperses pigment physiologically. Pigment dispersal correlates to its attention and camouflaging function. Vasopressin aids in "retaining" both memory on a brain level and fluid in the kidneys. At this chemical level, physiology and emotion are truly inseparable. Obviously the chemical information system is a fascinating interface. All of these peptides communicate directly from cell to cell, traveling within the body's fluid circulatory system. They act without relying on the transmission of nerve impulses along fibers. As we delineate the importance of the chemical communication system, we might discover that less than 2% of what we have considered neurological activity actually occurs at the synapse from one nerve fiber to the next (Pert, 1997). Thus, an estimated 98% of neurological functioning might occur within the chemical activity of this "mobile brain." The peptides and other molecules that are involved in this mobile brain have been dubbed *information substances*. Therefore, I refer to the whole system as the *information system*.

Glimpses into the Brain

The vast complexity of the nervous system renders it difficult to observe. However, there are several basic frameworks that can be used to get a sense of the current state of the nervous system. The nervous system is an integrator. Sensory input regarding the external environment is coming in from each of the special sense organs—skin, eyes, ears, mouth. Simultaneously and equally continuously, sensory input is coming from the sensory nerves monitoring our internal functioning. The vestibular mechanism monitors our relationship to gravity. The golgi apparati in the muscles monitor muscle length. The proprioceptors in the joints monitor joint position. The enteroceptors monitor the state of the viscera. In addition, there are pockets of more specialized sensory nerves tucked away in various nooks and crannies throughout the body. All of this sensory input is balanced with an overall sense of function: What are we doing now? And this is in turn balanced with the output of response or behavior. All responses and behaviors are in essence some sort of movement, whether it is movement of our eyes tracking an object we are looking at, postural shifts, speaking, or movement in space. Rodolfo Llinas, an elder in the neuroscience field, points out that nervous systems evolved to support movement. Thus, movement is essential to all neurological functions (Llinas, 2001).

The balance of movement between input and output is what we are intuitively tracking when we unconsciously test the nervous system of others. Examples of balance and imbalance of input and output can be seen in the flow of listening and responding in a conversation. Subtle shifts of posture occur as the world moves around us and we integrate those perceptions. In particular, slight shifts of head position tell us that a person is, in one moment, listening, in the next seeing, in the next thinking, in the next engaging with the world. These subtle movements in the head, face, and eyes, including pupil dilation and contraction are the key aspects of observing the nervous system. More prolonged placement of the head can indicate concentration on one neurological function, or it can indicate the disintegration of neurological dysfunction, such as processing difficulties, depression, fear, or shock. On the other hand, overly quick movements of the head sometimes indicate dysfunction as well, as in the more frantic orienting movements of anxiety or the jerky movements of disorientation.

Similarly, the subtle movement of the face and eyes tell us volumes about the state of the nervous system. Schore described the eye as "the visible portion of the central nervous system" (1994, p. 75). Dilation of the pupils can tell us that what has just occurred is exciting or frightening in some way. A flat gaze can tell us that this person is cognitively preoccupied. Similarly the face holds many neurological clues. A slight push forward in the jaw can tell us that a decision has been made to disbelieve what is being said. A minute slackening of the cheek muscles can indicate disengagement. As mentioned earlier, regarding the observation of all the body systems, our ability to perceive others at this level is innate. It has definitely been an evolutionary necessity to read the bodies of our fellow animals. What is unusual is to develop the ability to consciously articulate what is observed. As civilized and socialized animals, we have been trained to consciously disregard the minute shifts we observe in the nervous systems of those around us. It has been considered invasive to comment on these shifts, thus, we have become less conscious of them. However, the practice of psychotherapy is not bound by social protocol. Responding to these minute shifts of the nervous system can allow us to interact with some of the most basic, important, and somewhat hidden aspects of the client. To see the muscles of the throat constrict and ask, "What just happened?" allows both the therapist and the client access to less than conscious thoughts and feelings. Acknowledging minute shifts is a primary mode of BMP intervention with the nervous system.

Autonomic Arousal

Observing the nervous system is particularly important in terms of arousal levels within the brain. The autonomic aspect of the nervous system balances the focus of outer attention with internal functioning. The sympathetic nervous system mobilizes the skeletal muscles for action, increases the heart and respiratory rate, increases excitation hormonally, and heightens the sense perceptions and response time. Conversely, sympathetic arousal shifts the physiological emphasis away from digestion. Sympathetic arousal may be observed by flushing of the skin that accompanies increased peripheral blood flow, increased muscle tone, dilated pupils, and a general increase in alertness and responsivity. Parasympathetic arousal mediated by the vagus nerve has traditionally been thought to shift our organismic attention toward vegetative functioning, facilitating digestion and lowering heart rate.

Stephan Porges (1995) has added to our understanding of parasympathetic functioning and the vagus nerve with his **polyvagal theory**. He distinguished between two branches of the vagus nerve originating from two different nuclei in the brain stem. The ventral aspect of the vagus nerve originates from the nucleus ambiguus and related nuclei (Figure 2.9b). This ventral aspect of the vagus has a more recent evolutionary history and exists only in mammals, and is thus sometimes called the mammalian vagus or the "smart" vagus. The dorsal aspect is more ancient and is found in reptiles. The dorsal aspect of the vagus nerve originates from the dorsal motor nucleus. While Porges agreed with the traditional understanding of the sympathetic nervous system as primarily mobilizing the organism, he divided the parasympathetic functioning into the "engagement" function of the ventral vagal complex and an "immobilization" function of the dorsal vagal complex. The ventral vagal state of engagement can be characterized by a relaxed connection to the environment, head tilting that accompanies listening, higher tone and movement in the facial muscles, greater momentary variations in heart rate, breathing rate, and pupil dilation and constriction. The immobilized state is characterized by extremely low heart and respiratory rates, slackened cheeks and jaw, very low muscle tone, and minimal pupil dilation. This state allowed reptiles to survive underwater for prolonged periods and is less effectively integrated in humans. The immobilized state might be described as an extreme state of parasympathetic shock. This is different from the so-called freeze state which is characterized by high sympathetic arousal, including high heart and respiratory rates.

The autonomic nervous system functions through a continuum of various balances between the sympathetic and the parasympathetic branches. Allan Schore (1994) noted that the sympathetic and parasympathetic can function in a coupled and reciprocal state in which their arousal level varies reciprocally; that is, as sympathetic tone increases parasympathetic decreases. These functions can also be uncoupled and therefore vary independently. Furthermore, in fairly extreme states of shock, the two systems may be coupled and function in a parallel manner. Whether this is physiologically possible is currently a matter of scientific debate. If possible, this coupled state would be characterized by high tone in both systems. This might be the state of "playing dead" that prey animals resort to when they find no other way out. In this state the animal appears immobile, but internally their arousal level is very high. Given the opportunity, they can instantly rise from their seemingly near dead state and make a dash for it.

In the human being, the most common scenario in response to an external stressor is to initially raise sympathetic tone and decrease parasympathetic tone. As the stressor increases, the arousal might continue in this direction. At the point at which the person is unable to respond effectively to the external situation, one could say that the sensory input is overwhelming the ability for motor response. This state might be described as **sympathetic shock** (Emerson, 1999). If the external stress continues, the dorsal vagal tone might increase alongside the sympathetic tone. This state might be best described as a "high arousal immobilization." Finally, at some point the organism might give up the sympathetic arousal and stay in a collapsed, withdrawn state of high dorsal vagal tone. This state might be described as **parasympathetic shock** (Emerson, 1999). It aids the clinician to realize that these extreme states can shift from second to second or get frozen into an ongoing state over time. Helping clients track their own arousal levels and learn to modulate their arousal levels within a healthy range is one of the primary tasks of psychotherapy.

Relaxed Alert

Brains function best in a state that has been dubbed "relaxed, alert." This is intuitively obvious and has also been confirmed through neurofeedback in which the rhythm ranging from 12 to 15 hertz is called the sensorimotor rhythm (SMR). SMR lies within the upper range of the so-called alpha brain state, which is relaxed but awake (8 to 12 hertz) and the lower end of the beta range (13 to 30 hertz), the range of normal waking consciousness. SMR has been studied in a variety of contexts with both animals and humans, in both stringent studies and more questionable ones. It has been said to correlate with better neurological functioning and, increased resiliency to strokes and head injuries (Robbins, 2000). It is also likely that Porges's state of engagement with relatively high ventral vagal tone is an aspect of this relaxed alert state. While the importance of SMR is under scientific debate, there is no question that a balanced arousal level within the nervous system is important for optimal functioning. Additional evidence of this was found in Porges's research, which indicated that higher ventral vagal tone was potentially helpful in a variety of neurological dysfunctions, particularly autism (1996).

As therapists, we can support our clients to find and strengthen their ability to stay within an optimal arousal range, both through education and interaction. Educationally, to initiate clients into an awareness of their neurological state can be extremely helpful. In her book, *The Highly Sensitive Person*, Elaine Aron (1996) introduced the concept to the lay public that a significant portion (15 to 20%) of the human species has evolved with a particular neurological sensitivity. Aron points to the evolutionary efficacy of having a small number of clan members who are able to perceive stimuli more acutely than the average person. This increased sensitivity would be helpful in detecting both physical phenomena, such as the sound of an approaching predator, or interpersonal phenomena, such as subtle manipulation in a negotiation. So many clients in therapy have been trained to feel bad about themselves because they are "too sensitive." Reframing and understanding this sensitivity can aid clients in being better able to protect themselves from overstimulation and in cultivating greater appreciation of the positive aspects of their sensitivity, such as compassion for others or artistic sensibility.

Supporting clients to recognize and modulate their neurological states can also improve their relationship to themselves and their functioning in the world. Learning how fatigue and overstimulation affect their states can lead to changes of lifestyle and self-care. On a more moment to moment basis, tracking arousal level during the course of the therapy session can encourage the client to more actively self-regulate. Most fundamentally, we can support our brains to develop in a healthy direction.

The Developing Brain

Human brains change throughout the life span. There are two forms of brain growth: the growth of new neurons and the growth of new dendrites. In addition, there are continual prunings of dendritic growth as well as continual neuronal death. These may occur in a specific brain area due to stress, disuse, or aging. There are also periods of development in which major pruning is genetically programed to occur for all humans. All of these brain changes result in developmental spurts, changes of focus, and behavioral changes.

The first two years of life include the most dramatic phase of brain development. During this time, our brains are developing so rapidly that our ability to learn is unparalleled. Interaction with other human brains is essential for stimulation and regulation. Adult brain functioning and structure are significantly affected by patterns developed during the first two years. Following this period, major development of the brain occurs in spurts throughout the life span. The seventh year is significant for cognitive functioning. The sixteenth year sees a similar leap. In late adolescence and young adulthood there are periods of minor brain growth, but also major prunings occur. These prunings can be correlated with early onset psychotic behaviors, and the like. There are minor periods of brain growth throughout midlife. In addition to these phases of programmed growth and pruning, periods of change occur in response to experience. Raising children, learning a new language or musical instrument, and engaging in psychotherapy have all been documented as stimulating brain growth. Recognizing the plasticity of the human brain can aid psychotherapists in understanding behavioral change.

Interactive Psychobiological Regulation

As discussed in Chapter 2, Schore's (1994) idea of interactive psychobiological regulation described the manner in which two brains interact with regulatory rhythms from each other. Our cycles of excitement, anxiety, and recuperation are shared, exchanged, and modified in our interactions with others. Basic templates of excitation, engagement, and withdrawal are established during infancy in our interactions with the caregiver. They form the basis of adult cycles of energy, both individually and in relationship. Understanding the particular templates that were established in infancy can further the psychotherapeutic process. Moreover, developmental neuroscience is encouraging psychotherapists to recognize the repatterning of these cycles as a basic function of psychotherapy. This recognition can allow the therapy to focus directly on these energetic states and the relationship, thereby intervening at the root source rather than more peripheral behavioral symptoms. Finally, understanding the connection between these early patterns and their contribution to later resiliency or vulnerability to trauma lends support for seeing interactive regulation as primary in the treatment of complex traumatic stress.

Schore encouraged a clinical focus "not on mental states but on psychobiological states . . . " and defined empathy "as not so much a match of verbal cognitions as a nonverbal psychobiological attunement" (1998, p. 1). BMP training in observing the body through posture, breath, movement, and voice tone, is excellent preparation for tracking and responding to the state shifts of our clients. Specifically, BMP trains **interactive psychobiological regulation** in the following ways.

1. Through training in acute sensory awareness we strengthen the connection between cortical awareness and lower brain functions. This training strengthens a feedback loop important in autoregulation and thereby potentiates the therapist's ability to autoregulate. Therapists' conscious development of their own autoregulation becomes the experiential basis for educating clients in both autoregulation and interactive psychobiological regulation.

2. Through consciously experiencing the links between emotions and sensations, as well as the "emotional tone" of sensations, we are strengthening the cortical-lower brain link, specifically in the areas of affect.

3. Through working with mindfulness and awareness practices of every variety (mindfulness of sensation, breathing, somatic activity from internal viscera to blood flow to muscle tone, somatic awareness), we are developing a propensity for awareness states which inherently tend toward sympathetic-parasympathetic balance. This contributes to therapists' cultivation of a restful alert state, which is clearly related to the psychoanalytic "evenly hovering attention."

4. Through working with emotional expression and containment, we expand our tolerance of stimulation, as well as potentially expanding the range of our own optimal levels of arousal.

5. Through the sequencing and dialoguing of conflicting sensori-affective material, we are better able to respond authentically to our clients through eye contact and vocal tone.

6. Through tuning our own bodies to finer gradations of perception and expression, we are honing the skills of interactive psychobiological regulation.

Schore (1994) saw the psychotherapist as a potential interactive psychobiological regulator for clients with "early forming right hemispheric primitive emotional disorders." This could apply to a wide range of diagnostic categories from depression to anxiety to posttraumatic stress disorder (PTSD), as well as obsessive-compulsive disorder (OCD), phobias, and attention deficit disorder (ADD). In addition, I have found these principles to be highly applicable in regulation issues within family systems pertaining to parenting, intimacy, and sexuality.

As psychotherapists, a great deal of our work is about educating clients both explicitly and implicitly regarding self-regulation. Schore's work is an articulate reminder that our greatest tool in the education of our clients is through our selves, through our psychobiological interactions with our clients. I experience this to be true on the level of modeling as well as within the transferential relationship. Affective neuroscience, in general, and Schore's model of interactive psychobiological regulation in particular, are strong reminders to body psychotherapists to thoroughly marry the relational and somatic aspects of our work. I propose that **relational somatics** are fundamental to any psychotherapy that truly aspires to interactive psychobiological regulation.

Relational Somatics

Relational somatics is a specific aspect of interactive psychobiological regulation. In rhesus monkeys, mutual grooming is an interaction used in stressful situations to mutually calm through lowering heart rate (Judge & Waal, 1997). I find much of the mechanical work of somatics to be similar to the grooming behavior. Whether we are adjusting alignment or discussing breathing patterns, there is the potential for the same sort of intimacy as in grooming—brief light contacts (possibly including touch, but not necessarily) focusing on another's body. Attention to the client's sleep patterns, eating habits, posture, breath, internal sensations, all can be used as relational tools. As we become aware of our clients' state, it supports their own awareness of themselves. As our clients become conscious of their own subtle state shifts, they develop a deeper relationship with themselves. The following case illustrates the process of relational somatics leading to greater self-mastery.

Hank was a charming and light-hearted young man with a couple of restraining orders lurking in the background and a bad track record with rage mismanagement. He became enraged when his girl friends distanced themselves from him. He engaged in minor physical violations and gross verbal and spatial ones. He was an intelligent young man and knew that he had "problems" that prevented him from being able to "keep a girl friend." His parents were teenagers when he was conceived and not fully able to parent an infant. His early history included semiabandonment by his father after his parents' divorce when he was 3 years old. His father had been rageful toward his mother. At age 13, Hank began acting out enough with mom to be sent to live with dad. He was eager to bond with his estranged father, but soon found that his father's emotional energy went into frequent and noisy sex with a constantly rotating cast of short-term girl friends. Hank's adolescent experience was marked by excruciating loneliness, trying to get dad's attention, and having to listen to dad have loud sex with his girl friends several nights a week.

Hank and I worked for about a year reviewing his history, establishing a relationship, teaching him to notice feelings of anger in his body, and learning to both sequence and contain those feelings.

After a year, Hank had some understanding of his early attachment issues and how they triggered the rage. He was maintaining a decent job and was off probation and all restraining orders had been lifted. We had a no-rage contract, excluding even verbal rage. The agreement was that he would call and talk to my machine when he was "on the edge of raging." If necessary, I would call back. This had worked fairly well for about six months. Then independent of any external circumstance (he was between girl friends) his rage became activated for a period of about 10 days. We met twice during those 10 days. These two sessions were both extremely simple and immediate.

Hank would lie or stand and breathe while feeling the rageful impulses in his body. He described the sensations related to these impulses as "hot, fast, pressure everywhere in my body," a sympathetic arousal. I would sit about one foot away and gently reassure him that I was there, that I believed he could get through these feelings without raging. Periodically, he would escalate, and move toward exploding. At those moments, we discovered that his diaphragm was constricting. I would encourage his awareness of his breathing and his abdomen. When his thinking accelerated, he would continually insist that he could not tolerate the sensations, that he had to lash out. At these points, I would bring him back to his body awareness. At other times, we would pace my office side by side as I simply stayed in contact with him and encouraged him to stay in contact with his own bodily experience.

We worked with grounding and parasympathetic breathing into the lower abdomen, but primarily it was my simple embodied presence that was the fundamental tool. I did not go into my own sympathetic arousal in response. Instead through voice tone and presence, I helped him experience that he could have contact with himself and with me during these rageful states and that the physiological states would both shift and eventually pass. Through this he learned to metabolize these states, not only employing greater parasympathetic inhibition of the rage, but also lowering his arousal level.

I asked him to look at me often throughout this process. He would look, with hardened pupils. Often I just said, "Hi," at those moments. His pupils and breathing would soften a bit. As he felt the contact those moments provided, he would resist them more, "I can't, I can't look at you." These moments were deeply imbued with transferential feeling. "Yes, you can," I'd say barely audibly, "I'll wait till you can." And then he would.

Within 24 hours after the second session his rage subsided. He felt very proud of himself for getting through. He teased me a lot about saying "Hi," when he looked at me. He said that I was "being like a little kid." I heard this statement as, at least partially, projective. I let myself be teased and told him that I thought it was good when adults were able to be soft and vulnerable with each other.

Hank and I continued to work for two more years. He remained free of any legal charges or restraining orders during that time. His relationships matured and deepened and we terminated on an optimistic note.

These sessions with Hank illustrate the heightened marriage between the somatic and the relational aspects of the therapeutic alliance. During those two sessions, there was a stark quality in which nothing else existed but *relational somatics* or *interactive psychobiological regulation*. There was no content, no chatting, no education. Just the moment to moment labor of birthing a more mature version of Hank's self. Clearly, changes in patterns of brain functioning were required for this change. It is possible that structural brain changes occurred as well.

Brain Care

Our brains are often the source of a great deal of our psychological and physiological suffering. Since our brains do not have sensory nerve endings, we do not readily notice when they are stressed. Modern life and the extremely high level of stimulation it brings, results in an epidemic of neurological overstimulation and brain fatigue. Since our brains thrive on repetition and so readily habituate, they become attached, at times addicted, to states of overstimulation. Addressing overstimulation is fundamental in working with many of our modern syndromes, particularly ADD, ADHD, head injuries, anxiety, and depression. Introducing brain care requires becoming acquainted with brain distress. The clinician can help in pointing out relative shifts in and out of brain distress, as observed through all of the tracking devices mentioned earlier. Through developing a sensitivity to brain functioning, the individual can consciously seek a balance of the nervous system—a balance of rest and activity, mental and physical activity, internal and external foci, input and output.

Draining the Brain

The simplest framework for balanced brain functioning is to track the basic directional flow of input and output. Brain input arises from the peripheral nervous system, up the spinal cord, up through the brain stem, and then generally moves through several brain centers for processing. Optimal brain functioning often involves the coordination of nearly every center of the brain. As the brain processes the input and formulates potential responses, relays of communication occur between different brain centers. When the processing is complete, a response directive is relayed down, through the center of the brain, into the brain stem, down the spinal cord, and out the peripheral nerves.

Since there are no sensory nerve endings in neurological tissue, we do not sense our neurological activity directly. However, we do sense it indirectly through surrounding tisssue, particularly the blood vessels of the brain, the connective tissue surrounding the brain, and the muscles and joints of the head and neck. In addition we are aware of our ability to think more or less clearly and to respond in a relaxed, alert manner. Through these indirect indicators, we can learn to sense the balance of flow through our brains. One aspect of this optimum functioning could be some sort of harmony in the rhythm of firing between neurons in different parts of the brain. Llinas (2001) described oscillations that occur within neurons, minute variations across the cell's enveloping membrane. Furthermore, he stated that neurons "that display rhythmic oscillatory behavior may entrain to each other via action potentials. The resulting, far-reaching consequence of this is neuronal groups that oscillate in phase—that is, coherently, which supports simultaneity of activity" (p. 10). This coherence of firing occurs within the overall directional flows of brain functioning. Sensory information moves up the spinal cord and brain stem and, then processing moves within various brain centers, and finally a flow of response moves out of the brain, through the brain stem, into the spinal cord, and out into the periphery of the body. By attending to this flow, we can optimize our arousal levels and neurological functioning.

□   □   □   □

Take a position that allows free movement of the head and spine, either lying supine without a pillow, standing symmetrically, or sitting upright so that no portion of the spine is bearing weight. Take a moment to attend to the sensations of the head, face, and neck, including the mouth, throat, soft palette, and eyes. As you feel these sensations, breathe gently through the nostrils into the head, remembering that the sutures between the cranial bones are designed to shift minutely with fluid pressure changes within the head. As you breathe gently and sense your head and throat, allow the head to rock gently as if floating on the spine. Feeling the sensations as you breathe and gently rock your head, sense areas in your brain that might feel agitated or pressured or other areas that might feel frozen or numb. Visualize, imagine, sense a balanced easy flow of neurological activity that moves rhythmically through the whole brain, unwinding any imbalances and sequencing down and out of the brain stem and spinal cord. The soft palete provides an excellent landmark for sensing the brain stem which lies just above and behind it. To locate the soft palate, press gently upon the hard palate, the roof of the mouth with the tongue or a finger. The soft palete begins at the back of the hard palate. Allow your soft palate to pulsate gently with your breath. As you breathe, sense, and rock your head gently, allow any tremors or twitching that might occur as the nervous system sequences out the periphery of the body.

□   □   □   □

Variations or portions of this exercise might be used both to promote awareness of the nervous system and to regain neurological equilibrium. Particularly in cases of anxiety or PTSD, brief moments of sensing the brain and allowing it to unwind, might occur regularly throughout a session as the client becomes hyperaroused. This tool can be added to the standard abdominal breathing for client's self-care and anxiety management outside the therapy session.

The fundamental support for the brain is to allow it to be integrated back into the rest of the body. All of the other tissues and functions of our bodies can offer support to the brain, if they are allowed to. The irony of the BMP focus on the brain is that we focus on the brain, so that the brain can become less of a focus. By aligning the head on the spine, the rest of the body can structurally support the brain. By attending to nonmental aspects of ourselves, autonomic regulation and recuperation can occur. The fluids of the body can offer a soothing support to the brain, particularly the cerebral spinal fluid. A few moments of sensing the inherent fluidity of brain tissue and the buoyancy provided for it through the intrinsic and surrounding cerebral spinal fluid can also calm an agitated brain, flailing for safety. Thus, in general, awareness and activity of the rest of the body can support the nervous system to not become overzealous and overwhelmed.

Chapter 9

Systems of Experience

The Skin, Fluids, Fat, Viscera,

and Endocrine System

While the systems discussed in Chapter 8—the muscles, the skeleton, and the nervous system—structure our experience, the systems explored in this chapter fill out that structure with many layers and textures of subtle sensory experience. These systems are, in a sense, more personal and less extroverted in their functioning. For this reason, they are often neglected in the busy focus of modern lives. Through this neglect, their experience may become subconscious and blend together to form an inarticulate backdrop of experience a climate which we may rarely notice, but within which we live our lives. Exploring some of these systems may be a bit more ephemeral than the previous ones. In that case, proceed slowly, make an initial acquaintance, and recognize that this strange system is a large part of your daily life.

SKIN

Our skin forms the largest organ in the entire body. In utero, during the first differentiation of tissue into the three basic tissue types, the ectoderm is the outer most tissue layer. Both the skin and the nervous system evolve out of the ectoderm, thus, defining their inherent connection. The skin contains such an abundance of sensory nerve endings (thermal, mechanical, and noxious) that it is clearly seen as an extension of the peripheral nervous system. Psychologically, this sensitivity forms an important aspect of the skin's somatic quality. This sensitivity can become habituated toward either pleasure or invasion.

Boundary formation is the other psychologically relevant aspect of the skin. The skin is the clearest physical boundary of our selves. We can observe others as being comfortable "inside their own skin," "filling out their skin," or "shrinking within their skin." In order to feel comfortable with the boundary formed by one's skin, it is necessary to trust the ability of your limbs, speech, eyes, and brain to protect the self from invasion. This ensures that the skin has only to define the boundaries within its scope. Without this protection, the skin becomes either hypersensitized or desensitized to touch.

We can observe others' relationship to their own skin through the fullness of their bodies. Does their breath and movement seem to include the skin? Indirectly, we can observe their relationship to boundaries in general. And most directly, we can observe their habits of touching themselves. Do they ever indulge in self-touch that is light and caressing, or is their self-touch only conveying pressure, or is there no self-touch at all?

Self-touch is a powerful means of communicating with oneself, both to establish a sense of self and boundary and to self-soothe. Encouraging self-touch of various qualities in the client can allow them to deepen into their own relationship with their bodies, and to gain a sense of intrinsic safety, and a sense of having the power to give themselves pleasure and safety. Many somatic approaches to psychotherapy utilize techniques in which the therapist touches the client. In BMP, self-touch is used for much of this, as a way of empowering the client and avoiding enmeshment between therapist and client.

Self-touch can be used to wake up a part of the body that has become dissociated. Self-touch can be used to reassure parts that are frightened. Teaching clients to use a quality of touch that is reassuring and feels good can be a major turning point. This is especially true with clients with a history of early sexual abuse, in which there is learned confusion between nurturing touch and arousing or invasive touch. In our culture in general, that confusion seems to be spreading into our overall understanding of sexuality. Touch that is purely intended to arouse tends toward objectification. Touch that is communicative and acknowledges the subjectivity of the other has a quality of nurturance whether arousing or not. Creating an environment of self-respect and self-care can culminate in cultivating the ability to touch oneself in a loving way. The following case vignettes illustrate the importance of this sort of touch.

Dorothy was a newly divorced, middle-aged woman with an adolescent son. She was somewhat lonely, but also somewhat invigorated by her first forays into the career world. She was in a mode of discovery that spanned from craft projects, to taking classes, to learning to have an orgasm. She felt it was about time to have an orgasm! She had gone to a bookstore and found a self-help book, but was getting a bit frustrated. As our rapport grew, we discussed the degrading sexual treatment she had received from her husband. She was shamed for wanting an orgasm, and generally treated like a masturbation device. Having come from a family in which her father regularly degraded her, she had not questioned her treatment. It was to her credit that she had been able to keep up her self-esteem as well as she did.

I encouraged Dorothy to imagine what it might be like to actually feel love for herself. We started with her experience of loving her cocker spaniel. She visualized him running toward her and felt the front of her body soften—warmth and openness seeming to spread from her heart area. She noted these bodily expressions of love. The first time she experimented with directing these feelings toward herself, she actually flinched. She realized that it had been dangerous to attend to herself in this way, inviting the ridicule of her father or her husband.

Over the period of a few sessions, she was able to sustain thoughts of loving herself and stay relaxed and present in her body. I encouraged her to place her hand over her heart as she breathed, felt the sensations in her heart area, and contemplated loving herself. She became so accustomed to doing this, that she often did it spontaneously in our sessions. We began to discuss approaching masturbation from this point of view, backing off of the orgasm focus so intensely, and actually focusing more on making love to herself. She was fearless in her experimentation and her willingness to discuss details with me. I showed her anatomical pictures of the female pelvis and pelvic floor area and taught her Kegel exercises to strengthen her vaginal muscles and increase blood flow to the area. She was successful in achieving orgasm. She scheduled another appointment, but canceled it later, reporting that she felt good, and I never heard from her again.

The following case vignette is similar to Dorothy's focus on healthy self-touch, but the context is different in several ways.

Will had a history of repeated physical beatings throughout his childhood. As he grew older his sexuality mixed with the abuse in difficult ways. He began to fuse the abuse into his sexual fantasies while simultaneously seeking refuge in a series of intensely idealized romantic relationships. At the age of 40, Will had had three excruciating divorces and was full of hatred for women. Will had been in therapy for several year-long stints which he said had been extremely helpful. He knew a great deal about himself and had a shrewd understanding of human relationships. He was ready to take the next step. He had a tendency to fly into traumatic rages when he felt discounted by a lover. We worked to understand that these were not righteously justified by his lovers' lack of wisdom and understanding. We worked with developing an ability to track his own arousal level and stay out of the danger zone. Having made progress in these areas, he was ready to embark on romance again. In discussing this step, he realized that he was very traumatized around his sexuality. He remembered a homosexual experience with older boys that had become violent. This experience seemed to have planted the trauma from his childhood physical abuse into his genitals. We worked to resolve this memory.

As he began to get closer to a woman he was dating, he decided to wait until he felt ready for intercourse. He reworked his attitudes around male performance. He began to realize that his genitals were terrified of having intercourse.

As we had worked with self-touch during the trauma resolution and arousal modulation, he felt comfortable touching most of his body during our sessions. I suggested that his penis might need the same reassuring touch that had helped his head and his belly. He grinned and told me that I was really outrageous. I reassured him that other men had been okay touching their genitals in my office. We talked about safety, clarified boundaries, and he ended the sessions comfortably cradling his penis. I encouraged him to spend some time with his genitals, breathing, feeling, touching, talking, and listening to them each morning or evening in bed. He did this and worked further with his performance anxiety in this way.

We discussed what it might feel like to enter his next sexual relationship from a ground of safety and self-love. He and his new girl friend waited three months until they had genital contact and six months until they had intercourse. After they had intercourse, Will felt very comfortable with their sexual relationship and had no need to discuss it again.

Both of these case vignettes illustrate the complex relationships between skin, boundaries, self-love, and sexuality. The fact that both these vignettes are sexual is somewhat circumstantial. Working with self-touch is pertinent to any issue involving self-soothing or self-love, as illustrated by Dorothy's touching her chest to feel her heart more fully. However, the vignettes involving sexuality most readily delineate the full range of issues encompassed by the skin. Skin is an untapped area of strength and delight in our culture. Self-touch solves so many of the dilemmas that reside around the use of touch in psychotherapy. If the psychotherapist is patient enough to cultivate the client's relationship to it, great rewards can be found.

FLUIDS

Our bodies are composed of at least 70% fluid. The first life on this planet was little more than a primitive membrane surrounding seawater. As multicellular life evolved, it evolved from this basis, so that even the most complex of life forms can be seen as a series of membranes containing a continually circulating body of fluid that has as its basic constituency the same molecular elements as seawater. In prevertebrate organisms, the circulatory system was the basic communication system. As vertebrates developed sophisticated nervous systems, neurological activity continued to rely on the communication provided by the circulatory system. Biologists Dianna and Mark McMenamin (1994) developed a theory about the viability of terrestrial life, called *hypersea*, which explains the dependency of terrestrial life on the continual circulation of fluids via a network between all organisms, relying heavily on parasites, fungi, and viruses. Thus, terrestrial life lives within a virtual marine environmental matrix, the hypersea. All of this is to underscore the fundamental importance of fluid to the very existence of life.

Beyond the physical importance of fluid, there is the psychological importance of flow. Theoreticians from fields as divergent as sports psychology and organizational design agree that the psychological state of flow is the essence of optimal performance. Mihaly Csikszentmihaly devoted an entire volume, *Flow: The Psychology of Optimal Performance* (1994), to this state of grace. Perhaps, as organisms that are primarily composed of fluid, we do best when we are closely aligned with fluid dynamics. Most proponents of the "flow" experience encourage cultivation of this state through visualization, meditation, diet, exercise, and self-talk. Many clinicians are not aware of the access to a flow state that can be provided by an awareness of the actual fluids that circulate in our bodies.

□ □ □ □

Give yourself a few moments to sink into your body. Take a
comfortable position and focus generally on the practice of em-

bodiment. Feel the sensations in your body, and give those sensations permission to move and breathe and sound however
they like. As your attention shifts, follow it wherever it goes
and feel those sensations. After a few minutes of this, step back
and notice the patterns of sensation in your body. They form
an energetic map, marking areas where there is a great deal of
activity, stagnant areas, and areas that are relatively still or
empty. From this vantage point, contemplate the reality of being mostly fluid. This body is mostly fluid that is pulsing and
oozing, streaming and resting, but continuously circulating
through your body. This fluid bathes each cell, bringing nutrients and information, carrying away messages and wastes. Feel
the reality of fluidity in this body. Let go into being fluid. Allow
your solidity to float. Allow your breathing and movement to
arise out of fluid movement. Notice how this attention to fluidity changes your energetic map. Imagine that the parts that feel
moist and flowing seep or pour into the drier parts. Spend a
few minutes this way, continually resting into an overall sense
of flow.

□   □   □   □

In BMP, therapists begin by cultivating fluid awareness in their own
bodies. With time, this allows an embodiment of flow and an identification with the philosophy of flow and its fundamental sense of acceptance and trust. As an experience of flow and an identification with
fluidity deepens in the clinician, it allows the exchange of interactive
psychobiological regulation to more deeply convey that most fundamental message of the holding environment, "that everything is truly
okay right now."

Beyond this intuitive level of communicating flow, the clinician is
able to track the client's flow, acknowledge that, and support the client to develop it. Flow is observable through every human function—
speech, movement, decisions. While some people adopt a superficial
veneer of flow, it has a decidedly different feel. A somatic experience
of directly feeling flow and allowing one's behavior to be based on
that flow conveys a sense of easy vitality. In Chapter 6, we discussed
the relationship between the sense of self and an experience of flow
through the core. Observing clients shift away from their centers and
into more fragmented, less fluid states can be responded to in much
the same way as discussed previously. Encouraging clients to come
back to themselves and a sense of flow through their core can be the
beginning of restoring flow throughout their whole system.

FAT

Just writing the word in italics, in bold, alone on a line, has a power to it. Our culture generates a great deal hatred and fear of fat. We have very little understanding of it. For this reason, fat takes on an especially important role in many people's psyche, an area in which the culture seems to condone self-aggression. Socially there is some encouragement to be gluttons, and at the same time, to hate our fat. In the name of purely cosmetic effects, we legally allow and openly advertise self-mutilation of our fat.

Fat has very few sensory nerve endings and no motor functions. In that sense, it is one of the hardest systems of the body to observe. Certainly we can observe where and how a person carries fat on their body. We can observe what they report about their relationship to food, eating, and body image. And when the time is right, we can ask about their relationship to fat. Discovering how a person thinks about fat, feels about discussing fat, and receives information about fat is perhaps the most revealing way to observe someone's relationship to fat. This is often a very charged topic that will result in exploring family history. Within this, I find it important to educate people about the role of adipose tissue in the body as a storing of resources, the importance of fat reserve to general health, survival of illness, neurological functioning, and menstrual health for women. Discussion around this sort of issue can offer further diagnostic information regarding the client's relationship to fat. Often much of the work is desensitizing the aversion to fat and introducing the positive roles of fat in the body. If this is accomplished, it is possible to move on to the psychological importance of fat. Fat nurtures, warms, protects, and insulates. When the therapeutic process is focused on an eating disorder or body image issues, the client's relationship to fat may come to the forefront. Otherwise, it might rest in the background, just being lightly touched upon from time to time, as the client works with larger issues of self-acceptance and nurturing. The following case vignette illustrates this process.

Joan came to therapy afraid of a serious depression that arose after a major career disappointment. As a 25-year-old woman, she was still learning about herself, her values, and the nature of human interactions. As a side issue she mentioned her concern about her weight and her desire to be more disciplined regarding exercise. Joan was an incredibly passionate person with high standards for herself and a well-thought out philosophy of life. She did not have much tolerance for her own failings and negative emotions. We worked primarily with bridging the gap between who she really was and who she expected herself to be. Slowly over time, Joan learned to allow herself to feel whatever she was feeling. She became able to distinguish between her thoughts and her feelings. As she did this, she learned to allow herself to cry, to feel angry or afraid, and to give herself time to process feelings in therapy, with friends, or through writing in her journal. As these abilities developed, her depression lifted and she felt increasingly more confident over time that the next wave of sadness was not going to lead to months of depression. Throughout this process, her concerns over her weight and exercise came up periodically. I encouraged her to work toward accepting herself and creating a healthy lifestyle, rather than dieting. As Joan felt better about herself, she became serious about a man she was dating.

By this time, Joan had a cognitive desire to accept herself and challenge the self-criticism that was keeping her from letting her partner fully see and enjoy her body. This cognitive acceptance formed the basis for actually experiencing her fat. In sessions, we would talk about the positive aspects of fat: softness, energy reserve, nurturing, protection. As we did this, I would encourage her to touch her arm, for example, and feel her fat. At home, she practiced indulging in the sensual softness of her body both alone and with her lover. She spent time looking at herself naked in the mirror, breathing, moving, and talking to herself about what she liked that she saw. Finally, she talked to her partner about her issues around her body image. This presented a further challenge. He was fairly phobic about fat himself, and confirmed that he saw her as slightly overweight and that most of the women he had dated before were quite slender. On the positive side, he reaffirmed his love and appreciation for her. Joan was taken aback, and did not know how to react. Her resources rallied. She reframed the fat issue as a feminist issue, and became more militant in her campaign against fat phobia. She challenged herself to wear a bikini at a beach party and over time became more and more convinced of her fat-friendly rhetoric. This experience became an almost symbolic focus for all of her empowerment issues in relationship. She and her partner became engaged and began phasing out of therapy shortly after resolving this crisis of fat.

Joan's relationship to fat was fairly easy to address through education. In the following vignette, Lizzy has a serious medical challenge.

Lizzy was diagnosed with diabetes as a young girl. She was insulin dependent from that time on. At 45, she was in a stable but unsatisfying marriage and the mother of two teenagers. She was also 100 pounds overweight. Lizzy had been overweight since childhood. She seemed to have inherited the stocky body type that characterized her mother's side of the family. The diabetes also necessitated eating regularly and seemed to make it easier to gain weight. By middle age, Lizzy had tried everything. She exercised regularly and tried to control her portions as she had learned through Weight Watchers. She had done some metabolic testing and tried a few supplements to shift her metabolism a bit. She even maintained some of the supplements that a naturopath had recommended to her. Her weight seemed to be stable. Though she was significantly overweight, Lizzy had a relatively mild eating disorder. She would get discouraged about her weight and binge a bit once every week or so. She also hid her eating from others to a certain degree. For the most part, however, she had learned a great deal from Overeaters' Anonymous about a healthy relationship to food, and strove to practice this to the best of her ability. Therapy was yet another attempt to resolve her weight issues.

Initially, we explored the difference between coming into therapy to lose weight and coming into therapy to accept herself as she was. She recognized a lifetime pattern of denying her needs and accommodating others. Out of this, she began to become more assertive. We began to look at her relationship to her feelings. She realized that she did not allow herself more than a brief recognition of most negative emotions. The exception to this was discontent with herself regarding her weight. We practiced emotional expression and she developed an awareness of the somatic feeling of allowing emotions to sequence through her body. Through this she experienced the difference between holding onto her emotions and the feeling of letting go. She sensed a relationship between this and holding onto her weight.

Lizzy called a family meeting and told her family that she was going to change her behavior. When she was mad, she was going to practice saying so. There were going to be more times when she would say no to their needs. When she was sad or frightened, she was going to allow herself to feel these feelings as well. She warned them that they might not like her behavior as much this way, but that this is what she needed to do to feel better about herself. Her family was a bit leery of the whole process, but she forged ahead. Her project of self-care took off in several directions. She got a part-time job. She went out to lunch with friends. She began to exercise more. She recognized that she had been somewhat depressed. She lost a few pounds in this process, but began to accept that maybe her weight was not going to change significantly. It had never occurred to her before that she might need to be this weight to be healthy, that there might be some kind of balance there. This seemed to help her relax with the issue somewhat. We explored cultures in which women her weight were seen as extremely sexy. She really responded to this and experimented a bit with her appearance. Overall, she adopted a much more proactive approach to herself and her life.

Both Joan and Lizzy were healthy enough to be able to benefit from explorations of the positive aspects of fat. Clients with extreme eating disorders are usually dealing with much more complex psychological issues. In those cases, while it may be educational to present the physiological facts about fat, it is most important to continually bring the focus to the psychological issues that are symbolized by the physical issues. Ultimately, the process is one of freeing the fat from the emotional projections.

THE VISCERA

The viscera comprise the largest portion of our core (Figure 9.1), filling our throat, thoracic, abdominal, and pelvic cavities. We experience the viscera most directly through an extensive system of enteroceptors—sensory nerves specific to the viscera. The autonomic nervous system needs to keep a constant dialogue going with the viscera so that we can maintain our internal functioning and balance. Information from the enteroceptors to the autonomic nervous system can continue on to the prefrontal cortex and become conscious as that information is sought. However, in our highly stimulating culture, the fast-paced sensory input coming from the external environment seems to demand all our attention. We are not encouraged to attend to our internal sensations, but rather seek to minimize that input through external stimulation. When internal sensations become pronounced, we often seek medical consultation and attempt to stop the sensations as quickly as possible through medication and surgical procedures. Our autonomic nervous system is so intricately connected to our emotional processes that many sensations coming from our enteroceptors are, at least partially, emotionally initiated. Through attending to these gut sensations we can gain information about our emotional state and any imbalances between our internal processes and our environment. However, if these initial sensations are ignored, the stress that they reflect may develop over time into medical conditions. Stress is indicated as a factor in so many disease processes today, from heart disease to gastrointestinal distress to any immunological impairment, including cancer. In the case of disease, BMP can be highly effective in unraveling the emotional factors and supporting physical healing.

Nathaniel was a 40-year-old lawyer, married with two children. He was youthful, intelligent, and physically fit. He had been suffering

FIGURE 9.1 THE INTERNAL VISCERA

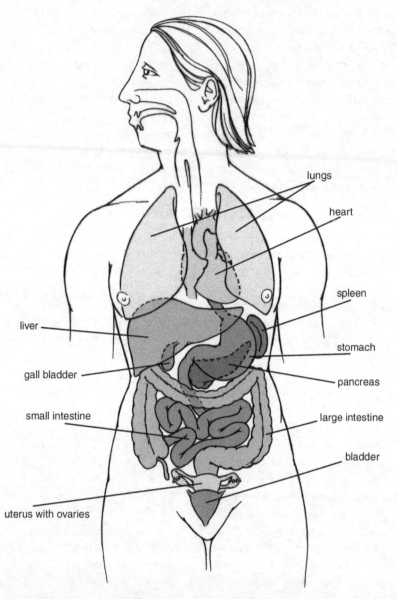

from esophageal refluxing for over a year. His physician had prescribed medication which had alleviated some of the discomfort, but not all of it. His physician suggested that stress might have been exacerbating the condition, and on the advice of a family friend Nathaniel decided to try counseling. We began by just feeling the area of greatest discomfort, his lower esophagus, around his diaphragm. We explored his desire for the sensations to go away and he was able to recognize that this thought was accompanied by a constriction of his diaphragm area. Nathaniel recognized that this constriction was counterproductive. Breathing into this restriction, Nathaniel resigned himself to working with his condition in a gentler way, rather than just trying to get rid of the sensations.

We began a practice of sensing and breathing into this area. Nathaniel discovered that he had a great deal of impatience when he attended to his body in this way. He felt that he had an internalized message to "get out there and keep going." He related this message to his family of origin and his mother in particular. The whole family was very oriented toward accomplishment. They had been proud of Nathaniel's abilities and pushed him to excel. He had enjoyed the process for the most part. However, he had begun to question it after having children and watching his wife with their children. When they snuggled in her lap, he realized that he had never had that kind of nurturing and felt a longing for it. Though he had a decent relationship with his wife, he did not feel that they were able to connect in the same intimate way that she connected with their children. I suggested that perhaps he needed to learn about this nurturing with himself first. Over the next few weeks, Nathaniel spent a few minutes a couple of times a day breathing into the burning in his esophagus and relaxing the whole area. He felt a very significant decrease in the pain to the point where it almost completely disappeared. He also realized he could predict when it was going to happen based on his stress level.

Nathaniel also noticed a vulnerable feeling that would arise when he did his breathing practice. He was uncomfortable with this feeling and sought my advice on how to get rid of it. We laughed about his constantly trying to get rid of things in this part of his body. Was there anything worth keeping there, I wondered? Indirectly, two answers arose to that question. One was spirituality. Nathaniel's wife was involved in a meditation group and she had dragged Nathaniel to a meditation gathering. He had resisted it, but recognized something there that he was seeking, something he was "hungering for." With this phrase he gestured with his hand right to the spot that often pained him. Perhaps this spot was reminding him of his spirituality. How was the vulnerability connected to spirituality? Nathaniel was able to get a sense of this and began adding moments of chanting and prayer to his breathing practice. At this point, Nathaniel's change process heated up. He discontinued his medication for the refluxing, asked his wife to go on a vacation with him, and began attending the meetings of her meditation group. After 10 sessions, he felt that he had gotten what he needed from individual therapy and was ready to go. He discontinued individual therapy and was anticipating that he would need to do some therapy with his wife in the future. His refluxing had not reoccurred within a two year period after discontinuing therapy.

Nathaniel experienced his visceral organs through the initial pain of his condition. As therapy progressed he was able to sense more subtle emotions in that area. I was able to observe his posture, initially he was folding in around this area, and later opening up that constriction. I was able to observe his breath not moving into his abdomen initially and then later moving through this area. Nathaniel's voice changed when he attended to his esophagus. It softened and deepened in pitch slightly. His behavior and attention shifted toward internal values, such as spirituality, vulnerability, and nurturing. He unconsciously gestured with his hands toward the area in his viscera that was feeling and processing his emotions. This process of slowly recognizing the presence and importance of our visceral self is common to adults in our culture.

A second important factor in this case is the process of **intrasubjective intersubjectivity**. In the psychoanalytic world there is interest in exploring the intersubjective space between two individuals. This refers to a shared, mutually created aspect of relationship and includes intimacy. I use the term *intrasubjective intersubjectivity* to acknowledge the internal relational space that we can create by attending with one part of ourselves to another part. In Nathaniel's case this was a relationship between himself and his upper gastrointestinal tract. With Nathaniel, as is so often the case, by developing a relationship with an important and ignored part of himself, he developed a greater ability to create intersubjective space with others.

Nathaniel's therapeutic process pointed immediately to the viscera through his medical condition. More commonly, there is more of a lack of feeling rather than an excess of feelings, that draws the attention there.

Beth was a large woman in her mid-30s, very intelligent with a generally reserved demeanor, though there were occasional flashes of humor through her eyes. She had a history of repeated hospitalization for suicide gestures and depression in her late teens and early 20s. After her last hospitalization, she became dissatisfied with the mental health field and decided to find ways to help herself. She discovered fitness training and EST-like self-help groups. Through these vehicles she felt she had taken responsibility for her life and avoided further hospitalizations. She felt she was generally able to handle her emotions through exercise, but occasionally cut herself, not as a direct attempt at suicide, but as a means of stopping emotion. She had broad social connections and became involved in volunteering with AIDS patients. She came to therapy because she had become attached to an elderly AIDS patient, Jim, who had died recently, and she found herself quite depressed in the wake of this loss.

The only child of a single mother, Beth reported a lack of bonding between them. She experienced her mother as constantly anxious and only interested in survival and appearances. She recalled no tenderness and affection between them and repeated shaming and insensitivity. Beth displayed no affect in discussing her mother and they maintained a cordial, though distant relationship. Beth acknowledged that her mother did the best she could and Beth's desire was to move on and take responsibility for her own quality of experience.

In discussing Jim, Beth's eyes teared up and she talked about how special it was to love and care for him, how fully she gave herself to their friendship, and how wonderful it felt to finally bond with someone. She described herself as dysfunctional after his death. While there were moments of affect in telling this story, there were many moments of flatness, holding her breath, constricting her chest, and gazing blankly away. We acknowledged this and I encouraged her to breathe into her heart and chest area as she spoke. She acknowledged that she dissociated a great deal and appreciated that I was encouraging her to "come back." As Beth breathed into her chest and went more deeply into her feelings, she also went more deeply into a dissociated state. She began to feel a numbness and a tingling in her face and hands, and her eyes and thoughts lost contact with me. This happened in a matter of moments. I encouraged her to get up and walk around the room, feel her body, and come back to herself, the room, and contact with me. She struggled to do so and said that this was the kind of feeling that induced her to cut on herself. We made a plan for her to go to the gym after the session.

In the next session, Beth and I agreed that in order to proceed with talking about Jim and actually feeling the feelings that would arise, she would need to be more grounded in her body. She asked if I had anything that she could hold in her hands as we talked. I gave her two small balls that fit into her palms. I suggested that she sit on a large physioball to talk and she decided to take off her socks to do so. In this way, she stayed in contact with her hands through the small balls, her feet through contact with the floor, and her pelvic floor through the physioball. I applauded her creativity, and pointed out that she also needed to stay in touch with her trunk. She had been practicing breathing into her chest and had made a definite improvement in her ability to do so. I found that even making such a small step as

*this illustrated remarkable self-motivation. However, with her chest a bit more open,
it was even more apparent that her abdomen was very pulled back as she sat on the
ball. We practiced rocking forward on the ball so that her weight moved through
her abdomen. This allowed the beginning of a connection through all of her viscera,
both thoracic and abdominal. Having practiced all this, she was able to tell me a
bit more of the story of her relationship to Jim and his death without dissociating
so much. However, I had to interrupt her very frequently, at nearly every sentence,
and encourage her to feel inside.*

Her intense depression dissipated after this session, and slowly,
overtime Beth was able to tolerate more breathing, energy, and emotion through her trunk. She remembered the intense feelings of emptiness that she experienced throughout her childhood and young
adulthood. We contrasted those feelings with the "amazing feelings of
really loving someone else." She was slowly able to touch those feelings in her chest and belly without dissociating. We spoke of this as
Jim's legacy, and Beth became ready to discontinue therapy, eager to
integrate this legacy on her own.

The viscera are involved on a physical level with our most basic
needs—oxygen, water, and food—in a nutshell, basic nurture. This
means that they are directly involved in the earliest exchanges between fetus-infant and caregiver. Thus, the viscera are deeply affected
by that earliest attachment and carry into adulthood remnants of early
infantile needs, frustrations, and attachment styles. Because of this, the
therapist's slow, gentle, and repeated interest in how the client is feeling
"inside," provides the client and the therapist with a direct interaction
with some of the most primitive relational patterns. The repetition of
interest in these internal experiences is also augmented by the prolonged attention lent to these areas, as discussed in Chapter 6 in the
section entitled "Listening and Allowing." By staying with the visceral
sensations and feelings, the relational message is that these most personal of feelings and their concomitant needs are important and val-
ued in the relationship with both self and others. This is another
example of relational somatics. This often flies in the face of the original attachment style that communicated frustration, neglect, or lack
of attunement to these same sensations and their expression.

Psychoanalytic literature has been intrigued with the subtle emotional
responses that flit across the analyst's face in a matter of nanoseconds.
Beatrice Beebe, a leading psychotherapist and infant researcher at Columbia University, stated that interactions involving facial responsivity
occur in .25 seconds. Based on this and other nonverbal aspects of

communication, Beebe wrote, "We need to expand the playing field of adult treatment to include nonverbal behavior, and we need to teach ourselves to observe ourselves and our clients at this level" (Beebe, 1999).

In working with sequencing through the viscera, one readily discovers the strong link between the viscera and the face. Without higher level inhibition, the face naturally expresses the visceral experience. This means that emotional processing occurring in the visceral naturally sequence into facial expression.

Both Schore's (1994) and Porges's (1995, 1996) work affirmed the basic relationship between the neurological mechanisms involving the face, the emotional exchange in relationship, and the autonomic nervous system, with its functional link to visceral regulation. In an overarching analysis, Tucker (2001), at the University of Oregon, delineated an in-depth sequence of neural structures relative to meaning in language. He posited fundamental neurological networks linking the limbic brain structures, those generally assumed to be central to emotional processing, to the brain structures in the brain stem relating to the viscera. Through the work of all of these neurological researchers, the link between relationship, emotion, the face, the autonomic nervous system, and the viscera is becoming clearer and clearer. In addition there is the influence of the gut brain or enteric brain discussed earlier, which links emotion, digestion, and overall well-being or malaise. In any case, there is ample support in the current research to imply that the viscera are an important area of study for psychological clinicians, both to increase their own level of awareness and that of the client. In BMP training clinicians become conscious of the input from their own enteroceptors, the sensory nerve endings in the viscera, particularly how extremely effective they are in amplifying and concretizing the clinicians' sensitivity to their own emotional processes and those of their clients. I call this work **enteroceptive training**. It is based on the general approach to embodiment, but is focused on the viscera. A basic understanding of the location of particular visceral organs (Figure 9.1) in one's body is helpful. From there it is a matter of attending to sensations in those areas and including them in embodiment practice.

THE ENDOCRINE SYSTEM

The endocrine system consists of a series of endocrine glands located in the trunk that produce and secrete hormones directly into the bloodstream. The endocrine system has a complex function, revolving around the influence, regulation, and control of metabolism, growth, reproduction, and other cycles. The list below presents a simplified introduction to each of the endocrine glands (Figure 9.2).

Pineal gland: Cone-shaped gland within the brain at the inferior, posterior aspect of the third ventrical that secretes the hormone melatonin, which may synchronize biorhythms with day/night cycles.

Pituitary gland: Located in the brain, connected to the hypothalamus. The pituitary sends hormonal signals to other endocrine glands, initiating growth and reproductive cycles. The pituitary secretes growth hormone, antidiuretic hormone, prolactin, and oxytocin.

Thyroid gland: Located anterior to the larynx. Produces the hormones thyroxin, triiodothyronine, and calcitonin, which regulate metabolism, body heat, and bone growth.

Parathyroid glands: Four small glands embedded on the posterior side of the thyroid gland whose hormones regulate the use and function of calcium and phosphorus.

Thymus: Located posterior to the sternum, secretes thymosin which stimulates white blood cell production.

Pancreal Islets of Langerhans: Small bodies within the pancreas that regulate blood sugar level through the hormones insulin and glucagon.

Adrenals: Located above the kidneys, they regulate autonomic activity through the hormones epinephrine, cortisol, and aldosterone.

Ovaries: Produce estradiol and progesterone, produce eggs and influence reproductive and sexual cycles and female characteristics.

Testes: Produce testosterone, stimulating sperm production and male characteristics.

In addition to these endocrine glands, other organs of the body produce hormones. These include the hypothalamus and other brain structures, the heart, the stomach, and the intestines. The endocrine system is a part of the information system discussed as part of the nervous system, and is inextricably linked to neuropeptide functioning. The endocrine system is also intrinsic to autonomic functioning. Indeed the endocrine system and the nervous system are so mutually interdependent that they are often discussed together as the neuroendocrine system.

Similar to all of the aspects of the information system, the endocrine system acts through its chemical messengers that are received

FIGURE 9.2 ENDOCRINE GLANDS

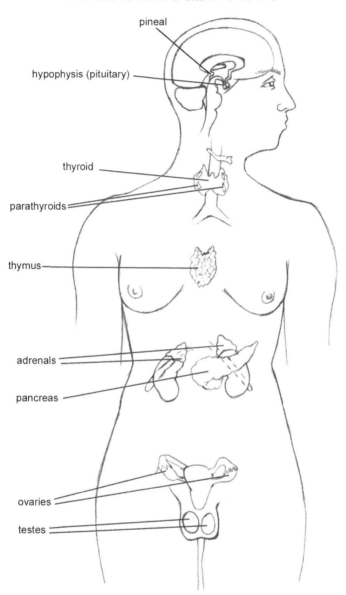

(From *Natural Intelligence: Body-Mind Integration and Human Development* by Susan Aposhyan (p. 137). © Copyright 1999. Lippincott William and Wilkins. Reprinted by permission.)

by receptors on the cell membrane. The endocrine system acts dramatically and affects mood, overall bodily state, and energetic balance.

Observing the endocrine system is again an indirect process. One perceives its footprint rather than local sensations in the endocrine glands. Occasionally, one might experience the initial flush of an endocrine gland in the process of a major secretion. This would be experienced as warmth or activity directly in the area of the gland itself. Generally, however, one experiences global chemical sensations throughout the body. Overall states of excitement or tranquility are healthy extremes of the endocrine system. On a continuum of pathology, we could cite anxiety and depression. Clearly these states are neuroendocrine functions which parallel autonomic states. Nevertheless, energetic states may fit into an overall pattern that is more significantly endocrinological than autonomic. Taking a history of information pertinent to the endocrine system can help reveal these patterns. Areas to be explored include: the level of anxiety and stress the mother experienced during gestation; the degree of trauma surrounding the birth; significant stress or sedation in the childhood home; the history of puberty and sexuality; drug or alcohol use; history of spirituality, artistic activity, or thrill seeking.

This history may reveal significant turning points in which certain states emerge or disappear. These turning points provide significant clues regarding the client's developmental process. Particularly significant are the personal and familial relationship to excitement, inspiration, tranquillity, bliss, anxiety, agitation, depression, and drug use. A history of sexuality, including age of puberty and menopause is also quite relevant. Drug use greatly affects endocrine balance and can also reflect attempts to create certain states that the endocrine system craves; for example, to heighten artistic or sexual states. Alcohol and drug use can be used to self-medicate endocrine imbalances, with drugs being somewhat more relevant to the endocrine system, while alcohol may be somewhat more relevant to the nervous system. Understanding the endocrine system and its influences can allow some control over the global energetic states engendered. The following case vignette differentiates between local sensations of the viscera and their related psychological issues, and the global sensations of the endocrine system. In this case, local sensations refer to sensations that occur in a particular location in the body, for example in one organ. Global sensations refer to sensations felt throughout the body. The client's interest in art, spirituality, and passion typify an individual who is very sensitive to and greatly affected by hormonal states.

Susette was an artist in her late 20s who spent most of her time painting in her studio. She had not fully differentiated from her parents who gave her emotional and financial support. She began to develop symptoms of agoraphobia, avoiding social contacts and having mild anxiety attacks when she had to go out to do errands. At the encouragement of her parents, Susette sought psychiatric help, was diagnosed as bipolar II, and began attempting to find a suitable balance of medications. The psychiatrist also encouraged Susette to begin psychotherapy. During the course of psychotherapy, Susette explored basic issues of maturation and individuation. Independent of psychotherapy, she became extremely resistant to the idea of medication and after a couple of months refused to continue. This refusal was related to her work with a nutritionist to counteract a rather extreme case of candida.

At this point, I encouraged her to begin to chart her mood swings, her menstrual cycle, and her diet. She began to see relationships between depression and her menstrual cycle. She also found that extremely stimulating events such as art openings and love affairs were often followed by a cycle of depression independent of her menstrual cycle. She began to be more sensitive to her chemical state. Through tracking subtle, global, vibratory sensations, she was able to become aware of shifts in her chemistry. She learned specific coping behaviors for both the more manic phases of her cycle, as well as the depressive phases. When she sensed herself in an overall state of excitement, joy, or slight mania, she practiced not believing that all her fantasies were real. She practiced grounding through her belly, pelvic floor, legs, and feet. When she sensed herself in a fearful, withdrawn, depressive state, she checked her menstrual chart and reviewed her recent activities for any causes of this state. She learned to gently nudge herself to eat well, exercise, and have easy contact with friends. She learned to remind herself that each state would pass. She also found that particular kinds of breathing practices were effective in balancing her chemistry. The foundation of all of these management skills was her ability to feel her chemical states. Through this, she learned to manage her mood swings sufficiently to maintain stability without medication.

This aspect of Susette's work relates to the manifestation of global emotional states of the neuroendocrine system. Often, however, we experience emotion as localized. These emotions are more often muscularly or viscerally expressed. Joy might be experienced as an uplifting lightness in the heart; anxiety as a churning of the gut or burning in the gall bladder; fear as constriction of the shoulders. We will continue to use Susette as an example of this.

As Susette was sorting out her conflicts around a love affair, she found several localized emotional experiences. Her womb felt contracted and pulled back. She interpreted this as feeling afraid of betrayal by her lover. Her heart felt open and drawn to this man. As Susette became aware of where she felt these different responses in her body, she learned to use the tools of somatic dialogue between these two parts. She was able to create more continuity of movement sequencing between the two.

Localized emotion and global emotions can be overlapping and are certainly mutually influencing. The term **localized emotions** refers to emotions experienced in one or two particular locations in the body, via localized sensation. The term **global emotions** refers to emotions experienced throughout the body via globalized sensation. In Susette's case, when she was in a more manic phase, she tended to ignore her fear and just went with her heart's feelings. When she was in a more depressive phase, she became obsessed with focusing on her womb's feelings. Both the heart and the womb were expressing emotions felt in those locations. However, her depression and her more manic states were experienced more globally, throughout her whole body.

Both localized emotion and global emotion can be influenced by our cortical perspective on the emotion, through the process of mutual feedback loops. Reassuring cortical messages can slow down an anxiety or fear response. An apprehensive cortical response can escalate them. Conversely, a cynical attitude can diminish joy, whereas a welcoming response can allow joy to blossom. In Susette's case, she practiced touching into an awareness of her whole body in both manic and depressive states. She practiced dialogue between her heart and her womb. This allowed her to integrate these levels of emotion. In somatic clinical work, it can be helpful to differentiate between local and global emotions.

Since the endocrine system is so thoroughly integrated with the nervous system and other systems of the body, it illustrates well the interrelationship between the systems. This is always the case in working with the body systems. However, it is helpful to explore them independently by way of introduction.

The endocrine system is also interrelated with the nervous system by way of beliefs. Although there are no good studies documenting this, it has been my clinical experience that core beliefs seem to create particular physiological patterns, most readily through the endocrine system and other aspects of the information system. For example, many people are raised with the notion that they are "too much" (i.e., too energetic, active, emotional, expressive, or the like). I have witnessed people find greater hormonal balance after resolving their internalized beliefs that their basic way of being was somehow wrong. For example, Susette believed that she was "too sensitive and too emotional." On a practical level, it is clear that this belief greatly affected her behavior and thereby exacerbated her depression. However, it is clear that beliefs have a direct physiological effect as well. This is particularly true of the endocrine system, which is both sensitive and volatile and therefore has a great potency, both for health and for confusion.

PART IV

ANCHORING CHANGE
IN THE BODY

Chapter 10

Energetic Development

The Interaction Between Early Motor
Development and Psychological Development

Energetic development refers to the interface of psychological development and physical development. The template of early motor development gives us a framework for tracking energetic development.

As a culture, we have explored psychological development from a variety of perspectives. At this point we can continue to examine how nurture interfaces with our nature to create character and self. This approach supports an integration of biology and psychology and a body-mind approach. Body and mind are clearly mutually effective in the process of development.

In understanding psychological development, we have historically relied on the clear stages formulated by Freud, Piaget, Maslow, Mahler, and others. Contemporary neurological research has given us much more information about the shaping of the basic templates of our nervous systems during the first two years of life. Schore (1994) and others have helped us understand the interface between attachment and this early and fundamental neurological development. Daniel Stern and colleagues (1998) have articulated the highly experiential nature of the world of the infant.

As developmental study focuses on early, preverbal experience, the importance of the body becomes paramount. During this period, our bodyminds experience the world and formulate our earliest responses. These early perceptions and responses form a template through which later experience is mediated. Thus, this template becomes the basis of our character structure and clearly influences the expression of the self. Early motor development is a particular template that allows us a means to articulate distinct states in this process, as well as a way of somewhat distinguishing the basic differences between character and self. However, before we embark on a detailed look at energetic development and early motor development, let us begin with defining character and self.

CHARACTER AND SELF

Damasio defined the self as a composite of bodily state and autobiographical memory. "You rise above the sea level of knowing, transiently but incessantly, as a *felt* core self, renewed again and again, thanks to anything that comes from outside the brain into its sensory machinery or anything that comes from the brain's memory stores toward sensory, motor, or autonomic recall" (1999, p. 172). To further clarify the core self, Damasio wrote:

> I have come to conclude that the organism, as represented inside its own brain, is a likely biological forerunner for what eventually becomes the elusive sense of self. The deep roots for the self, including the elaborate self which encompasses identity and personhood, are to be found in the ensemble of brain devices which continuously and *nonconsciously* maintain the body state with the narrow range and relative stability required for survival. These devices continually represent, *nonconsciously*, the state of the living body, along its many dimensions. I call the state of activity within the ensemble of such devices the *proto-self*, the nonconscious forerunner for the levels of self which appear in our minds as the conscious protagonists of consciousness: core self and autobiographical self. (1999, p.22)

In BMP, self is seen as an amalgamation of past, present, and future. The past component is that of our memory of our bodily and environmental circumstances; the present component is our current sense of the state of our bodies, and our future projection of this body, its abilities, and circumstances. Character, on the other hand, is a more functional and transactional construct. Whereas self includes an internal sense of capability in various circumstances, character implies external behavioral patterns, how we manifest self and interact with the world. This distinction will become clearer as we explore the basic neurological actions, our template for early motor development.

EARLY MOTOR DEVELOPMENT

Our understanding of early motor development is based on the basic neurological actions which arise from both evolutionary studies and neurodevelopmental therapy. Body-Mind Centering has developed a precise method of looking at early motor development and the following description is derived from that work. As human infants progress from infancy through the first year, culminating in learning to walk, we recapitulate the basic patterns used by progressively evolving species for locomotion.

We begin our movement with the **pulsating motility** of single-celled and simple multicellular organisms. This movement is fundamental to all life, through all levels of complexity. It is this pulsing motility that is the basis of the experience of flow described in the previous chapter.

The next stage of animal evolution brings us to the branch of the animal kingdom called *radiata*, simple multicellular creatures that have a center and are arranged concentrically around this center. This stage of life exhibits the first prevertebral, rudimentary nervous systems. Some phyla of the branch radiata, such as hydras, have netlike nervous systems (see Figure 2.8). They continue to move with a pulsating motility, although this conforms to a certain directionality implied by their body shape. Other members of the branch radiata, such as the starfish and other echinoderms have a central nerve ring with radial nerves and a modified nerve net in each arm (see Figure 2.8). These prevertebrates move by pulsating contractions, beginning in their centers and radiating out. This **radiation** is the second phase of prevertebral locomotion.

The next phases of evolution are all generally characterized by some sort of bilateral, rather than radial body shape. A bilateral animal not only has a top (dorsal side) and a bottom (ventral side), as in the radial starfish, but a head end and a tail end, and thus a left and right side. Prevertebral animals with heads and tails move from their heads to their tails, through a **mouthing** sort of movement. This parallels the **spinal movement** of vertebrates (Figure 10.1a). Vertebrates without fins use purely spinal movement. The next distinct level of neurological action is the **homologous** movement of the amphibians (Figure 10.1b). Picture a frog leaping; upper limbs move together, lower limbs move together. Next, we have the **homolateral** movement, which is

FIGURE 10.1a SPINAL MOVEMENTS OF VERTEBRATES

FIGURE 10.1b HOMOLOGOUS MOVEMENT OF AMPHIBIANS

FIGURE 10.1c HOMOLATERAL MOVEMENT OF REPTILES

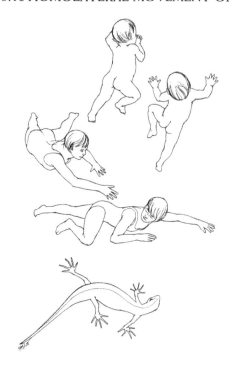

FIGURE 10.1d CONTRALATERAL MOVEMENT OF MAMMALS

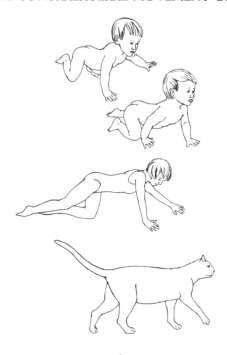

an innovation of the reptiles (Figure 10.1c). Lizards represent homolateral movement most clearly. In homolateral movement, the limbs
on the right side move together, antagonistically to the limbs on the
left side. Finally, with mammals, we add **contralateral** movement to
our repertoire, movement in which the right upper limb moves in con-
cert with the left lower limb, and vice versa (Figure 10.1d). Contralateral movement is the movement that humans use to walk, run, and
do the freestyle (Australian crawl) swim stroke. These four stages of
movement developmen and organization were articulated in neurodevelopmental therapy by Temple Faye (Wolf, 1968).

These stages of locomotion follow the same basic order in our early
motor development as they did in evolution. There is a basic neurological template through which the human infant's motor development
follows a basic evolutionary blueprint. The human being begins utilizing the pulsating motility action as a zygote. As each phase of movement emerges, the earlier stages serve as foundations and supports for
the more advanced actions. This is a fundamental principle of developmental movement, that the primary actions are integrated into and
provide support for the later actions. Pulsating motility forms the
foundation of flow and connection throughout life. In that sense, the
more basic the action, the more influential it is in a person's energetic
development. The movement of radiation begins with implantation of
the fetus and the formation of the umbilical connection with the
mother. This movement of radiation is basic to a person's sense of
center. Mouthing and other spinal movements begin in utero and are
clearly of primary importance throughout development, moving the
core of the body and forming the basis for the core self. Homologous
movement and homolateral movement also begin in utero, but are not
thoroughly explored until after birth through interaction with gravity
and a supporting surface. While contralateral movement may occur
randomly during gestation and in the early months of life, it does not
generally appear as an organized form until later in the first year of
life. Gravity assists in the development of spinal movements as well.
During the first year of life, the infant engages in a developmental dance
that involves squirming, pushing, sliding, rolling, crawling, reaching,
and creeping and results in the ability to stand and begin walking,
generally around the first birthday.

These basic patterns of movement can be diagrammed in simple
ways. Pulsing motility is basically centerless and involves the whole
organism. Radiation is organized around a center. Spinal movement is
bipolar. Homologous movement differentiates the upper and lower
halves. Homolateral movement connects the upper and lower and dif-

ferentiates the right and left sides of the body. Contralateral movement connects the limbs diagonally through the core.

In BMP, we use the term **endpoints** to refer to the face (head),
pelvic floor (tail), hands, and feet. Through their extensive sensory
nerve endings, their small intrinsic muscles, and their being free ends
of the skeleton, the endpoints of the body are able to both sense and
respond to the world with accuracy and sensitivity. Neurologically our
movements are most organized when initiated at the endpoints of the
body. Both the animal and the infant, as they interact with the world
through the endpoints do so by using five fundamental actions: yield,
push, reach, grasp, and pull. These actions were articulated by Bonnie
Bainbridge Cohen (1993) and form the building blocks of locomotion.
Yield refers to an action of moving into contact with a force, either
external and internal. Yield may involve a softening, a release into
gravity, or may be more a psychological allowance of an internal
force. Yielding is more contactful and aware than collapsing. The
other four actions are more self-explanatory. However, in BMP, as we
look closely at how each of these familiar movements is initiated and
sequences, their complexity is revealed. Bainbridge Cohen added
these five actions as performed by each of the various endpoints to
develop the 12 basic neurological actions.

TABLE 10.1 TWELVE BASIC NEUROLOGICAL ACTIONS

Spinal Push from the Head
Spinal Push from the Pelvic Floor
Homologous Push from the Hands
Homologous Push from the Feet
Homolateral Push from the Hand
Homolateral Push from the Foot
Spinal Reach from the Head
Spinal Reach from the Pelvic Floor
Homologous Reach from the Hands
Homologous Reach from the Feet
Contralateral Reach from the Hand
Contralateral Reach from the Foot

While each of us is neurologically compelled to experiment somewhat with each of these 12 movements, we vary tremendously in how
fully we develop, utilize, and form neurological frameworks around
each action. This variation in our early motor development corresponds
with the tremendous variation in human psychological development
during the first year of life.

ENERGETIC DEVELOPMENT

At the same time that this instinct-driven flurry of early motor exploration takes place, the infant is exploring and developing herself and
her environment, particularly the relationships with her primary caregivers. As Stanley Greenspan (1997) pointed out in his seminal work,
Growth of the Mind, none of the infant's development proceeds in isolation. It has only been our professional limitations and biases that have
formed the artificial boundaries between aspects of development. Thus,
it is logical that there is a strong and formational interaction between
the infant's experiences of self and interaction with caregivers that
forms the basis of psychological development and each infant's unique
experience of early motor development. In fact, it is obvious that
through the infant's experiences of yielding, pushing, reaching, grasping, and pulling with both caregivers and his or her environment, that
a sense of self and character is formed.

In clinical observation of individuals of any age, we can, in fact,
characterize their psychological profile fairly completely by describing
their relationship to the basic neurological actions. The following description serves as an illustration to this.

*This individual has a very strong push upward through the head that also
involves the forehead and the eyes. This push extends downward through the cervical
spine, but is then almost completely truncated at the top of the thoracic spine. There
is very little vitality in the arms, including a relative absence of yield; the arms
hang limply by the sides with only the slightest hint of grasping. This minute grasp
is homologous through the upper limbs (involves both arms), sequencing through the
chest, heart area. There is a quite adequate homologous push from the lower limbs
(a push that involves both feet and legs) that sequences clearly from the feet through
both legs into the trunk and up to the ribcage. Minimal homolateral or contralateral
movement are evidenced.*

Translating the above paragraph onto your own body, while requir-
ing a bit of effort, will teach you a fair amount about energetic development. This description is styled after a classic figure from literature
and cinema. Can you guess who it is? Psychologically, this character

would tend to be focused and determined with little variation in focus. The character would be relatively self-sufficient with minimal need or ability to contact others. Does this fit with your impression of Frankenstein?

MOVEMENT ANALYSIS

While it takes a bit of an investment to learn this system of movement analysis, the effort is minimal relative to the abundant yield of clinical insight. This insight falls into two primary areas. One area is an immediate sense of the bodily role in character style, psychological state, and psychological development. The second area is an in-depth understanding of the developmental edge that is pertinent to the individual at that time and will afford the clinician the greatest leverage for focused change.

Observing the actions is to observe both the shape and the fullness of the pathways involved. These pathways comprise the connections from one endpoint to another (Figure 10.2). Based on these observations, one can surmise which fundamental action is being used, and combining this with the pathway, one then knows which basic neurological action is occurring. For example in the description above, we first observe the exaggerated push in the head. This would relate to the spinal push from the head. Then we observe a grasp in both hands. Second, one can observe the sequencing of an action along its' pathway. Once the action sequences from the initiating endpoint all the way to another endpoint or endpoints, that action can be said to be sequencing fully. However, generally in adult movement, we find that many, if not most actions are more or less truncated, that is, not fully sequencing along their own pathways.

Therapeutic use of the observations of energetic development fall along three different lines. The first has to do with discovering the developmental edge (Figure 5.1). Through the developmental edge we observe where clients are and are not sequencing in their bodies. This edge of sequencing can be analyzed according to the basic neurological actions (BNAs) involved. It can also be analyzed in relationship to the psychological issues at hand.

The second and related use of observations regarding the BNAs is in reconciling the psychological developmental issues that are occurring in the client's life with the current sequencing of the BNAs. This can render a more developmental understanding of the client's character structure, an understanding that is at once dynamic and implies emergent qualities. This is in contrast to approaches to character analysis that tend toward a more static and pathological view. The third

FIGURE 10.2a THE SPINAL AND HOMOLOGOUS PATHWAYS

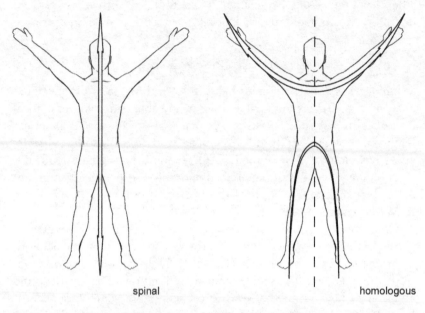

spinal   homologous

The first two of the four basic pathways through the body based on neurological stages.

FIGURE 10.2b THE HOMOLATERAL AND
CONTRALATERAL PATHWAYS

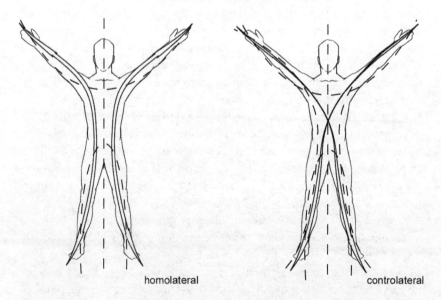

homolateral   controlateral

The second two of the four basic pathways through the body based on neurological stages.

aspect of observing the current sequencing of movement is the possibility of supporting clients' awareness of their direct experience of interacting with the world, feeling the developmental edge, and practicing the newly emerging movement options.

The following case studies illustrate the interaction among various actions.

Benjamin was a middle-aged engineer, raised by British parents of Indian descent in South Africa. Benjamin greatly admired his mother's beauty and intelligence, but felt unloved by her. His father was alternately loving and rageful to the point of minor physical abuse. Benjamin was raised by a black South African nanny whom he loved and by whom he felt somewhat loved in return. However, his nanny would disappear for long periods of time when she returned to her native village. When Benjamin was 18, he followed her to her village and was welcomed into a celebration there. During this visit, Benjamin became sexually involved with a young African woman. When her brothers discovered them, Benjamin was severely frightened. He ran off into the night and made his way home on his own in a state of disoriented traumatic stress. He was hospitalized after this experience and was unable to sleep alone for several years. He gradually stabilized and accompanied his parents when they immigrated to the United States He was able to work part-time as an engineer but he never established a long-term intimate relationship. He longed to travel to India and live on an ashram with an Indian guru that he followed, but he did not feel he could tolerate the anxiety that such a move would provoke.

At 37, Benjamin began BMP after having been in one form of therapy or another for most of his adult life. Benjamin had an excellent understanding of his psychodynamic history and recognized that he had an insecure attachment with his mother.

He needed to internalize a feeling of being loved and supported by a mothering woman. He felt that he needed me to physically hold him. I resisted his urgency and invited him to join me in forming a emotionally secure relationship that would allow us to explore his needs.

Benjamin alternated between a victimized, helpless stance and a rageful, demanding one. Physically he enacted his victimization by pulling (grasping) all his endpoints in toward his center and reaching toward me helplessly with fearful eyes. From this place, he quickly transferred a familiar feeling of dependency onto me. He experienced my unwillingness to physically hold him as a fundamental rejection and would become rageful at my denial of his basic needs. In this rageful state, there was a very spinal strong push that came through his head and eyes and voice. However, that push was held at both ends by a grasping at both endpoints—in the forehead, eyes, and mouth, at one end, and in the entire abdomen, from the diaphragm through to the pelvic floor, at the other. There was also a strong homologous push from the hands that would come up with this rage. This homologous push was truncated by a grasping in the back thoracic area and in both hands.

Our work was very precise in the beginning, and involved constant negotiating. I was on trial and continually acknowledged my inadequacy. Benjamin thoroughly explored all of my neurotic tendencies and basic flaws. I allowed him to express anger directly to me by psychologically pushing me away thereby supporting his homologous push. At times, Benjamin felt that he wanted to physically push me away but realized that this was too terrifying to him. Nonetheless, he was able to continue to experiment by verbally and psychologically pushing me away. As he began to trust that I was accepting of his anger and his boundaries, and that he could not drive me away with anger and setting boundaries, he became able to physically push me. We would stand facing each other, hand to hand, to push. As this realization reached a certain saturation level, we moved into a new phase.

Slowly, Benjamin's terror surfaced. He was afraid to feel and afraid of my abandoning him. As this happened, his jaw would quiver slightly. This involuntary movement terrified him. Over a period of several months, I continually reassured him that I was not frightened about his jaw quivering and that I thought if he allowed the quivering to happen that we could work with it in a safe way. Allowing this quivering to happen, allowed him to diminish some of the grasping he did in his jaw and his head. Over the next year or two, Benjamin became so comfortable with this quivering that it ceased to be something he noticed and he could even let it happen on the rare occasions when he cried alone. With the small amount of freedom that came with the quivering, Benjamin had a bit more access to his spine and core. This was a release of a part of that initial grasping in his head. This allowed a greater degree of spinal yield and spinal push to emerge.

At this point, Benjamin's desire to rage became his focus. He was simultaneously terrified to rage, fearing that his father would annihilate him for asserting any power, and felt urgently compelled to assert himself. This conflict manifested in a complete loss of any awareness of his spine or trunk when he would begin to rage. While he was very frustrated by going slowly and convinced that only a cathartic explosion of the highest degree would be healing, he was willing to practice expressing his rage in increments, but only because he was literally unable to do otherwise. He sensed my bias against his desire to cathartically explode and greatly resented that. Nonetheless, he worked incrementally to the point where he was soon able to practice looking at me with a sense of power in his eyes. This felt like the beginning of allowing his spinal push to express itself relationally. He discussed beginning to believe that there was room for both of us in our relationship. He recognized that he had not felt that he was allowed to exist in his family. His mother was rejecting of his needs and his father was threatened by any of Benjamin's strength.

With this newfound ability to push through his hands and his eyes, Benjamin began getting into more power struggles at work. We were constantly exploring the edge between pushing others and pushing to support himself. When he pushed others away, he noticed that he had grasped the muscles of his pelvic floor. When he pushed to support himself, he allowed the push to sequence through his pelvic floor.

All of the earlier therapeutic themes were continually reemerging and being woven back together, but there was an interchange between learning a psychological action and then a greater enactment of that pattern physically. In this last round with anger, Benjamin had learned to feel his pelvis and allow that to push. This push from the pelvic floor is in some ways the most basic assertion of one's existence. It was as if he had come to believe in his own existence. He began to be able to breathe into his pelvic floor and use his awareness of his pelvic floor to calm himself and feel supported within himself. At this point, we often sat together on physioballs. Benjamin would rock from his pelvic floor and feel the movement go up his spine and through his head. With this rocking he was able to tolerate greater and greater levels of emotions without dissociating. With this support, he was able to actually stay present through extreme states of terror that he had previously avoided assiduously. He was actually able to reexperience his night of fleeing through the veldt and soothe himself through that without panicking and dissociating. Benjamin experienced this as a major victory and began to use this tool to venture out beyond his previous limits. He took more challenging projects at work. He experimented more sexually, and he traveled within the United States to a retreat with his spiritual teacher.

As the spinal push integrated itself, a deeper level of rage emerged. This time Benjamin was able to experience much more intensity without dissociating. He was able to look me in the eye, push me away physically, and tell me how angry he felt without becoming anxious, blaming, or stopping himself. At this point, the developmental edge moved down into his legs. He began using his legs to support himself more as he related to the world. He felt that he was being supported by his own strength, that he did, in fact, have some strength.

We began discussing the possibility of Benjamin taking a trip to the ashram for two weeks. He was terrified and excited. At this point, he had a variety of ways to use his body to soothe and support himself. He practiced using all of those. With all of the yielding and pushing that Benjamin had learned, he was beginning to be able to reach into adult contact to a small degree. Finally, he actually embarked. He had psychopharmacetical support on hand, and we had arranged several phone contact times. The trip was stressful, difficult, but generally successful. He returned less desirous of moving to India, but more desirous of continuing to work and consolidate some of the gains that he was beginning to recognize within himself. I emphasized that I saw the trip as a huge step toward health.

Benjamin's process focused primarily on yielding and pushing through the spinal pathway, and a homologous path through the arms and chest. The focuses arose organically out of Benjamin's process. The energetic developmental perspective provided (1) support so he could learn to feel his bodily experience; (2) an articulation of the organization of that experience; and (3) suggestions of physical activities that might support his development process. This is always true in working with energetic development. The fundamental principle is to track what is already emerging from the client's life and bodily experience, see the connection between the two, and support that process through awareness and activity. This is in contrast with a remedial approach in which one might notice what movements are weak or nonexistent and help the client strengthen them. This fundamental approach should be evident in the following case as well.

Christina came into therapy because she was terrified of her new habit of taking several of her kitchen knives with her to bed at night. She would place some of the knives on her chest and abdomen and lie in bed, while tracing lines on her arms with the points of other knives. As a young woman steeped in the popular psychology of her time, she was convinced that she had been sexually abused as a child and that this was the source of her obsession with suicide. She sobbed profusely and was unable to speak during much of our initial session. In order to manage her emotions, I asked her to stand at times and walk around my office, look out the window, and breathe slowly into her belly. Somehow, between sobbing bouts, I was able to get a tiny bit of history. Newly graduated from college, Christina had undergone brief therapy at her college clinic. She had tried antidepressants at that time, but "hated them," and "would never, ever try them again." She had never been hospitalized or attempted suicide. Her paternal grandfather had recently committed suicide due to terminal cancer, but she did not know of any real mental illness in her family, though she felt that her parents were weak and confused people. She did not want to kill herself, but did want help in working with the sexual abuse she hypothesized was the source of all of her problems. She was currently living with her boyfriend whom she hated because she had recently aborted a pregnancy and she blamed him for wanting to have sex. She felt that his insistence violated her basic reluctance to either have sex or say no to having sex. She was initially reluctant to see a psychiatrist because of her fear of medication, but agreed to get an evaluation. She readily signed a suicide contract in which she agreed to contact me before harming herself in any way.

Christina and I began to work biweekly to get her stabilized. Initially our work was just to stabilize her mind and contain her emotions. Much of it consisted of me asking her to sit up, walk around, or look me in the eye when she became hysterical. Her basic posture was collapsed with very little spinal support. She kept herself upright by pulling herself up by her shoulders. Breathing into her abdomen helped to shift her awareness lower into her body, provide some support for her spine, and move her out of the hysteria which seemed to be a sympathetic nervous system activation.

In a month or so, she stabilized enough to begin working. She quickly accessed a tremendous rage toward her boyfriend, the sexual abuser that she imagined though could not consciously recall, and her father. Her rage would move up through her chest and into her eyes and mouth. There was some quality of spinal push from the head in that, but at the same time, she would grasp and pull in through her chest, neck, and shoulders, effectively truncating both the spinal push and any potential homologous push that she might access. She wanted me to support her in raging endlessly in this way. She believed that raging in this way would heal her sexual abuse. Through feedback and supported exploration, Christina slowly came to realize that it was scary to her to rage in this way, and that she felt frightened and out of control underneath that. She realized that she was being motivated by her belief that raging would be healing. We began to explore feeling the anger and staying physically present and grounded. She would stand and bend her knees, gently pushing homologously with both feet. At the same time, she pushed out into space with her hands as if in a martial art posture. Through breathing and holding this posture, the push began to fill her body and sequence through her spine and arms without being so extremely truncated.

Her boyfriend had no idea that she considered their sexuality violating. He was not forceful in any way. In regard to the sexual abuse, she came to be unsure whether she had been abused. Finally, she recognized that though her father's behavior was not overtly abusive, physically or sexually, she had felt frightened by him and repulsed by his overtly confused sexuality. We explored how she perpetuated this dynamic with her father through disempowering herself and projecting her sexuality and anger on others.

This began a phase of exploring her history and family dynamics. With less projection and hysteria, it was possible to understand herself, her childhood, and her family in a more sophisticated way. A central theme of differentiation emerged. The physical aspect of this theme was one of feeling herself, breathing into her core, and staying present. This was a slow process through which more spinal push began to develop. Parallel to this, some of the grasping in her trunk fell away.

She was constantly tempted to project, identify with her parents, and dissociate in some way. During these states, her spine and trunk were simultaneously collapsed and constricted. She would fidget, squirm, and twist herself into collapsed and contorted postures. In contrast, she began to experience staying with herself as an option that she could utilize more frequently. She accessed a sense of clarity within herself by pushing with her pelvic floor and head, thereby sitting up straight and breathing through her trunk. During this period, she broke up with her boyfriend and did not relate to men at all for the next few years.

At this point, many of Christina's push patterns were becoming integrated into her life; simultaneously, her boundaries and interactions were more appropriate. She was supporting herself more with her family, seeking to move out of dysfunctional exchanges and create healthy contact in which she felt boundaried and differentiated. She applied to graduate school, was accepted, and enjoyed academic success. She was able to discuss with me areas in which she was dissatisfied with our work. In terms of her basic neurological actions, her spinal pushes were accessible to her and she used them more and more. Her homologous pushes both with her arms and with her legs were in place. However, the more advanced patterns—homolateral and contralateral—were not a strong part of her repertoire.

This became evident when she graduated from nursing school and began work in a busy inner city hospital. At the same time, she began to explore her first relationship in the four years since she had broken up with her last boyfriend. Under these stresses, she regressed significantly. She experienced a great deal of repressed rage, felt victimized by her supervisors and her new love. She was angry with me because I was not helping her. She was convinced she would fail. The black and white quality of her world became quite acute. This is often the case with people who are arrested at a homologous level. There is no ability to relate to the complexity of situations, opening to some aspects and rejecting others. This behavior is dependent on the contralateral movement patterns—the ability to push with one foot, for example, and reach with the opposite hand. In Christina's situation, that would have meant the ability to support herself with a push during a stressful shift while still reaching out to her colleagues and patients. With her lover, that would have meant the ability to say, "No, I can't see you tonight. I'm exhausted. But how about this weekend?" This sort of negotiation remained difficult for Christina. She found that she had to monitor her stress level quite closely. However, with the support of therapy, medication, and a cultivated awareness of her body, she was able to function within the normal range. This was notable for someone with borderline characterological issues and a strong bipolar tendency.

Christina's situation is one in which her early motor development was probably normal in infancy, but her family was dysfunctional enough that her basic neurological actions were not strengthened and developed throughout childhood. This is generally the case with people with normal neurological functioning, but psychological difficulties.

Benjamin and Christina both illustrate the therapeutic leverage offered by energetic development. In both these cases, energetic development offers a clear sense of the developmental stage that a person is grappling with and a strong bodily focus to ground the work and create a behavioral protocol. By focusing on pushing with the hands, Christina was able to feel the possibility of differentiating and setting boundaries. By pushing with her feet and pelvic floor, she could experience the feeling of supporting herself and not abandoning herself to hysteria. By creating a spinal connection through her trunk, she had a sense of clarity and presence. These bodily focuses become a constant backdrop to the verbal aspect of the therapeutic exchange, and they also become a barometer of the real level of integration and development within the therapeutic process. It is clearly visible when the legs are pushing to support the trunk, and when this is not happening. These basic neurological actions provide a very different barometer from verbal reports. It is also a way of giving the client feedback about their state. "I know that you say you are feeling panicked, but as I look at you, I see you standing calmly on your own two feet. Remember how you used to feel so weak in your legs when something like this would happen; you felt as though you could barely stand up."

Having a bodily focus can offer clients a tool to use outside of therapy in their everyday lives. For many clients who are functioning at a relatively high level, yielding can be very helpful to practice during challenging situations. When clients realize, for example, that whenever they feel challenged, they constrict their bellies, breathing into the belly and yielding can offer access to new responses when under challenge. Similarly, pushing can become a instant source of support for clients who tend to become disempowered. Once a client has experienced reaching and is consciously choosing to extend, reaching actions can be utilized to make contact and take risks. In general, energetic development offers concrete tools for both the client and the therapist.

BODY SYSTEMS AND ENERGETIC DEVELOPMENT

In integrating the body systems with energetic development, one only has to realize that whatever actions (basic neurological actions) are sequencing through the body, are moving along a particular path and through a particular medium (body systems). For example, when people use their muscles to push with their legs into the ground, that action has a quality of strength and vitality. However, by allowing the fluids to circulate fully into the legs, and yield into gravity all the way through the feet, one can push through the fluids of the legs. This has a fuller and somewhat softer, but potentially more resilient quality. All the actions and all the systems are always used in conjunction with each other. Only the purpose of articulating each of their unique qualities necessitates separating them from each other. Benjamin was very mental in his approach to life and would overwork his nervous system, creating headaches and nervous breakdowns for himself. By becoming more fluid and allowing more expression of his muscular self, through martial arts and in other ways, Benjamin was able to use his nervous system in a more integrated fashion and literally soften the truncated, but intense pushes through his head. Christina, on the other hand, did not tend to lead through thought and logic, she was much more emotional and reactive. In this way, she was overly fluid. She also had a very sensitive relationship with her viscera and reacted intensely to feelings that expressed themselves there. By calming her hysteria, she strengthened her nervous system and was able to use her intelligence to see clearly without projection. This allowed her spinal push of the pelvic floor to come up through her neck and support her head. This also allowed her to feel the simple support of her skeleton that was unavailable to her when she was hysterically and reactively squirming and trying to avoid her life.

In using the interaction cycle, one focuses on what emerges most prominently out of the client's process. This means that at times there is more emphasis on the systems or the actions. In human functioning, the two methods of analysis are inextricable and overlap. If the therapist is able to track the client's body through both the body systems and energetic development, then a great deal of information becomes available in that manner.

In utilizing energetic development as a tool for analysis of psychological issues, it can, at times, be helpful to look at an individual's history of early motor development. This is so in situations where there are marked dysfunctions in the client's movement repertoire. A history of early development can also be helpful for the therapist utilizing energetic development to explore the subtleties of their own movement preferences as rooted in their own early motor development. The following interview (Table 10.2) can be used in either situation, as either a self-interview or as a guideline in exploring with clients. It is designed for use with adults for whom information access may be an issue. Gathering this information for children is generally much easier.

When you gather this information and combine it with an analysis of adult movement habits, you may perceive levels of movement preference or conditioning that were present from early infancy on. Possibly these preferences correspond with certain aspects of temperament. Though no research has been done to correlate the connection between temperament and movement style, clinically one finds repeated correspondences. In addition, one often finds movement preferences that persist throughout the life span. An individual who relished a particular movement in infancy may still exhibit a strong use of it in their adult movement repertoire. Such preferences might also lead to the omission of a particular stage of movement. For example, extremely visual, observant, intellectual people sometimes are not interested in the crawling phases of development and may, as infants, prefer the seated position that affords a greater visual field. At times, these individuals forego crawling altogether and scoot along the floor

TABLE 10.2 EARLY MOTOR DEVELOPMENT

For each of the following movements, first note if they were utilized at all. If so, at what age and for how long? Finally, what was the level of effort-enjoyment involved in the performance?

For adults, to gather this information, one may study photographs from the first year of life. In addition, one may gather information from the best living correspondent. Finally, as you perform these movements now, what is your intuitive sense of your early relationship to these movements. Does the information gathered correspond with your own intuitive experience? What are your feelings now in response to these bits of history?

IN THE FIRST YEAR OF LIFE

Rolling

Inch worming (homologous push from the feet)

Lizard (belly) crawling (homolateral push from the foot)

Crawling on all fours (contralateral reach from the hand)

Independent sitting

Walking

Speed of development and coordination

Family attitude (e.g., older siblings, floor is demeaning, hurry up and walk)

CHILDHOOD MOVEMENT

Injuries and major illnesses

Braces, corrective shoes

Level of physicality, involvement in sports or dance, specific memories

---

in a vertical seated position. This means that many of the early push patterns will be weakly developed. This may make psychological self-support more difficult to manifest.

Awareness of such lifelong preferences and an experience of their psychological implications can support people to better understand both their temperament and their early conditioning. This can support their ability to work with themselves as adults. In general the tool of energetic development has a number of useful applications. As with all somatic tools, embodiment is the key. As the clinician acquaints herself personally with this tool, the possibility for utilizing it expands.

Chapter 11

The Possibility of Transformation

Accessing Cellular Change

Often when people are in the midst of a major identity crisis, they will spontaneously talk about their cellular experience. While this may sound merely metaphorical, there is a certain accuracy with which we choose our metaphors. There seems to be a distinct quality of experience that is often present when people choose this metaphor of *the cells*. Accompanying this quality of experience, the cellular level of sensation and bodily experience is quite distinct from those arising from, for example, a tissue level. The case of Alex illustrates this.

"I can't keep going like this. It will kill me. When I think about accepting this position, I feel this hot, tight constriction. I feel it in every cell of my body. It's like a meteor—hot, condensing molten lava, or lots of them, all over me, like every cell is hot lava condensing, hardening. I can't do it. I have to say no." Alex had been a bright young star of the technology industry. He had risen within his growing company to the point where he was now being offered the CEO position. As he faced middle age, he found himself in an existential crisis. He had loved his work. He was married to a wife whom he knew he had once loved passionately. Now, he could no longer sleep and found it hard to concentrate on the tasks at hand. He was still performing adequately at work, but felt that it was only a matter of time until he was "found out." He fantasized running away to California or Mexico, becoming a surf bum, disappearing from this life.

TYPES OF SENSATION

Sensations can be grouped according to the level of the organism that is involved. When we are tuned in to our sensations that are occurring in a particular tissue of the body, the sensations have a distinct shape and location. They tend to involve a part of the body, rather than the whole body or a whole area of the body. Tissue sensations are produced by physiological activity in a particular type of tissue.

In contrast, fluid sensations are characterized by fluid movement either in one area or the whole of the body. Fluid sensations are created by the movement of fluid as experienced by the surrounding tissue. These sensations vary depending on both the type of fluid involved and the type of tissue that the fluid is moving through. However, there is always the obvious quality of fluidity involved.

Chemical sensations are a bit more subtle. They are the result of a particular type of chemical messenger traveling throughout the body. As these chemicals bind to receptors on cell membranes throughout the body, a particular experience is created. Chemical sensations are generally whole body or large area sensations. They are less local and more generalized than any other type of sensation. They tend to have a more pronounced energetic quality than any other type of sensation, a strong quality of mood. Metaphors like schools of fish, leaves on a tree, or herds of animals on the savannah describe the qualities of grouping and movement that characterize chemical sensations, that is, globalized sensations occurring throughout the body.

In contrast to all these other types of sensation, cellular sensations tend to have a pointilistic quality. As in the painting style of pointilism, cellular sensations seem to occur as discrete, but multiply replicated points of sensation throughout large areas of the body or the whole body. Cellular sensations are generally fairly globalized, like chemical sensations. Despite this broad spread, they retain a quality of existing in a particular location, and are not as mobile or diffuse feeling as chemical sensations or fluid sensations. While one has to be somewhat of a connoisseur of sensation to readily distinguish these, when an intense cellular experience is occurring, even untrained people often report it spontaneously, as in the case of Alex above.

THE THERAPIST'S PROCESS

There are really only two requirements for the therapist to work effectively with the cellular level of being, one of which is a basic understanding of the nature of cells. The second is an experiential sense of the quality of cells. This can be achieved by opening one's mind and being intimately introduced to cellular experience.

It is difficult to conceptualize that there are approximately 75 trillion cells in the body, and one must maintain an open state of mind to think about this. When one realizes that all of the important aspects of physiology take place on a cellular level, the vitality and importance of the cells comes into focus.

Generally, we ascribe intelligence to the brain, and specifically to the frontal lobe of the brain. The etymology of the word *intelligence* derives from the Latin, *legere* to choose among. One could argue that at the level of the cellular membrane, there is tremendous discrimination; the receptors on the membrane may be involved in *choosing among* the various ligands swarming around the membrane. The receptors discriminate as to whether or not to bind. Pert (1997) has described the interaction between receptors and ligands in various metaphors, from dancing to sexual union. Is there intelligence on this level or is it purely reflexive with no choice involved? Various theorists argue either side of the debate. However, there are astute neuroscientists who would argue that all brain activity is reflexive as well, having perhaps a more complex mechanism for the reflex, which seems to yield a more diverse number of outcomes, but is nevertheless reflexive. Granted, proponents of this persuasion would thereby view all human experience as reflexive, rendering free will an illusion.

Whatever the verdict regarding the intelligence of the cell, it seems clear from those experienced in cellular exploration, that when one is tuned into that level, a very particular quality of mind is present, characterized by the qualities we find at the cellular level. I have gathered this information in classroom and training situations, through the process of first describing cellular anatomy and physiology, and then showing slides of various kinds of cells, and then finally inviting people to tune in to their bodily experience, as you can do now.

Take some time to move and stretch, letting go of your breath and your voice, tuning in to the sensations in your body. Continue with this until you feel a certain degree of presence and openness. Now, contemplate the idea that our whole body is composed of cells and fluid, trillions of cells, filled with fluid, surrounded by fluid, with these very sophisticated membranes that allow some exchanges between the cell and the contents of the fluid surrounding it. Spend a few minutes moving in a way that allows you to sense your fluidity; approximately 70% of the human body is fluid. Let go into your own fluidity. Once you have an experiential sense that you are mostly fluid, this naturally opens the way into an experience of the cells. Approximately two thirds of our overall fluid content is inside the cells at any given moment. Two thirds of our fluid is cellular fluid. When you are ready, shift your attention into your cells, whatever that means to you. This can be done by verbally thinking, "cells," or by visualizing a cell or cells. Letting go of thoughts, allow your attention to rest in your own bodily sensations, and gently direct yourself to the cells, through your breath, and your thoughts, and your images. Come back, again and again to the cells; allow yourself to bathe in cellular experience without questioning yourself.

□   □   □   □

After an exercise like this, I ask people to describe their experience, both on the level of bodily sensations as well as their state of mind. From performing this experiment with hundreds of people, I have found that certain experiences tend to be very common, both on the level of sensation, that was described in the previous section, and also on the level of state of mind. The state of mind that is commonly described has the following qualities. First of all there is tremendous vitality and activity happening within our cells. For the relatively healthy animal, there are literally thousands of creative, metabolic, and physiological processes occurring every second within every cell. Second, there seems to be some quality of tranquility or contentment on that level. It seems that cells do not argue with their experience: they do not argue with living or dying or changing. These two qualities—tranquility and vitality—do not always coexist, but when they do combine they create an experience that is often described as blissful. Even as I write this, I feel the particular, delicious quality of cellular experience creeping into my body. I would speculate that by doing this sort of meditation, we are both giving the cells more attention, which allows their quality to become highlighted, and also allowing them more leeway to express themselves directly rather than being more subjugated to tasks and intentions from other quarters.

This experience of cellular consciousness and the accompanying state of mind seems to enhance intelligent behavior and thinking. Many people experience increased confidence in their abilities, more trust in their lives, and greater ability to creatively engage with the world. For some people this experience is incredibly profound. I have experienced professional, grown men who were very resistant to the body, crying after this experience. One person said, "I can finally feel myself. All my life, something has been missing. It is this experience of myself."

Training fluency in the cellular level of experience is an even more subtle and esoteric process than working with cultivating awareness of the body systems. Nevertheless, it is possible to do with anyone with an open mind and a modicum of bodily awareness. The goal is to become familiar enough with the state in yourself so that you can recognize it in others. This occurs first through the therapist's own kinesthetic perception of her cellular state, second through visual and auditory cues regarding the client's state, and finally through the verbal cues pointing to a cellular experience.

Visual cues that may accompany a cellular state might include a somewhat fluid state of yielding in the body. The client's gaze will tend to be softer and more diffuse, though still clear. Voice tone may likewise have a fluid softness to it. Verbal cues that signal a cellular attunement include the obvious references to cells themselves. In addition to that, there may be verbal content that signals a very basic level of being, globalized sensations, and identity shifts, such as, "I feel that I am changing on a very deep level." The verbal cues are secondary, and without the accompanying atmosphere of vibratory, cellular experience, would not in themselves suggest an attunement to the cellular level.

CELLULAR LEVELS OF CHANGE

Cellular functioning represents an extremely fundamental level of functioning. Cellular change has a very profound effect on the functioning of our whole organism. Cells can change in a variety of ways. While much is unknown regarding the communication between cells, there is some indication that often groups of cells, and perhaps at times, most of the cells of our body, go through a change process in a relatively simultaneous manner. That is to say, that perhaps there is some level of "group mind," on a cellular level in which the whole group shifts together. This is obviously a mechanism in basic metabolic and immunological shifts. Based on that, one might assume that this communication mechanism could function in other types of change. One mechanism that might facilitate this level of communication could occur at the level of the integral proteins embedded in the cellular membrane. These proteins are long molecules which change shape radically in response to changes in the electrical field surrounding them

(Lipton, 1993). If an electrical field containing a large group of cells or even the entire body fluctuated, then a shift within many cells might occur simultaneously.

Receptor Behavior

Such a shift in integral proteins is one example of the first level of change that can occur in cellular functioning, changes on the level of the membrane. Such changes involve receptor behavior. Each of our cells can have millions of receptors on its cell membranes. Minimally, each cell would have 70 different types of receptors, with 10,000 to 100,000 individual receptors of each type. Pert described receptors as sensing molecules, scanners that "hover in the membranes of your cells, dancing and vibrating, waiting to pick up messages carried by other vibrating little creatures, also made out of amino acids." (1997, p. 23). As the state of the organism and the state of the cell vary, the receptors also vary tremendously with how active they are in the communication process, what they respond to, and how intensely they respond. Receptors not only respond to electrical changes as described above, but channels and gates bind with extracellular molecules and either transport them into the cell body or maintain a bond in the membrane that affects internal functioning (Figure 2.7).

Cells function in basically two states, a state of receptivity and a state of minimal functioning. When cells are minimally functioning, their state could be likened to a coma in which all processes necessary to stay alive are maintained, but any functions beyond that are suspended. Cells can maintain this level of functioning for long periods of time, more or less indefinitely. Perhaps when we do not want to feel a particular part of our bodies, whether due to physical pain, or emotional pain or fear, we might, over time, shut things down on a cellular level in that area. Certainly, there would be other mechanisms that might occur first, such as a constriction of blood flow to that area, or a neurological blocking of those sensations. Beyond that just avoiding breath or movement in a particular area can shut things down. Out of these more peripheral mechanisms, the final stage of shutting down would be for the cells of a certain area to shift into a coma state.

I often suspect this has been the case in clinical situations in which as the client comes into contact with a certain part of the body over time there is a distinct physiological shift in the functioning of that body part. Most notable are the growth or diminishing of cysts, fibroids, or tumors. This is something that I have experienced a handful of times, not enough to form any conclusions. One can only wonder.

Less dramatically, there can be major shifts in the physiology of a particular area, apparent through changes in mucous production, digestive ability, vitality, eyesight, or hearing.

Population of Receptors

The next level of potential change occurs in the population of receptors. Although, we are not able to monitor this level of change at a very discrete level, there is a variability in the numbers of receptors of each type on any given cell at any given time. Perhaps, when a cell has been in a minimal functioning, coma-type state for an extended period of time, the number of receptors begins to decrease. Perhaps a certain number or ratio of receptor types supports a particular mode of functioning. As our habitual states shift it is possible that receptor numbers and ratios may change as well.

Genetic Expression

The changes of functioning on the membrane will change the level of internal activity in the cell. The nature of internal activity seems to be able to change for a variety of reasons, most of which we do not understand. Fundamentally, the internal functioning of a cell reflects the process of genetic expression. Our genes are an archive of possible cellular behavior. It seems that individual genes are turned on to express themselves by a wide range of factors. This is illustrated by the differences between identical twins and clones. Those differences do not reflect fundamental differences of genetic makeup, but differences in genetic expression. What we are expressing genetically affects and is affected by everything about us—our health, our state of mind, even the actual shape and structure of our bodies. It is possible that psychological change could correlate in some way with genetic expression. The mechanism for this would be on either the chemical or the electrical levels.

Mutation

Finally, the last level of change possible on a cellular level is that of mutations. Mutations are occurring randomly in individual cells all the time. Darwin (1859/1968) postulated the theory that random mutation is the foundation of evolutionary change. As this view has taken hold of our understanding of cellular functioning, this indirectly seems to negate the possibility of directed mutation. However, directed mutation has never been ruled out. There is truly no reason to believe that this not a possibility, albeit an infrequent occurrence. Perhaps this is a factor in miraculous changes.

Evidence for the possibility of directed mutations comes from a study by John Cairns and colleagues at Harvard University (Cairns, Overbaugh, & Miller, 1988). Cairns and colleagues starved a group of lactose intolerant bacteria and then gave them a lactose-based food source. Subsequent genetic testing revealed that an unpredictably large number of these bacteria mutated toward being lactose-tolerant. This possibility of directed mutation can lead to an almost magical sense of intentional transformation, which might be misused by the "wish away your cancer" camp. Nevertheless, it is a real possibility. Now that we have completed the mapping of the human genome and are beginning to decipher its parts, we are much closer to understanding the nature of mutation. Whether random or directed mutation may have any role in the psychological change process might be something we can determine in this century.

HEART, BRAIN, AND CELLS

The general discoveries of psychoneuroimmunology and behavioral medicine make it clear already that cellular functioning and psychological dynamics are absolutely connected. Psychologist Paul Pearsall (1998) cited a 1993 study under the direction of the United States Army Intelligence and Security Command in which lymph cells obtained by gently scraping the inside of several subjects cheeks were placed in petri dishes. In the first round of the study, the subjects sat in an adjoining room, watching a video. When the video portrayed violent, disturbing imagery, the lymph cells began to move about in an agitated manner. This experiment was later expanded to include longer separations both in time and distance. Some behavioral connection between the lymph cells and their donor was exhibited up to two days after removal from the body and up to 50 miles in distance. Certainly this seems to indicate an intense interaction between cells and the psychological state of their organism.

Our human organism has a level of complexity that makes its organizational design difficult to define. Who is in charge? Clearly our cultural preference is to believe that the frontal lobe of our brain is in charge. In Western cultures, we feel comfortable with ascribing both leadership and intelligence to that part of ourselves and only that part. In most Asian cultures, the heart is seen as the center of leadership. Pearsall (1998) likened our confusion regarding leadership between the heart and the brain to our 15th-century confusion about the sun and the earth. In both cases, we seem to be fooled by immediate prominence. The heart's electromagnetic field is 5,000 times as strong as that of the brain. Electromagnetic fields naturally entrain each other. Thus, the heart is clearly in the position of resonant leadership. Restoring the heart's leadership role has been refined into a simple technique for stress management and problem solving by a consulting group called HeartMath (Paddison, 1997). In this technique, one focuses one's attention and breath for a short period of time to the heart area or the center of the chest. After only a short period of time, one can note shifts in a variety of measures, including brain wave (EEG), heart rate variability, and respiration. These shifts have been associated with such diverse variables as increased immune function and enhanced conflict negotiations. HeartMath has been successful in working with a range of corporate and governmental groups through this technique.

Perhaps the mandate is to shift from regarding the brain as the monarch of our beings to regarding it as a consultant. The brain has a tremendous amount of information-processing and problem-solving ability. However, when it is placed in a position of unilateral power, it can easily lose touch with the rest of the body. There is one simple reason for this: The brain does not feel. In addition, the brain has a tremendous predilection for control and perseveration. It has a great deal to offer, but its activities need to be tempered. I recommend shifting the brain into the role of consultant, rather than ultimate decision-maker. For this, I would suggest that we can learn from Asian cultures and most indigenous cultures and reinstate the heart to its throne in the center of our being. From this position the heart easily consults with the brain as well as listening to the rest of the body.

The cells seem to easily fall into line with any leadership that is offered by either the heart or the brain. The cells are extremely receptive both chemically and electromagnetically. The integral proteins that extend through the cellular membrane change their shape as the electromagnetic field around them changes (see Figure 2.7). This in turn changes the internal cellular activity. However, the brain's tendency to overly focus and control can limit the potential of the cells. With the heart in the primary leadership role, the cells might be allowed to exercise more of their potential and create a powerful, chemical and vibratory harmony throughout the whole body. In order to do this, the brain must relinquish control and any attempts to micromanage. This is evident in the types of life-changing processes that seem to innately involve the cells such as divorce, close proximity to birth or death, or major psychological shifts. In those cases, a person's experience seems to overwhelm their beliefs about the world and their

sense of habitual control. An implicit trust and surrender to the unknown elements may arise. This allows the cells full empowerment to
create a symphony of physiological transformation which can contribute greatly to both physical and psychological health. This might take
a primarily psychological form, such as a major change of lifestyle or
attitude. It might also involve radical improvement in physical health.
It seems that the cells need very little to do this, beyond simple permission.

Facilitating Cellular Experience

Generally the therapist's role is purely to notice when the client is
experiencing or hovering close to a cellular level of experience. This
is noted through the client's change in state. Some qualities of the
cellular state are the sense of vitality and tranquility, a physical lightness combined with fullness, an acute awareness that is both focused
and diffuse. This state is extremely seductive and will easily spread
between client and therapist. Thus, as the therapist senses and aligns
with the cells, the client's state is augmented and enhanced. This
awareness of the cellular state is the therapist's most important task.
The ability to resonate with it allows it to grow and develop. If there
are cognitive resistances to dispel along the way, the therapist can
gently open these gates.

There is generally no need for the client to label an experience as
cellular. However, it is important that the client has some sort of image or label to remember and tune back into this state of transformation. The therapist can use this label to remind and reinvoke this state
as needed. To observe this, we can continue with Alex's work at the
beginning of the chapter.

*As Alex contemplated this turning point in his life and felt the excruciating sensa-
tions that he described as lava in each cell, I encouraged him. "Alex, this is a really
important process and it is happening in you right now. What if you stop struggling with this and just breathe right into the center of it? Breathe into that feeling
of lava in your cells. What if something important is trying to happen right now?
Let go and let it happen. If you feel these sensations without judging them, what do
you really feel now?" Alex lay back into his chair and breathed for a few moments.
After a while, he began to speak. His eyes were closed and he spoke quietly, with
frequent pauses. "It's very intense, but if I don't fight it, it's almost pleasurable."
After a few moments longer, I asked him, "From this place that you are in now,
how does this turning point in your life look? What wisdom does this state offer
you in your decision?"*

Alex: Let go. If I let go, it's like little volcanoes exploding all over my body. I don't feel the hot, hard feeling anymore.

Therapist: Great, breathe that idea of letting go into your body.

Alex lay slumped back in his chair for five minutes, just breathing. As I watched him rest, I relished what I observed in him and what I felt in my own sensations— the scintillating luxury of cellular change.

Though somewhat bewildered by this experience, Alex was able to touch back into it and let it guide him over the next couple of weeks. He asked for more time to respond to the job offer. He and his wife took a trip to Hawaii. I coached him on working with his wife to uncover the connection that had brought them together. They had difficult confrontations, but were able to work through them with the help of a phone session from Hawaii. They swam and made love and began to envision their future together.

When Alex came back, he continued to develop a vision that would entirely revamp his company's organizational structure, marketing policy, and mission statement. His proposals were accepted; he took the job, and embarked on a new phase of his life. His memory of his cellular experience became a fond touchstone that he chuckled about later, "What was that anyway?"

Chapter 12

Specific Clinical Issues

A Body-Mind Psychotherapy Approach

The basic principles of BMP were presented in Chapter 3. These principles form the basic attitudes of working with others, and they inform our actual interventions in working with others. In addition to these, I want to add the principles of applying specific BMP techniques. These principles will inform not only our attitude, but shape our actions and interactions.

PRINCIPLES OF BODY-MIND PSYCHOTHERAPY TECHNIQUE

The first principle has to do with integrating BMP techniques with other techniques that the therapist is working with. BMP does not offer a complete way of working; it offers a *ground*. In psychotherapy it is necessary to integrate further cognitive and relational pieces as well. While BMP informs how we work cognitively and relationally, it does not offer a full education in those areas. In order to direct our work, the first BMP technique is to assess the client at a particular moment regarding the priority of his or her needs to *think, feel,* or *do*. What needs to happen most? Or first? This issue was thoroughly discussed in Chapter 6.

The second assessment has to do with self and relationship. Is this issue primarily or immediately *internal* or *relational?* While all issues are both internal and relational, which level needs to be addressed first? Through the techniques of sequencing and attending to the **core self**, one can work very directly with internal processing. By adding the technique of circular attunement, one can stay with the core process and develop a relationship. Finally, through sequencing and energetic development, one can rectify or develop the necessary connections between the inner self and the outer world.

The next and third principle of BMP techniques shows up in all lists of principles so far, a reflection of its importance: **embodiment**. The therapist's embodiment affects the choice of techniques, the timing, and the quality of communication in applying the technique. This principle includes the use of **embodied speech** and **embodied listening**.

The fourth principle is that of *less is more,* allowing the client to discover as much as possible on their own. Again, embodiment supports this because we can communicate nonverbal support and not have to spell out as much to the client. Also, to the degree that we are supporting the client's embodiment, the client has multiple intelligences operating and will have access to more information than if they were just functioning cognitively.

The fifth principle guiding the use of BMP techniques is *seamlessness:* Allow the intervention to arise naturally out of what is already occurring. Do not go anywhere new or do anything fancy and out of context if it is unnecessary.

The sixth and final principle is that of tracking the **developmental edge**, both psychologically and physically. A clue here is that the two (psychological edge and physical edge) have to interface for it to be a real developmental edge. The psychological edge will relate to what the client wants, as in the interaction cycle, and what they need to develop next psychologically to move toward what they desire. The physical edge is the edge between the area that is sequencing and an area where less is sequencing. Tracking the developmental edge involves assessing both the basic neurological actions involved as well as the primary body systems that are part of the pattern. Working with the developmental edge also means not jumping ahead to the next logical step, but rather waiting for the bodymind of the client to fully work through the developmental process at hand. In this way, the next edge emerges on its own.

Working with all of the tools and principles of BMP allows the practitioner to address extremely potent and challenging situations with a simplicity that is at once concrete and subtle. The BMP therapist strives to communicate in the simplest manner, addressing the issue as directly as possible without added complexity. While the human change process is often inherently slow and indirect, BMP tools and principles can allow the client to recognize a concrete path of moving toward their desired changes.

BEGINNING AT THE BEGINNING

We begin our physical existence as a particular sperm and a particular egg coming together, generally, in our mother's body, as a result of a particular sexual exchange between her and our biological father. The physical and emotional components of this moment would seem logically to have a profound effect on the rest of our lives. What was the emotional state of the mother and the egg? And the father and the sperm? How did they interact? Beyond that, what was the climate in the mother's womb? What was the atmosphere in the mother's life? How did this impact the climate in the womb? What was it like to live for nine months, creating a body for ourselves inside our mothers? How did we approach birth? How did the labor begin? How did it unfold? What happened to us during delivery? How did we cope with that? What happened in the moments and minutes and hours and weeks after delivery? What was the atmosphere in our families? How did we interact with that?

Despite the obvious profundity of this earliest history, our culture has decided to ignore this phase of life. In our confused debate regarding the effects of nature and nurture, we have deleted the history that occurred before our narrative or explicit memory developed. Explicit memory is memory that is consciously recollected as words or images. Explicit memory retrieval is accompanied by an awareness of remembering. The central nervous system does not develop sufficiently for explicit memory to take place until the second year of life. The ability to organize and consolidate explicit memory is not perfected for a number of years after that. Thus, from an extreme point of view, linking explicit memory with psychological awareness, most of early childhood is psychologically insignificant.

There is another kind of memory that is foundational to explicit memory. The nervous system has implicit or procedural memory from the moment it begins to function in utero and it is functional throughout our life span. Implicit memory retrieval does not come with an experience of remembering. Instead it is associational and often behavioral. It links a particular sensory stimulus with an emotional state or a behavioral response. A particular smell evokes feelings of safety.

A particular color of the sky evokes fearful, isolating behavior. A particular environment or type of person evokes a state and behavior. A particular state leads to a particular behavior or mindset. We do not sense that we are remembering, but rather feel we are reacting to the immediate environment. In our early years, as we are constantly learning from the environment, we are constantly developing implicit memories. Our earliest experiences form particular patterns of connection throughout our brains. These later emerge as states and behaviors in response to particular stimuli.

To understand how this works, we need to look again at a basic framework of neurological functioning. The nervous system operates very much in terms of repetition. As noted earlier, Hebb (1949) made an important contribution to our understanding of the nervous system. He stated in essence that any two cells or systems of cells that are repeatedly active at the same time will tend to become associated, so that activity in one facilitates activity in the other. This has become known as Hebb's axiom and forms the basis for our understanding of neural nets, the networks of neurons that interconnect in a particular pattern for a particular function. In this way our earliest experiences form templates upon which later experiences are evaluated. Repetitive experiences strengthen these neural networks, and in this way, our characters are formed over time. Perry and colleagues communicated this succinctly in the title of their paper, "Childhood Trauma: the Neurobiology of Adaptation, and 'Use-dependent' Development of the Brain: How 'States' become 'Traits'" (1995, p. 1). Clearly the nervous system is being patterned long before the advent of explicit or narrative memory.

In addition to early implicit memories, our experience of life begins at conception, before we even have a functioning nervous system. To understand the imprinting of that period, we must look beyond even implicit memory and the central nervous system. We need to go back to the information substances of the mobile nervous system. A brief glance at evolution will help to contextualize the relationship between the nervous system and the chemical communications of the information substances. If we view memory as the result of learning from experience, this capacity existed long before multicellular life and differentiated neurons. Single-celled organisms and simple multicellular organisms do not have nervous systems. They use chemical communication to interact with the environment and internally within themselves. Basic chemical substances, many of which have maintained their central roles in the biochemistry of more complex organisms, convey information, trigger intracellular and extracellular responses, and monitor the results of these behaviors. As multicellular life evolved, these same chemical substances continued to be instrumental in the communication and functioning of all organisms, including human beings. As discussed earlier, some neuroscientists believe that this chemical information system may be responsible for the vast majority of communications that we are mistakenly attributing to the structural nervous system.

The chemical information system is active in the functioning of any living cell. This includes, of course, the egg and the sperm during conception. A third component of the chemical information system at conception is the chemical environment of the mother's womb or in unusual circumstances the lab in which conception takes place. All of the chemical substances are involved in patterned behavior, and these patterns are impacted by the interactions between the various elements. It could be argued that these patterns of interaction form the basis of the evolving chemical structure of the new being—a template upon which the chemical functioning of the developing person is based. While the subtleties of such preneuronal patterning are beyond the scope of current scientific inquiry, we can postulate the possible mechanisms. In a sense, it is a matter of keeping a metaphorical foot in the door, preventing the dismissal of the impact of the very beginnings of life.

Seeking to understand a human being is such a complex thing, whether it is ourselves or another. So much intuition and speculation is involved. The relevance of any particular experience is primarily intuitive and the resulting understanding is much more a working hypothesis than a fixed truth. In BMP, we rely heavily on the utility of any working hypothesis; that is, if looking at one's life in a particular way *feels* true and leads to further development and empowerment, then we will continue in that direction. On the other hand, we do not introduce any hypotheses that are not necessary to achieve the goal at hand.

In this spirit, the earliest experiences of life often provide fundamental clues, yet need not become the central focus of the therapy. The therapist can use the client's history to develop hypotheses regarding the developmental issues at hand. This may or may not involve pre- or perinatal experiences as central or explicit themes. Clients may draw these themes from their own experience. The therapist can introduce only what is necessary to achieving clients' goals and that can be introduced in the manner that is most helpful and least overwhelming to clients. This relates to the BMP principle of working with simplicity.

The field of pre- and perinatal psychology has developed an understanding of this phase of life and experimentally documented its significance. For example, early research comparing children who lost their fathers while in utero to children who lost their fathers during the first year of life reveals a greater psychological impact to the first group (Huttunen & Niskanen,1978). Clearly this supports the impact of chemical and implicit memory, and discredits the notion that they were too young to remember or know what was going on, so therefore, there is no impact. Instead, we find that the earlier in our lives an event occurs , the more profound the impact may be.

The earliest phase of our life from conception through the first year of life revolves around basic experiences of feeling wanted, understood, loved, supported, engaged, and nourished. Obviously these issues are fundamental to our sense of self and our sense of the world. In addition, the experience of labor and delivery are possibly the most potent endocrine experiences of our entire life span, therefore there is a strong potential for imprinting those experiences upon later experiences which require the navigation of tremendous intensity. Did we feel supported, loved, and engaged during that intensity? What was the cycle of excitation, exertion, and soothing like? In an intense situation, the potential for either transformation or victimization is vastly increased. In these situations the prefrontal cortex is often more or less overwhelmed, which creates a greater than usual need for somatic sequencing.

In BMP, the clinician does not focus on these early experiences more than the client is interested in doing so. However, through personal exploration of these early life events, the clinician is sensitized to their energetic signature. When this sensitivity is activated, the clinician may explore a bit through simple questions—e.g., "When do you think this pattern began?" If the client goes back to a postverbal time, then it might be helpful to check further. Sometimes people feel that only the explicit memories of postverbal time are worth reporting. By asking, "So you don't think that you felt that way before then?" the client might respond, "Oh, yes, I just can't 'remember' anything earlier." In this way, one can tap into a sense of implicit or preverbal memories. By supporting clients in trusting their intuition, the therapist may get a sense of whether or not this is a preverbal pattern. In either case, the exploration can continue, "What do you think that time was like for you?" "What do you think that was like for your mother? What was going on with your father? How do you feel in your body as you think about this?" The following interview is provided to stake out the range of pertinent information.

TABLE 12.1 PRE- AND PERINATAL INTERVIEW QUESTIONS

Note: For adults, gathering this information may be difficult. One may write the hospital of birth to see if any records exist. This is more likely for those under 35. One may seek to gather information from one's best living correspondent. This might be a frustrating or emotionally challenging situation for both interviewer and interviewee. It is often surprising how little may be remembered or how much emotional defensiveness may obscure the information. Low expectations and a relaxed attitude can produce a significantly greater yield of information. Skimming through a family photo album often provides a relaxed venue. Beginning with stories and then going to specifics can be helpful. At times, information gathered is blatantly contradictory or false. How does the information gathered correspond with logic, intuition, and the subject's felt experience? Finally, what are the feelings now in response to these bits of history?

CONCEPTION
- Any family or parental stories dating from around this time?
- Your fantasies about each parent, nature of the relationship, and
    family at this time?
- Conscious, was there a sense of having conceived?
- Was the sexual interaction voluntary or forced?

PREGNANCY
- Mom's overall experience
- Significant health concerns for you or mom
- Significant family events
- Smoking, drugs, alcohol
- Mom and dad's relationship
- Stories

BIRTH
- Birth story
- Labor induced or spontaneously begun
- Medication to speed up labor
- Mother's level of sedation (local or spinal or general anesthesia)
- Labor (what was it like? how long did it take?)
- Stages of labor, contractions, pushing (how long? quality?)
- Breech
- Cesarean
- Problems with chord entanglement or breathing
- First few hours/days with mother or nursery
- Early traumas

EARLY FEEDING
- Your responsiveness
- Mom's attitude
- Breast or bottle (how long? On demand?)
- Colic

The above list is only guideline. Furthermore, there are no specific meanings or implications to any of the answers. The information gained through this inquiry will provide a stepping stone for the client to directly experience the impact of these early events. It is important that the therapist thoroughly explore these areas for themselves before approaching them with clients. In exploring this time through open-ended questions, the client might stumble into the energetic seed of the pattern.

At 28, Ellen had become frustrated with her ability to develop meaningful work for herself. Raised by two physicians, with older and younger sisters who had either become physicians or were on their way, Ellen was not interested in academic learning. Instead she dabbled in the arts, traveled, and worked as a nanny. Ellen felt extremely judgmental of her seeming inability to "make a niche" for herself in the world. She could be scathingly sarcastic about her life. Eventually, Ellen was able to see the quiet, but institutionalized family standards through which she judged herself. Though no one in the family openly criticized Ellen, she became able to see the subtle way in which such thoughts were engrained in family life. As Ellen stopped attacking herself, she began to explore her interests, her emotionality, and her values with a spirit of fresh inquiry. She began to develop a philosophy that supported her as the kind of person that she was, rather than who she thought she should be. Amidst the enthusiasm of these new discoveries, Ellen fell into a depression.

It was a surprise to us both and led me to encourage her to consider medication once again. As we looked for possible triggers to this depression, Ellen mentioned her birthday that had just passed.

"I always get depressed around my birthday. I think about how old I am and what I should be doing at that age. I was so proud of myself for not doing that this time. I don't know, maybe, I did it again subconsciously." As we discussed this, we both became quietly convinced that this was not the case.

Therapist: Is there anything else about your birthday?

Ellen: [with a brief shiver] It's always so cold. [She drew farther into herself, though it was quite warm in the room.]

Therapist: What are you feeling right now?

Ellen: Cold. Alone. Afraid. [then with a disgusted voice] How I always feel on my birthday. I was born prematurely. I was in an incubator. [again, with disgust] I couldn't even get born right.

Therapist: [firmly] Stay with yourself now, Ellen. What do you feel when you imagine the incubator?

Ellen: Cold. Scared. [Ellen curled into herself even further.]

Therapist: Give yourself lots of permission right now. Stay with yourself.

Ellen curled up into a ball. After a few moments, she began to cry softly. The rest of the session was spent this way. Ellen would talk about what she knew of her first few weeks of life. She would cry a bit. I worked to keep her thinking simple and nonintrusive and her experience of her body alive. Ellen began to feel a connection between her early postnatal experience and her depression. Fearful that she might use this to fall more deeply into a depression, I encouraged her to be kind to herself about this new awareness. We developed the idea of adding to her postnatal experience by reassuring herself with thoughts and images of a warmer, easier postbirth experience. I encouraged her to put her hand on her belly and keep it warm and connected.

At the next session, Ellen came in full of enthusiasm. She had contacted the hospital and requested her birth records. Her depression was nowhere in sight. We continued to explore her experience of the depression coinciding with the postnatal review. Ellen felt that the aloneness was key. She felt she had really imprinted on this experience, and that it contributed greatly to her struggles to relate to others. She also identified a feeling of "not belonging anywhere." This seemed very connected to her inability to "find a niche."

When the birth records arrived, she poured over them with relish. She brought the records to me and delighted in details that the nurses had recorded. It was as if she were reclaiming herself. Over the next year, as the depression arose, she would tell me about it by saying, "I'm back in the incubator." She learned to treat herself with the kindness required by a newborn. She kept warm and fed. She paid special attention to her belly. She imagined herself in warm, creative wombs connected to strong, nurturing umbilical cords. The depressions came and went more quickly and more easily.

Ellen began to understand her own vulnerability and need for human contact. She saw her tendency to isolate herself in a new light, and retrained herself to seek and receive contact more easily. Opening up to her early postnatal experience provided Ellen with a richer and kinder relationship with herself. She reexamined her frustration and passivity in creating a "niche for herself."

With Ellen, the postnatal experience arose spontaneously, but it required a spacious attention to her sensations. The BMP principles of embodiment and simplicity allowed this experience to emerge. The BMP therapist recognizes and supports any intensification of patterns of sequencing within the body systems and along the pathways of the basic neurological actions and encourages awareness at those moments. In Ellen's case, the curling into herself was a pulling in around the umbilicus. This movement expressed her developmental edge. Later she learned to receive along that pathway in a more yielding manner. BMP takes a similar approach in working with any phase of pre- or perinatal work.

BONDING

In the same way that our conception, gestation, and birth form basic templates for our lives, so too do our early bonding experiences with our primary caregivers. The quality of the relationship between the earliest and most primary caregivers teaches us about ourselves in relationship. In fact, because the human being is born dependent upon others, modern developmental psychology is arguing that the self is inherently relational and cannot be accurately observed outside the context of relationship (Stern, 1985). The quality of this early bonding becomes both a template upon which future relationships are based and a benchmark to which all future relationships will be compared. In the psychological world, much research has focused on the quality of our early attachment to our parents. Basic patterns have been delineated. A secure attachment is loving, sensitively attuned, and allows the child growing autonomy. An insecure attachment might result in either the need to cling or the need to avoid relationship altogether.

In looking at the nature of the attachment, one needs to explore the child's innate temperamental tendencies. In order to feel securely attached, different types of children have different needs. Temperamentally shy, sensitive children require particularly sensitive parenting. This evokes the issue of the temperamental fit between child and caregiver. While a caregiver may be able to create a secure attachment with one type of child, this might be difficult with another type of child. Understanding the body systems can greatly aid this type of exploration. By analyzing the dominant body systems of both the mother (or other primary caregivers) and the child, one can understand more of what worked and what did not work in the relationship. For example, a child who is extremely muscular needs to vigorously engage with the world. If that child's mother is quite sensitive and expresses herself primarily in mental ways, they might have a more difficult time working with each other. In addition, understanding the primacy of our somatic nature and the intense need for touch, one can analyze how communication was transacted in the relationship. Discipline and affection are particularly significant. Children vary greatly in terms of what communicates effectively to them. All of these early experiences interact with our basic temperament to form our character structures. These become structured in the body through the habitual use of particular sequencing through the basic neurological actions and through particular patterns of organization in the body systems. While attachment and character are not solid entities and can change over time, it is clear that our early experiences do become somewhat structured into our bodies in general, our nervous systems in particular, and our behavior overall. Understanding this can allow for more skillful means to work toward change.

Miles was a successful executive who sought coaching from time to time to enhance his negotiation skills. Overtime, he had come to notice a feeling of emptiness, a lack of confidence within himself. This was in contrast to his outwardly assured and poised manner. As he explored a difficult transaction, he recognized those feelings.

Miles: There they are again.

Therapist: What?

Miles: The feelings. I think the whole deal is going to fall apart.

Therapist: What do you feel in your body?

Miles: Uuuhhh. It's in my belly. I feel sick, empty.

Therapist: What is the emotional tone of those feelings?

Miles: I'm afraid. I'm afraid the deal is going to fall apart.

Therapist: But the deal didn't fall apart. It went well and it's done and over now. Let yourself be with these feelings in a more open way. Forget about this deal. Just feel these feelings. [Miles relaxes into himself. Takes a deeper breath.] Good. Just breathe and give these feelings permission to move, imagine, speak, sound, whatever they want to do. . . . So what's happening in your belly now?

Miles: It's moving. I'm mad. I'm so mad. It was always like that. No one knew how much I hated my mother. She didn't care about me. I tried so hard to please her. Nothing worked. [Again, Miles shifted. His belly contracted back into himself. His spine slumped slightly. His face became more somber.] My belly's not moving again. It's tight. I feel hopeless. Like a little boy. Alone. I want it to go away, then I'd believe in myself." [He took a fuller breath into his lower body as he said this.]

Therapist: Fine, feel that. Believe in yourself. Say it again and feel what happens. Keep saying it and keep feeling what happens. How does your belly feel? What's happening in your pelvic floor?

As Miles felt a state of believing in himself, his visceral organs relaxed, and his pelvic floor pushed gently, supporting him in a more upright position. I helped him recognize and understand this. He became clearer about his mother's narcissism and the fears of intimacy it had engendered in him. He began to cultivate a state of openness in his viscera, supporting his viscera with a gentle push from the pelvic floor. He began experimenting with feeling his viscera and pelvic floor as support for intimacy with his family and friends. The results were enriching. Slowly this support and connection to himself began to serve him even during difficult business transactions.

Miles's situation, though relatively mild, illustrates the basic process used in BMP with early bonding issues. The difficulty was identified and felt. Out of that the interaction cycle was employed and completed. For people with serious disruptions in their early attachment experiences, a similar process may require years of delicate renegotiation.

In terms of the BMP technical principles, Miles had spent enough time thinking about the situation, so that he was clearly ready to feel more. After considerable time feeling, he began "doing," by cultivating this state of openness during business transactions. The work Miles did with his breathing and his body were simple and direct enough that the body aspects of the work wove seamlessly into the more cognitive aspects. Miles was working with his developmental edge in his belly through embodiment.

By understanding the body systems and energetic development, we can see our early experiences, and our subsequent character structures can be understood and ameliorated more concretely and directly. For Miles, his mother's narcissism left him feeling empty in his viscera and lacking in support for his core. Other examples of using the body systems to understand developmental issues might include, a child with an extremely fluid nature who is adversely affected by a rigid school environment. Through this experience, he may come to hate his own fluidity and battle mightily against it, or conversely, he may reject anything remotely akin to rigidity and fall into a chaotic lifestyle. As another example, a very willful child needs to explore her ability to push against boundaries. If these impulses are continually squelched in an authoritarian manner the child may renounce push in favor of collapsing and have difficulty supporting herself as an adult. In this type of situation, awareness of one's nature and the opportunity to feel deep innate impulses toward pushing can open the door for characteriological change. Energetic sequences can be completed and new experiences developed. In situations involving major character disorders, working with the core self and circular attunement can give the client and therapist a concrete way of developing a stronger sense of self and the ability to feel oneself and be in relationship. This forms the basis for a healthy sense of self and the ability for intimacy.

INTIMACY AND SEXUALITY

Culturally, we have a distorted sense of intimacy. We see intimacy as a hazy blur of perpetual harmony. In order to create this kind of relationship, the individuals involved must necessarily sacrifice their own interests, needs, and even awareness of their unique sensations. All intention is invested in creating a union in which everybody wants the same thing all the time and is always happy. Of course, we fail miserably at this. Thank goodness.

True intimacy involves two separate and differentiated people. Differentiated people are willing to be different from the people that they are close too. They do not need to be the same, as in the enmeshed version of relationship described above. They know what they feel, what they want, what they like, and what they don't like. This takes a significant amount of core strength and ego structure. Without this core strength, it can be frightening to be different, we might be afraid of being annihilated or abandoned. We might be afraid of annihilating the other.

In the dance of intimacy, there is not a haze of perpetual harmony, but rather a constantly shifting tide, bringing us together and apart. The differentiated person capable of intimacy engages with others and then separates and is alone. The play between space and contact is negotiated between self and other, and space always wins. This is so, because in order for real contact to take place, two people have to *both* want to engage. If one person wants space, then space it is.

This is confusing in a committed partnership. If one person consistently wants more space, the other partner might feel that he or she is not getting the appropriate contact, and maybe feel that this is not "fair." Often the partner wanting space, compromises and interacts at times and in ways that are not what he or she really wants. At that point, a partner might disassociate from his or her experience a bit, thereby becoming less embodied. While there is the behavior of engaging, it is obligatory and not fully embodied. This is a type of enmeshed relationship. Other problems tend to arise out of this, and the whole relationship can degenerate from this breach of integrity. There seem to be two real and embodied solutions to this dilemma of different contact needs. One is to recognize the differential between contact needs, accept it, and meet those needs through your relationship with yourself or others outside the relationship. The other is to recognize the differential and evaluate it as too great to be satisfactorily reconciled, and dissolve the relationship. Either solution allows both partners to maintain their integrity. The basis of embodied relationship is staying in touch with yourself, that is, continuing to feel your-self, while in relationship. This can also form the basis of a healthy sexual exchange.

As with intimacy, our sexual exchanges are strongly influenced by cultural stereotypes. Rather than staying in touch with our own sexual-ity—what we are feeling moment to moment—and interacting from there, we seek to create an idealized sort of sexual exchange. As with false intimacy, this creates a dissociated, disembodied foundation and the potential for a general deterioration. Instead, the BMP psychother-apist encourages clients to feel the sensations in their bodies moment to moment and allow their sexual behavior to arise out of this embod-ied awareness.

Why is sex so important in our lives? Beyond the possibility of enormous pleasure, bonding, and perhaps spiritual awakening lurks the strongest biological drive that exists—procreation of the species. The BMP emphasis on biology can help clients understand the strength of this drive, so that they can work to integrate it into their lives.

In the human animal, sex is uniquely linked to pleasure, particularly physical pleasure. As neotonous animals, we also have a strong affinity toward play and pleasure. Clearly this has become confused in modern human culture. Through cultural influences repressing our sexuality, we have denied our physicality and sensuality as well. Sexuality is a unique way of cultivating flow, creativity, and life in our bodies through skin, fat, muscles, fluids, brains, and hormones—a renewal of pleasure. Sexuality can be a bridge to spirituality, taking us from the personal to the transpersonal and back. Orgasm can function as a physiological reset button for the whole organism. However, because sexuality is such a powerful tool in these ways, we can overemphasize its importance, making it our sole connection to the physical, rela-tional, or transpersonal. In this sense it is important to integrate plea-sure and sexuality throughout our lives. The integration of sexuality into our everyday lives is often the final fruition of the embodiment process, the key to full embodiment. The fruition of embodiment is moving through the world in the process of continual lovemaking be-tween ourselves and the world, literally making or generating physical love, regardless of the situation.

In BMP, we support our clients in feeling their bodies and making contact with the world—embodied relationship. While this sounds simple, it is much more difficult than one might imagine. It requires that the therapist be quite sensitive to the client's subtle shifts of pres-ence. Out of this the client and therapist must establish a common goal of increasing presence. Finally, tremendous patience and vulnera-

bility is required on both the client's and the therapist's parts to practice moments of opening and connection. In this way, we can strengthen
our ability to be present and in relationship. Clearly embodied relationship is fundamental to healthy sexuality. And there is such a strong
and historical link between disembodiment and our cultural denial of
sexuality. Due to negative familial or cultural imprinting or outright
trauma, many people are frightened of sexuality and have developed
energetic patterns that make the literal mechanics of sex difficult. It
may be difficult for such people to feel a flow of sensation through
the core of the body. Two parts of the core might be disconnected
from each other, say the heart and the genitals for example. There
might be difficulty breathing through the whole core. Or finally, a
surprising number of people are literally desensitized around their
genitals. In one way or another, they have learned that it is not safe
to feel their genitals. In any of these situations, BMP can be particularly helpful in assessing both the physical and emotional issues that
are obstructing full sexual expression. In no area more than sexuality
is it obvious that the physical and emotional issues are overlapping
and most be addressed together. BMP is perfectly suited in its ability
to provide simple and integrated methods of working through these
challenges.

Patty was a young attractive woman, married for 10 years. She
came to therapy due to her frustration with her marriage. Her relationship with her husband had degenerated a number of years ago in all
areas. Through psychological exploration, she realized that she had
maintained a constantly angry front to keep him from expecting sex.
She felt so alienated from him in every way, that she had no desire to
be sexual with him. Yet, she felt that she could not connect to him in
any way or he would expect that connection to lead immediately to
being sexual together. Finally, to complicate the situation further, she
felt tremendous guilt about denying her husband sex, and regularly
engaged in obligatory sex with him. A complex, but not so uncommon
situation.

First we began by rethinking sexuality. Why would a good wife be
obligated to "give her husband sex?" What is the relationship between
sexuality and intimacy? Patty was able to conceptualize the possibility
of intimate, mutually desirable sex. Patty discovered that when she
thought about sex at all, she constricted her diaphragm and her pelvis.
She identified these feelings as fear. We began to review Patty's sexual
history. She wanted to enjoy sex and have a healthy attitude about
her own sexuality. By noticing her habit of constricting her lower
trunk out of sexual fear, she began to work with herself around this

fear. She would breathe, place her hands on her belly, and talk gently to herself. She also created a safe environment for herself at home.

She told her husband of her new belief that she did not owe him sex. Together they agreed to reinvent their sexual relationship. He agreed to her request that they not have intercourse for a number of weeks. With this boundary in place, Patty was able to relax enough to be affectionate with him. Soon she wanted to revise the boundary. The new agreement was that he should not "expect" intercourse, no matter how sexual their affection became. This agreement allowed Patty to experiment with whether she wanted to have intercourse or not. Within three months, she felt sexually empowered to the point that she could initiate and ask for whatever sexual activities she wanted. She also felt free to accept or decline her husband's initiatives.

At this point, Patty began to want more intimacy in her relationship with her husband. She felt that though they were much closer, their sexuality was mechanical and overly orgasm-focused. With encouragement, she began to look at her husband and talk to him more during sexual exchanges. She began to ask him questions about his experience and to ask if he was interested in hers. While Patty felt really good about her ability to do this, she felt that her husband was not "really there." Some of the intimacy issues at the root of their problems surfaced and they began couples therapy. It was a difficult process and Patty was not optimistic that their marriage would survive, but despite all this she was thrilled about her new relationship to herself, her own vitality, and her sexuality. In the midst of the worst struggles in her marriage, she bounced into my office, radiant and with a big smile, "Even with all this going on, I still feel great in myself. I can't believe how different I feel when I'm not shut down sexually. You should write me up. I'm a success story."

All sexual intimacy reflects the overall patterns of intimacy in the relationship. These in turn often reflect our early bonding experiences. In any intimate relationship, our primitive bonding needs will surface to a certain degree. While early psychological theory expected adults to be adults all the time, it is clear now that "normal, healthy adults" want to be babied or parented or mentored at times. If there were early needs that were not fulfilled, there may be some dysfunctional patterns around these needs that make it difficult to meet the needs, and thus create neediness out of basic needs. This problem is exacerbated if it is not recognized or if it is judged. Particularly in a sexually intimate relationship, our earliest needs for bonding, suckling, protection, and nurturance will definitely surface. The parallels between infancy and sexuality are too great to avoid this for long or completely.

Being naked, sharing love, having no tasks to attend to, are the simi-
larities between sexuality and infancy. When infantile feelings emerge,
it is possible for two mature adults to attend to them in a simple,
healthy, and balanced way. This can be as simple as asking to be held,
and allowing oneself to feel loved. When there were some early deficits in the infantile experience, the old feelings will surface. The feelings could result from feeling abandoned: "You don't really love me.
You don't want to give to me. I am repulsive. How could anyone really want to be close to me?" Or they could result from feeling
invaded: "You're trying to suffocate me. Get away." Or they could
alternate: "Come close. Go away." When both partners are aware of
their own early needs and willing to work with them in a balanced
way, sexual intimacy can be one of the most healing contexts for these
issues. Sexual intimacy can provide a context in which the need can
come up, the emotions be expressed, the need be met directly and
physically, and all of this move into a mature, empowered exchange.
When there is not an awareness and a willingness to work through
these issues as they arise, then the relationship will inevitably come
to a crash. The emphasis in BMP on feeling your body, respecting
what arises, and moving through it in an embodied way can support
this sort of sexual healing in a powerful way, as illustrated in the following case vignette.

John and Sue were at the end of their rope. The couples counselor
they had been seeing suggested that their work together had hit a
dead end. When I met with them, I had to agree that their relationship
was in a very sorry state. There was continual flatness in their exchanges, punctuated by brief spikes of rageful animosity. Underneath
this, I had the distinct impression that they had never bonded. I
shared this perception, asking for their responses. They both agreed
that they had never been really close to anyone, including each other.
However, with further conversation, a beacon of attachment emerged.
As they spoke about their children, a boy, Jack, age 3, and a girl,
Gelsey, age 5, both their demeanors softened. Their voices became
more resonant. These parent-child relationships became our baseline
for the experience of bonding. Together we practiced having them
think of the kids and feel what happened in their bodies. They were
both aware of the softening that happened. They both reported a
warming as well. For Sue, it was primarily around her heart, and for
John, it was located in his belly. As they became adept at feeling this
state. I encouraged them to move directly across from each and feel
it together. Eventually, they were able to look at each other and hold

hands and feel it. Finally they could sustain the feeling during a hug. We called this the "bonding project."

As they experimented with bonding with each other, the early childhood issues surfaced. John had felt unloved, rejected, and attacked in his family. He was overtly terrified of invading Sue and underneath that even more afraid of attack and rejection. Sue had felt responsible for everyone's needs in her family. Beyond this, she had been unprotected sexually and had suffered from sexual abuse. These unresolved issues created tremendous strife in their domestic life and made sexuality literally impossible.

John learned that when he held back out of fear of invading Sue, she felt that she was all alone and was responsible for their sexual relationship. He learned to walk the fine line between actually invading her and offering her sexual contact while taking a leadership role. By observing subtle shifts in Sue's posture, facial expression, and breathing, John learned to watch Sue's somatic cues to inform his choices. Sue practiced softening and letting John into her inner world. John easily felt rejected or attacked and Sue became compassionate toward his struggles and learned to appreciate him in a way that was very healing to him. Slowly they were able to progress from hand-holding, to hugging, to sexual fondling, and finally to intercourse. The step back toward full sexuality after 6 years was both reinforcing and intimidating to John and Sue. Here they had to encounter the early issues more dramatically. For both John and Sue, it was challenging to let John take a fully empowered masculine role. For Sue, it was terrifying to surrender to John. They learned to address these issues within a sexual exchange, telling each other of their fears and their desires. Often lovemaking moved away from intercourse and into holding each other, talking and crying.

Overtime, they grew much closer and developed a greater understanding of each other's issues. Many of these issues began to fall away. John and Sue experienced the ebb and flow of intimacy in their relationship. At the beginning, they would often panic when there was distance between them, assuming this was the end of the relationship. Overtime, they began to see the natural rhythm of moving together and apart in their marriage and in their sexual exchange. Eventually, I taught them the practice of circular attunement. John commented "That's a good exercise." When we terminated, their marriage was still shakey, but they had the tools they needed to continue their work.

The overlap between early bonding experiences, our character structure, our tramatic history, and our ability to be intimate and sexually empowered is an intricate dance. Untangling these complex issues is always delicate. The technique of directly feeling our bodies can give us a foothold to begin and practice the new behaviors required.

TRAUMA

Trauma can be defined as anything that overwhelms the organism, physically, mentally, or emotionally. Experiences are not innately traumatic or nontraumatic, it is our reaction to them that defines a traumatic experience. In a potentially traumatic reaction, the autonomic nervous system goes into an extreme state designed to protect the organism as fully as possible. It is important to note that the threat may not come in the form of an event, but is often the nonevent of neglect. Recent research indicates that childhood neglect may have more profound effects than actual abuse. What makes the situation traumatic is how successful we are at protecting ourselves from danger and then shifting out of the extreme state after the initial stimulus.

Sue Taylor and colleagues have delineated a stress response in women based on the neuropeptide oxytocin which they have dubbed, "tend and befriend." (Taylor, Klein, Lewis, Gruenewald, Gurung, & Updegraff, 2000). Clearly, there are many strategies such as this one that can both protect us from danger and stress to avoid traumatization.

Fundamental to recovering from trauma is the restoration of the feeling of safety in our bodies. Some therapeutic approaches are focused on "creating safety." This is tricky business, because from an empirical point of view, safety may not exist. For example, a plane might crash on the roof at any moment. Things happen that disrupt our outer safety. From a BMP point of view, the focus is on restoring the feeling of safety in the body. This is done is several ways: By identifying areas of safety in the body, those areas can provide literal support and protection to less safe areas. When centers of fear in the body are identified, the client can begin to listen to those fears, allow them to express themselves, and reassure them that the threat is over. By developing physical support and protection, the body becomes more convinced that future safety is possible. From the point of view of trauma, our experience of dangerous or even life-threatening situations is very subjective. For example, a client with complex PTSD wrote: "In one or more of those rageful moments, [my mother] would have liked to destroy me. I want to change the word *destroy* to *hurt*, but I can't." Her childhood experience of the rage was life-threatening, even though as an adult she assessed that this was probably not the objective reality. An objective observer would probably have said that the exchange was emotionally abusive, but only mildly physically abusive. Nevertheless, the client's experience was life-threatening. Almost 30 years later, that experience was so real that she could not edit it out of her writing.

Our autonomic nervous system is key in responding to danger. In a sympathetic response, our heart rate, respiratory rate, and muscle tone increase. This response readies us for action—fight, flight, or freeze. In a sympathetic response, this is a light freezing to orient ourselves or escape detection. We become very still, even holding our breath in order to hear more clearly or to not be heard. If we are able to successfully avoid danger in this way, we feel empowered and shake the sympathetic arousal off. If we are not able, our sympathetic responses might intensify and fragment, becoming dysfunctional. In this case, we become frozen. This frozenness is a much more extreme state than the momentary freezing above. It is more a feeling of being unable to move or vocalize, but feeling very aroused underneath that. If this state persists for any period of time without relief, than we shift to a parasympathetic collapsed response, in which our heart rate, respiratory rate, and muscle tone decrease dramatically and at times dangerously.

In BMP, we use the simple term **shock** to define these states for our clients. By naming the state, clients can learn to recognize their own traumatic response. The word *shock* works well clinically, because it is short, simple, and needs no explanation. It is important to name this state because there is an inherent dissociative element in this state. When we are in shock, we are not paying attention to ourselves and generally don't notice our state. In this way, shock is a self-secret; naming shock breaks the cycle. We can begin to recognize it in our bodies.

> *Therapist: What just happened?*
> *Client: I don't know. Things just got very quiet.*
> *Therapist: What do you feel in your body?*
> *Client: I don't know. Nothing really.*
> *Therapist: Do you think there might be a bit of shock here?*
> *Client: Yeah, maybe, I guess so, it's weird. You're far away.*
> *Therapist: Seems like it changed really fast.*
> *Client: Yeah.*
> *Therapist: Feel your breathing and see what happens.*
> *Client: I feel a little more real.*
> *Therapist: Sounds like you fell into a bit of shock.*

As the client slowly comes to recognize this state, it can be worked with more readily:

Therapist: What just happened?
Client: It's the shock again. As soon as I told you that, it started.

In this way, naming the state is a move toward embodiment. In this simplified system of naming shock, if the symptoms are more sympathetic in nature, i.e., elevated heart rate, respiratory rate, and muscular tone, then we might distinguish it further as **sympathetic shock**. If the state is more parasympathetic in nature, then we might designate it as **parasympathetic shock.**

If we have experienced trauma repeatedly or in an extreme situation that was not resolved, shock lingers in our bodies. Without attention, redirection, and completion, it generally does not go away on its own. This lingering nature means that shock can permeate our lives, being triggered by everyday events. BMP explores the effect that shock has on all the body systems, rather than just the nervous system. There can be agitation or frozen stillness in all the other body systems as a result of lingering shock. Generally, the autonomic nervous system has to find its regulatory balance first and then the muscles or the fluids can begin to release their shock and move back into full participation in life. This process is no different from any embodiment process. What is unique here is the possibility of checking in with all our systems to see if there is an experience of shock. The experience of shock is very subtle. The sensations often have a quality of numbness, sometimes vibration. It may only become evident over time through a process of contrast. By noticing how a part of the body feels when it is fully present, one can by comparison recognize a relative state of shock.

By educating clients to track their states, they can come to recognize a state of relative presence and embodiment in contrast to the static or fog of even mild shock states. Overtime, they may be able to distinguish between varying types and intensities of shock states. I encourage them to name their familiar states for easy recognition in the moment. Names like *the void, the dark place, caged tiger on Valium, crazed,* have been used. In BMP we use embodiment practice of some sort as a ground to establish presence, strength, and contact before entering into an area that is traumatic. Working slowly, we use the body, breathing, sequencing, and contact to reestablish a sense of flow in the body. The use of relational contact may enlist the ventral vagal and other components of Porges's "social nervous system," which constitutes engagement. Flow and engagement are both antithetical to shock. Particular somatic tools that are often helpful are nostril breathing, activation of the soft palate, micromovements in neck and head, belly breathing (to reverse sympathetic shock), chest breathing (to reverse parasympathetic shock).

Nostril breathing stimulates the frontal lobe of the brain and may literally cool the blood flow to the frontal lobes, which can enhance processing (Zajonc, 1982). Porges (1996) identified the *soft palate* as a key in the functioning of the social engagement system. Breathing up the back of the throat and lifting the soft palate may support the client to shift autonomic functioning. Often clients can hear when their voice becomes "flattened," a result of the soft palate having either collapsed or pushed downward. While it may be a bit tricky to help a client recognize their soft palate and shift it, once they have a relationship with their soft palates, it becomes an indispensable indicator of stress. First have the client locate the soft palate behind the hard palate. This may be done through sensing, touching with the tongue, or touching with a finger. After locating the soft palate, practice yawning in a way that pulls the palate up. For contrast, feel how stifling a yawn pushes the soft palate down. *Inner smile* is a term used in chi gong, referring to a slight lift of both the right and left back posterior corners of the soft palate. This image may assist the client.

In addition, *micromovement* of the head and neck can help shift our neurological state. By encouraging clients to feel their heads and sense their brain state, BMP uses the image of allowing the brain to unwind and drain down through the center of the brain. Along with the image of this brain drain, the earlier approaches of sensing, breathing, and movement are continued to facilitate this unwinding. In addition, the clinician might notice if the client is not allowing the head to rock backwards, forwards, or from side to side. The clinician might encourage gentle head rocking along a particular vector. It is possible that lack of head movement along a particular vector may indicate difficulty processing between two brain centers along that route. For example, to facilitate communication between the frontal lobe and the brain stem or cerebellum, place one hand on the forehead and one hand on the base of the skull. Gently rock the head slightly from forward to back. Sense the minute weight and pressure shifts that occur. Some clients are able to sense areas that feel congested or vacant. To connect the right and left hemispheres, place one hand on either side of the head, rocking gently to create small figure eight movements from side to side. Having explored these primary pathways, an individual may find that micromovement of the head along other vectors is satisfying. As always with any embodiment practice, encourage the client to do this in a way that feels good or relieving to them. As the nervous system begins to shift out of an extreme state, we can bring our attention to the sequencing through the rest of the body.

Lack of sensation or movement in other body systems may or may not be a residue of unresolved neurological shock in other body systems. If the BMP clinician senses that there may be a residue of shock in an area that the client is ignoring, she may first encourage him to let his awareness move all through his body. If this does not draw the particular area into participation, next suggest checking in with that part. If there is still no shift in sequencing, then share the hypothesis by asking if it feels as if there is still some shock in this part. If so, support the client to feel the subtle sensations in the area and allow them to come back to life. If the client does not feel there is residual shock, trust the client's sense of this, but continue to track the sequencing in that area.

In the final stages of sequencing out shock, it is important to use the muscles to restore a balance in the sensorimotor nervous system. Our peripheral nerves enter the spinal cord in two sets. In back the dorsal sensory nerves receive input. In the front, ventral motor nerves send out a motor response (Figure 12.1). By educating the client in the

FIGURE 12.1 SPINAL CORD AND PERIPHERAL NERVES

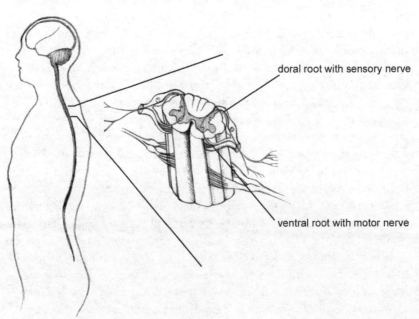

doral root with sensory nerve

ventral root with motor nerve

FIGURE 12.2 MOVEMENTS OF THE SPINAL COLUMN

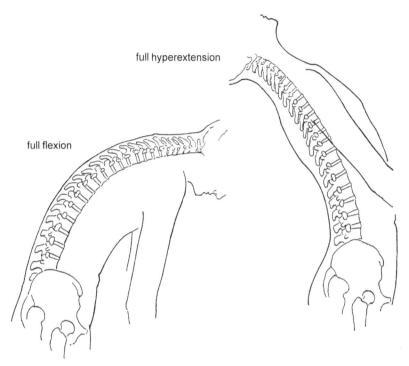

full hyperextension

full flexion

(From Wells & Luttgens, *Kinesiology: Scientific Basis of Human Motion*, 6/ed [p. 203], © 1976 Elsevier Inc.)

anatomy of this area and helping them sense the balance, we can use movement to reestablish a balance in the sensorimotor aspect of the nervous system. As we visualize sensory material moving into the spinal cord along the dorsal nerves, we can slightly extend our spines (Figure 12.2). Visualizing a motor response moving from the spinal cord out the ventral nerves, we can shift into a slight spinal flexion (Figure 12.2). This restores a sense of being able to respond effectively. This balance of sensory input with motor response is basic to a healthy response to any external stimuli.

An important final phase of completing a trauma response is to reconnect with flow in the fluids. Often the fluids are the last to know that it is safe to breathe and move, make noise, relax, and exist. There is often a residual stillness at the fluid level. By bringing clients' awareness to their contrasting states of becoming still and releasing into a relaxed sense of flow, a fuller sense of reconnecting with themselves can ensue. While the process of recovering from complex trauma can be a long-term process, the resource of embodiment practices can allow one to reclaim a feeling of safety as the norm throughout one's entire body. On a cellular level, our cells have two basic states, either they are moving toward life or are moving toward death. When we have felt that our lives are in danger, there are generally some parts of us that begin to slow down our life processes and prepare for death. Embodiment practice helps us go into all of the nooks and crannies of our bodies, into the backwoods, even into the cells, and proclaim that it's over, the threat of death has temporarily abated. Let the creativity of life resume.

Lisa had been in therapy for most of her adult life. At 40, she was both cynical about the possibilities of therapy and terrified to face her life without that support. She changed therapists fairly frequently due to dissatisfaction and a feeling that she was not "resolving her trauma." She had been exposed through the popular media to several approaches to trauma that convinced her that she could be rid of her crippling fears. Unfortunately, her attempts at these approaches had not yielded much. I talked to her about the misleading nature of such claims and the complexity of working with trauma that has its roots in early bonding difficulties. I stressed that our work would probably not be technically new to her, but that I might require her to work with herself outside of therapy much more actively. As we discussed this, Lisa's impatience was evident. I noted this and added a further requirement—for our work to succeed, Lisa would have to develop a great deal more patience. As our work proceeded, Lisa alternated between implacable anger and frightened withdrawal. When Lisa was in her implacable anger state, she realized that she could not think rationally. She dubbed this state "the wild animal," she agreed with my suggestion that there was probably some sympathetic shock involved. In her frightened withdrawal state, which she dubbed "the scared, little girl," she felt alone, invisible, and unable to defend herself—a somewhat paralyzed state.

Lisa and I established a new strategy. Whenever we identified one of these states, we stopped whatever discussion or activity we were involved in and began a conscious process of circular attunement. We would sit quietly and look into each other's eyes, breathing together. Initially, I often matched Lisa's rhythm of respiration with my own. Later on she would match her respiration to mine. In this way, Lisa began to recognize her shock states more readily, and learned to use this contact with me to soothe herself. As she got better at doing this with me, she was able to do it by herself by breathing and remembering doing it together. It took a number of months to progress to this point. Lisa was repeatedly angry and resistant, but I insisted that she had tried everything else and that this was the last tool that either of us could come up with. While her life continued to be frustrating to her, this simple tool made a dent in her experience of being neurologically overwhelmed.

Lisa's work illustrates the more relational use of embodiment in BMP. Later, she used her experiences of circular attunement to internalize emotional support and soothing. The overall focus of the work was very simple. By limiting the scope of the work, Lisa was able to make progress in an area in which she had been stuck. This illustrates the principle that "less is more."

DEATH

The paradox of being human lies within the polarity of attachment and death. It is distinctly human to become so strongly attached in this life, all the while knowing that death is a constant. In order to function creatively, we need to be fully and firmly anchored in life and not energetically consumed by the threat of grief and death. Yet, death is an integral part of life—an unavoidable reality. In indigenous cultures, death occurs in the home as part of community life. The death of creatures killed for food is frequently witnessed. Even birth is much more connected to death, without the extreme interventions of modern medicine to keep the maternal and infant fatality rate so low. However, in modern culture, we are shielded from the reality of death; we forget about death. We somehow forget that it is the norm. We are shocked and surprised by death, even somehow insulted by its unpredictability and finality. Yet death is still a great force within our psyches. It is undeniable that death brings to life its precious finiteness, both sweet and savory. How, in modern culture, can we reconcile to the reality of death in a healthy and balanced way? How do we support our clients to acknowledge and accept the influence of death in their lives?

For BMP death is a tricky subject. Freud relegated the body, sensuality, sexuality, creativity, and love of life itself to the drive of Eros. Clearly the natural affinities with embodiment lie in this camp. In contrast to that, Thanatos seems distant from the embodied process. How does embodiment relate to death? First of all, by facing squarely the biological reality of death, feeling the preciousness of our time in this body, we can find an embodied relationship to death. Second, we can recognize and stay present during all the minideaths with which we are constantly faced and allow our bodies to process our reactions to these minideaths. Endings, loss, disappointment, accidents, trauma, even near accidents, all of these represent minideaths. In French, orgasm is called the *petit mort*, little death. Even a sneeze elicits the customary blessing, an acknowledgement of a momentary glimpse of mortality. When we face death, our bodies respond. We feel it; we grieve; we move, biologically, if only for a moment, toward death. As this happens in our bodies and our unconscious minds, is our conscious mind fighting this process, pushing aside grief, loss, or the reality of death, creating a false front of eternalism? If so, our fear of death becomes the very root of our dissociative disembodiment. In a manner parallel to our fear of Eros, love, life, body, and sexuality, we are afraid of Thanatos, death, destruction, aggression, ending, loss.

The embodied alternative is that, in facing death, as in every other area, we can feel our bodily response to the death. We can breathe and allow our physiological responses to sequence through our bodies. We can strive to continue to feel our bodies in the presence of death. We can become aware of how we split off and become conceptual, less than present around any sort of death. In any transformation process, there is both a minibirth and a minideath. How do our relationships to birth and death affect our behavior toward transformation? By exploring our own patterns around beginnings and endings, we can come to a fuller presence during transitions, transformations, and terminations. We can use embodiment practice to sequence through these patterns to the fullness of completion that comes with both.

In the absence of this processing and creating a full relationship to death, we can flatten the process, make it black and white in some way, and miss the subtlety. In any change process, there is some death and subsequent loss involved. This is never more poignantly apparent than in working with childhood issues. To acknowledge and address the issues is to destroy the idealized childhood. That is a heartbreaking loss, albeit a healthy one. In any transformation process, some part is dying. When we avoid death and grief, we may suppress and avoid death ideation. In contrast, by facing suicidal thinking, one might ask, "What part is trying to die?" By supporting thoughts, fantasies, and even enactments of death (with healthy clients), we can differentiate the transformation process from actual physical death. This can be an invaluable way to reframe mild suicidality. In termination processes, we can acknowledge, allow, and fully communicate the pain and grief of the loss. We can review our history of endings.

Often in this process of integrating death, it is important to explore beliefs regarding death, an afterlife, and souls. In working with actual physical death, it is important to recognize it as an active physical labor. Embodiment can support this. Ultimately it is possible, with the

proper support and pacing in the dying process, for death to be perceived as a satisfying process that is more about yielding than grasping. Death can become an adventure and a surrender connecting us to
a deeper level of reality.

Luke came back into therapy in his mid-50s to cope with his mother's aging process. His mother lived alone in a small town an hour
from Luke's home. She had grown up in her home on a ranch, been
away only briefly as a young adult, and then moved back later with
husband and family to run the whole endeavor. Luke's mother was
87 and worn out from five children and years of hard work on the
ranch. Her eyesight was nearly gone and her heart was weak. She was
unable to walk upright due to disc pain, and she had begun to spend
the evenings with a bottle of scotch. And she was "damned" if she was
leaving her house, and would not consider any help. Luke was the
only relative left close by and he felt overwhelmed and confused.

The initial loss Luke experienced was that of his strong and competent mother. He arrived at the house to find it littered with garbage
and unwashed dishes. Empty bottles of scotch disturbed him further.
His mother seemed to have retreated into herself, not talking much
while Luke was there. At this point, Luke panicked, tried to provoke
her by yelling at her. This was unsuccessful. In therapy, we began to
explore Luke's beliefs about death, his relationship to his mother, and
his sense of her autonomy. When Luke recognized that his mother
was not going to cooperate with any of his plans, he felt a weakness
throughout his whole body, particularly in his muscles and his viscera.
Exploring this, Luke recognized how much strength he had always
drawn from his mother's character. As Luke breathed into these weak
feelings, fear and grief emerged. By spending time with these feelings,
Luke was able to differentiate a bit from his mother. He began to
understand that this was her way of aging and dying. As we explored
what Luke wanted in regard to his mother, he began to contact feelings of love and acceptance for her eccentric nature. He felt a softening and warmth emanating from his heart and spreading throughout
his body. He began to cultivate his ability to feel this state while with
her. Eventually, we were able to joke about her current lifestyle.

One Saturday, Luke arrived to find his mother unconscious in her
chair. He called the ambulance, and was able to sit quietly with her
during the half hour it took the ambulance to arrive at her out of-the-
way location. During this time Luke held his mother's hand and spoke
quietly to her. He stayed with her in the ambulance and she died that
evening in the hospital. Luke felt very satisfied with her death and was
able to be kind to himself during his grieving process. He was left

with a feeling of admiration for his mother and a sense of death that was more peaceful then he had previously imagined.

Through Luke's embodiment of his feelings around death, he was able to move from a fearful, angry stance to a loving, peaceful acceptance of death. Our bodies need time and attention to adjust to the loss of a loved one. In some ways, this is the culmination of the bonding process. Without body awareness and breath, grief can be both more overwhelming and more prolonged.

Birth, bonding, intimacy, sex, trauma, and death, all of these topics, discussed in this chapter, are central to our lives. They form the most basic aspects of life. While BMP does not offer a full education in any of them, it brings the perspective of embodiment to them all. The commonality between these topics is our crucial involvement with them all. The intensity of these experiences brings increased endocrine involvement, and with that a greater potential for either transformation or victimization. Our prefrontal cortexes are somewhat overwhelmed by all of these topics and experiences, thereby creating a greater than usual need for somatic sequencing. In this type of situation, the embodiment process itself can become a source of guidance, when clarity of thought is not accessible.

Due to this intensity, our brains shift into state specific processing. That is to say we think in a particular way that we have learned to think around trauma or death or birth or any intense situation. This kind of processing might be fear driven, or very simplistic. We might lose access to certain kinds of memory or rationality. At those times, a cultivated relationship to embodiment is an extremely helpful, even necessary resource. By cultivating embodiment and trust in our bodily intelligence, we can use these physical resources to move through intense life situations. Or we can use the embodiment to readdress past experiences that have become persistent patterns. Often in an intense experience, the template for future learning and behavior is laid more strongly, due to the extreme mobilization of physical and emotional energy. In this case, the patterns tend to be particularly persistent. In BMP, the question is how to touch original experience deeply enough to recognize, understand, and have empathy, but lightly enough not to engender further fixation on the pattern, as so easily happens when working with these potent areas. In this way, it is possible to sequence it out, rather than maintain the pattern. Embodiment practice provides an excellent inroad into seemingly intractable patterns.

This is a fundamental of body-mind integration, this ability to touch deeply enough to include the body, but lightly enough so that the mind opens and releases its fixed identity and view of the world.

BMP is a study in this sort of balance. Paradox is a hallmark of embodiment: Through embodiment, we can be simultaneously tender and strong, fierce and vulnerable, openhearted yet definite. This requires the clinician to hold a view in which paradox is recognized as essential, rather than adopting a fixed, mechanical approach. I hope that the details articulated in this book have contributed more to this sort of paradoxical thinking than they have to some kind of formulaic mechanization. The practice of BMP is based on giving fully without creating dependency. The BMP practitioner can be simultaneously precise in observations, yet retain a keen inquisitiveness. The key to this wisdom of the body, this living embodiment of polarities is to feel these qualities directly and not resort to empty personifications of them. May this book further the depth and breadth of embodiment, as it moves into this culture, into the helping professions, and into psychotherapy in particular—we sorely need it. And may this book honor the tremendous wisdom that is both around us and within us.

Glossary

Active imagination   Jung's method of encouraging the client to develop a particular theme through an artistic medium, such as drama, music, dance, or visual art.

Authentic movement   An approach to dance therapy developed by Whitehouse (1963) in which client is encouraged to follow their inner impulses into movement.

Breathing (into a body part)   Emphasis of a particular direction in the breath (i.e., up, down, back, front).

Breathwork   Literally any work involving conscious breathing.

Catharsis   Elimination of a complex by bringing it to consciousness and affording it expression. General usage within the psychotherapy field defines catharsis as an intense emotional expressive. Dissociative catharsis is catharsis in which the client is dissociated on some level during the cathartic expression.

Centering   Maintaining the core of the body as the center of one's attentional field.

Circular attunement   The process of allowing our perceptions of the world and another person to flow into us and through our core, thereby allowing a continual attention to ourselves and the world simultaneously, similar to a complex fountain, water coming in, going through, and going out, continually. This core flow allows us to balance our internal perceptions and needs with the external world.

Contralateral movement: See movement

Core healing   Attention to basic psychological issues as they are manifested as sensations in the core of the body.

Core self   The synergistic relationship between the physical core of the body, as represented by the central nervous system, the viscera, the cerebral spinal fluid, the central components of the cardiovascular system, and the endocrine system, with the most central experience of the self.

Development   6th principle of body-mind integration, recognization of the ability of the human organism to continue to develop throughout the lifespan.

Developmental edge   The border between our strengths and our challenges. It can be identified as a place in the body, or as a conceptualization of our abilities and their current limits, or as the distinction between behaviors that are mastered and behaviors that are untried.

Dialogue   4th principle of body-mind integration, cooperative communication between parts and aspects of the bodymind.

Dissociation   The state of being cut off from some aspect of one's process. Central nervous system dissociation limits one's ability to perceive, process, and respond to current stimuli.

Dissociative catharsis   Intense emotional expression which leads to dissociation.

Embodied listening   The ability to listen and feel one's own internal body sensations simultaneously. This would include the changes in sensation affected by what one is hearing.

Embodied speech   The ability to speak directly from one's own bodily experience as one feels it in the moment.

Embodiment   The moment to moment process by which human beings may allow their awareness to enhance the flow of thoughts, feelings, sensations, and energies through their bodily selves.

Embodiment training   The training of bodily awareness and the ability to allow bodily sensations to develop into movement, behavior, thoughts, words, and images.

Emotional operating systems   Functional neurological systems delineated by Jaak Panksepp which set-up fundamental brain-body states involving specific behaviors. The primitive emotional operating systems are seeking, rage, fear, and panic. Further socioemotional systems are lust, care and play.

Endpoints   The face and head, hands, feet, and pelvic floor. Each of these free ends of our skeletal is endowed with an increased concentration of sensory nerve endings and fine muscular articulation.

Energetic development The interface between psychological and physical development; the process through which we learn to interact with the world by yielding, pushing, reaching, grasping, and pulling through each of our endpoints, and thereby develop our psychological characters.

Enteroceptive training Training in becoming conscious of the input from enteroceptors, the sensory nerve endings in the viscera. Found to be extremely effective in amplifying and concretizing the clinicians' sensitivity to their own emotional processes and that of their clients.

Felt sense A term developed by Gendlin (1981) as part of the Focusing process, refering to a bodily awareness of meaning or personal significance.

Flow (through the core) The movement of life through the core of the body.

Focusing A process developed by Gendlin (1981) through which one accesses a felt sense to further self knowledge and emotional change.

Full participation 3rd principle of body-mind integration, empowerment of each aspect of the bodymind to shift in and out of initiatory and supportive roles as appropriate.

Global emotion An emotion whose sensations are experienced throughout the body.

Grounding Allowing the physical weight of the body to pass down into gravity.

Healing edge The balance between feeling the pain produced in the past and feeling the healing possibility of the future; experiencing the healing edge allows healing to occur.

Healing intention A conscious intention to heal, specifically in the case of reexperiencing emotions related to the past.

Homolateral movement See movement

Homologous movement See movement

Immobilization A state of immobility in response to life-threatening circumstances with no perceived escape in which there is a very low heart and respiratory rate, low muscle tone, and very little ability to think or respond to the world. When this occurs in the laboratory animal, the animal stops moving, goes limp, and defecates.

Implicit memory   Also known as procedural memory. Learned behavior or state that includes no conscious awareness of remembering.

Inclusivity   2nd principle of body-mind integration: cultivating participation by all parts and aspects of the bodymind.

Interaction cycle   A basic cycle of interaction which joins both the clients' and the therapists' awareness in a focus on what clients want and how clients are manifesting their developmental edge in their bodies.

Interactive psychobiological regulation   Schore's (1994) term referring to the dynamic by which we regulate our neurobiological functioning through interaction with others.

Intrasubjective intersubjectivity   Adapted from the psychoanalytic concept of intersubjective space—a shared, mutually created aspect of relationship. Intrasubjective intersubjectivity refers to the internal relational space that we can create by relating with one part of ourselves to another part.

Kinesthesis   Perception of movement.

Localized emotion   An emotion whose sensations are experienced locally, i.e., in one or two specific area(s).

Mirroring   A conscious or unconscious replication of the client's physical state on the part of the therapist.

Mouthing   Movement that begins in the mouth and sequences to the tail.

Movement,
    spinal   Integrated movement of the spine.
    homologous   Movement in which the upper and lower bodies each act as integrated wholes.
    homolateral   Movement in which the left and right halves of the body are integrated units.
    contralateral   Movement which crosses the mid-line of the body, connecting the left and right extremities.

Natural intelligence   A synergistic intelligence that combines all the creative resources of every tissue and fluid in the body down to a cellular level.

Neotony   A term borrowed by biology from evolutionary theory to describe species in which certain qualities of infancy persist into adulthood.

Parasympathetic shock   A term used by Emerson (1999); in BMP this term is used as a simple, subjective name for a state that is neurologically overwhelming, thereby causing dissociation, and is parasympathetic by nature, i.e., depressed heart rate, respiratory rate, and muscular tone.

Polarizing   A conscious or unconscious movement on the part of the therapist into a physical state that markedly contrasts or opposes that of the client.

Polyvagal theory   Developed by Porges (1995); postulates that social engagement is a basic strategy for regulating the autonomic nervous system.

Positional functioning theory   A BMP theory recognizing that the posture and movement range being utilized have a direct impact on functioning and the possibilities of behavioral and emotional change.

Prolonging attention   BMP technique of tracking client's breathing, postural changes, and eye movement to assess when the client's attention is beginning to shift away from self-awareness and using the therapist's breath, voice, or speech to direct them back to the internal process.

Proprioception   Perception of sensations.

Pulsating motility   Simple fluid movement of cells, tissue, and simple organisms.

Radiation   Movement that extends from the center of the body out to the periphery.

Relational somatics   The therapeutic practice of cultivating relationship through attention to the client's bodily functioning.

Respect   1st principle of body-mind integration: appreciation for the intelligence of the bodymind, its motivations, emotional tone, and responses.

Self-talk   The process of consciously speaking with oneself.

Sensory boundaries   Sensory feedback that activates when we move beyond our prescribed self-image, as a fence around a field. If we extend ourselves beyond our familiar range of activity, we encounter these sensory barriers, which may consist of many different kinds of sensation, such as trembling, nausea, or dizziness.

Sequencing   5th principle of body-mind integration. The uninhibited flow of energy within all parts and aspects of the bodymind and between ourselves and the environment. One of the principles of body-mind integration.

Shock   This term is used in BMP as a simple, subjective name for neurological overwhelm and dissociation in any system resulting from traumatic arousal.

Social engagement system   Postulated within Porges' (1995) polyvagal theory as the most evolutionary advanced strategy of the autonomic nervous system, involving the ventral root of the vagus nerve as well as other cranial nerves which activate social behaviors involving facial expression, vocalization, listening, and sucking.

Somatic dialogue   Communication between two parts of the body, which can be both verbal and nonverbal.

Somatic marker theory   A hypothesis postulated by Damasio (1994) in which a particular response option is marked by a particular gut feeling. Somatic markers are a biasing device which help us to weigh future benefits with current costs. When there is proper communication occurring between the brain and the body, somatic markers influence our decision-making process, even without coming to consciousness.

Somatic psychology   Psychological approaches that focus significantly on the role of the body.

Spinal movement   (See movement)

Staying in your body   Remaining aware of a significant portion of your bodily sensations from moment to moment.

Sympathetic shock   A term used by Emerson (1999); in BMP, it is used as a simple, subjective name of a state that is neurologically overwhelming thereby causing dissociation, and is sympathetic by nature, i.e. characterized by elevated heart rate, respiratory rate and muscle tone.

Sympathetic arousal response   Response to perceived external threat involving elevated heart rate, respiratory rate, and muscle tone.

Titration   Term borrowed from chemistry by Levine (1997) to denote the use of the smallest amount of activation that is manageable within trauma resolution, as in addressing one moment of an experience at a time.

Visualization   Formation of mental pictures.

Internet Resources

For more information about Body-Mind Psychotherapy:
  www.bodymindpsychotherapy.com

For the School for Body-Mind Centering:
  www.bodymindcentering.com

For the Body-Mind Centering Association:
  www.bmcassoc.org

For the United States Association for Body Psychotherapy:
  www.USABP.org

For the European Association of Body Psychotherapy:
  www.EABP.org

References

Ainsworth, M. D. S., Blehar, M. C., Waters, E., & Wall, S. (1978). *Patterns of attachment: A psychological study of the strange situation.* Hillsdale, NJ: Erlbaum.

Aposhyan, S. (1999). *Natural intelligence: Body-mind integration and human development.* Baltimore, MD: Williams & Wilkins.

Aron, E. (1996). *The highly sensitive person.* New York: Broadway.

Bateson, G. (1972). *Steps to an ecology of mind.* Northvale, NJ: Aronson.

Baxter, L. R. (1992). Neuro-imaging studies of OCD. *Psychiatric Clinics of North America, 15,* 871–884.

Beebe, B. (1999, August 24). *Organizing principles of interactions in infant research and adult treatment.* Presented at the Boulder Institute for Psychotherapy and Research, Boulder, Colorado.

Beebe, B., & Stern, D. N. (1977). Engagement-disengagement and early object experiences. In N. Freedman & S. Grand (Eds.), *Communicative structures and psychic structures* (pp. 35–55). New York: Plenum.

Bergin, A. E., & Garfield. S. L. (1994). *The handbook of psychotherapy and behavior change.* New York: Wiley.

Bowlby, J. (1969). *Attachment and loss: Volume 1: Attachment.* New York: Basic.

Cairns, J., Overbaugh, J., & Miller, S. (1988). The origins of Mutants. *Nature, 335*(8), 142–145.

Cassidy J., & Shaver, P. R. (Eds.) (1999). *Handbook of attachment: Theory, research, and clinical applications.* New York: Guilford Press.

Chaiklin, H. (1975). *Marian Chace: Her papers.* New York: American Dance Therapy Association.

Clarke, D. M. (2003). *Descartes' theory of mind.* Oxford: Claredon, Press.

Cohen, B. B. (1993). *Sensing, feeling, and action.* Northampton, MA: Contact.

Cohen, B. (1996–1997). Embodying cellular consciousness. *Somatics, 11*(1), 1–7.

Cushman, P. (1995). *Constructing the self, constructing America: A cultural history of psychotherapy.* Reading, MA: Addison-Wesley.

Csikszentmihaly, M. (1994). *Flow: The psychology of optimal performance.* NY: Harper & Row.

Damasio, A. (1994). *Descartes' error: Emotion, reason, and the human brain.* New York: Putnam.

Damasio, A. (1999). *The feeling of what happens.* New York: Harcourt.

Darwin, C. (1968). *The origin of species.* New York: Penguin Books, 1968. (Originally published 1859)

Davidson, R. J., & Kabat-Zinn, J. (2003). Alterations in brain and immune function produced by mindfulness meditation. *Psychosomatoc Medicine, 65,* 564–570.

Emerson, W. (1999). *Shock: A universal malady.* Petaluma, CA: Emerson Training Seminars.

Freud, S. (1961). The ego and the id. In J. Strachey (Ed. & Trans.), *The standard edition of the complete psychological works of Sigmund Freud* (vol. 19, pp. 3–66). London: Hogarth Press. (Originally published 1923)

Freud, S. (1966). Project for a scientific psychology. In J. Strachey (Ed. & Trans.), *The standard edition of the complete psychological works of Sigmund Freud* (Vol. 1, pp. 281–391). London: Hogarth. (Original work published 1895)

Freud, S. (1975). *Three essays on the theory of sexuality*. New York: Basic. (Original work published 1905)

Gardner, H. (1993). *Frames of mind: The theory of multiple intelligences*. New York: Basic.

Gendlin, E. (1981). *Focusing*. New York: Bantam.

Graf, S. (1988). *The adventure of self discovery*. Albany: State University of New York Press.

Greenspan, S. (1997). *Growth of the mind: And the endangered origins of intelligence*. Reading, MA: Addison-Wesley.

Goleman, D. (1995). *Emotional intelligence*. New York: Bantam.

Hanna, T. (1988). *Somatics: Reawakening the mind's control of movement, flexibility, and health*. Cambridge, MA: Perseus.

Hebb, D. (1949). *The organization of behavior*. New York: Wiley.

Hochheimer, W. (1969). *The psychotherapy of C.G. Jung*. New York: Putnam.

Hora, T. (1986). *Dialogues in metapsychiatry*. Orange, CA: PAGL Press.

Huttunen, H., & Niskanen, P. (1978). Prenatal loss of father and psychiatric disorders. *Archives of General Psychiatry, 35*, 429–431.

Janet, P. (1932). *La force et la faiblesse psychologiques*. Paris: Maloine.

Judge, P. G., & de Waal F. B. M. (1997). Rhesus monkey behaviour under diverse population densities: Coping with long-term crowding. *Animal Behavior, 54*, 643–662.

Juhan, D. (1987). *Job's body: A handbook for bodywork*. New York: Station Hill.

Jung, C. G. (1969). *On the nature of the psyche*. Princeton, NJ: Princeton University Press.

Kandel, E. R., Schwartz, J. H., & Jessell, T. M. (2000). *Principles of neural science*. New York: McGraw-Hill.

Keleman, S. (1975). *The human ground: Sexuality, self, and survival*. Palo Alto, CA: Science and Behavior.

Keleman, S. (1985). *Emotional anatomy*. Berkeley, CA: Center Press.

Keleman, S. (1986). *Bonding*. Berkeley, CA: Center Press.

Knaster, M. (1996). *Discovering the body's wisdom*. New York: Bantam.

Kurtz, R. (1990). *Body-centered psychotherapy: The Hakomi method*. Mendocino, CA.: Life Rhythm.

LeDoux, J. (1996). *The emotional brain*. New York: Simon & Schuster.

Levine, P. (1997). *Waking the tiger: Healing trauma*. Berkeley, CA: North Atlantic Books.

Lipton, B. (1993, October). *The biology of consciousness*. Paper presented at the International Association for New Sciences, Fort Collins, CO.

Llinas, R. (2001). *I of the vortex: From neurons to self*. Cambridge, MA: MIT Press.

Lowen, A. (1975). *Bioenergetics*. New York: Coward, McCann & Geoghegan.

Mann, C. (1991). Lynn Margulis. Science's unruly Earth mother. *Science, 252*, 378–381.

Margulis, L., & Sagan, D. (1986). *Microcosmos: Four billion years of microbial evolution*. Berkeley: University of California Press.

McMenamin, D., & McMenamin, M. (1994). *Hypersea*. New York: Columbia University Press.

Mindell, A. (1985). *Working with the dream body*. New York: Routledge & Kegan Paul.

Mindell, A., & Mindell, A. (1992). *Riding the horse backwards.* New York: Penguin.

Morgan, M. L. (ed.) (2002). *Spinoza: Complete works.* Indianapolis, IN: Hacrett Publishing Co.

Moyers, B. (1993). *Healing and the mind.* New York: Doubleday.

Murphy, M. (1992). *The future of the body.* New York: Tarcher.

Ogden, P. (1997). Inner body sensation. *Somatics, 11*(2), 41–42.

Ogden, P., & Minton, K. (2000). Sensorimotor psychotherapy: One method for processing traumatic memory. *Traumatology, 6*(3), Article 3. Available at http://www.traumapages.com

Paddison, S. (1992). *The hidden power of the heart: Achieving balance and fulfillment in a stressful world.* Boulder Creek, CA: HeartMath.

Panksepp, J. (1998). *Affective neuroscience: The foundations of human and animal emotions.* New York: Oxford University Press.

Pearsall, P. (1998). *The heart's code.* New York: Broadway.

Perry, B., Pollard, R., Blakley, T., Baker, W., & Vigilante, D. (1995). Childhood trauma, the neurobiology of adaptation, and "use-dependent" development of the brain: How "states" become "traits." *Infant Mental Health Journal, 16*(4), 271–291.

Pert, C. (1997). *Molecules of emotion.* New York: Scribner.

Porges, S. (1995). Orienting in a defensive world: Mammalian modifications of our evolutionary heritage. A polyvagal theory. *Psychophysiology, 32,* 301–318.

Porges, S. (1996). Physiological regulation in high-risk infants: A model for assessment and potential intervention. *Development and Psychopathology, 8,* 43–58.

Pound, E. (1969). *Confucius: The Great Digest.* New York: New Directions.

Reich, W. (1972). *Character analysis.* New York: Touchstone. (Originally published 1935)

Robbins, J. (2000). *A symphony in the brain: The evolution of the new brain wave biofeedback.* New York: Atlantic Monthly Press.

Rosenberg, J. L., & Rand, M. L. (1985). *Body, self, and soul: Sustaining integration,* Atlanta, GA: Humanics.

Schacter, D. L., & Singer, J. E. (1986). Effects of elaborative processing on implicit and explicit memory for new associations. *Journal of Experimental Psychology: Learning, Memory, and Cognition 12*(3), 432–444.

Schore, A. (1994). *Affect regulation and the origin of the self.* Hillsdale, NJ: Erlbaum.

Schore, A. (1998). Principles of psychotherapeutic treatment of early forming right hemispheric primitive emotional disorders based upon the interactional developmental models of *Affect Regulation and the Origin of the Self* (1994). Print out by author.

Some, S. (1999). *Spirit of intimacy: Ancient African teachings in the ways of relationship.* NY: William Morrow.

Smith, E. (1985). *The body in psychotherapy.* Jefferson, NC: McFarland.

Stern, D. (1985). *The interpersonal world of the infant: A view from psychoanalysis and developmental psychology.* New York: Basic.

Stern, D. N., Sander, L. W., Nahum, J. P., Harrison, A. M., Lyons-Ruth, K., Morgan, A. C., Bruschweiler-Stern, N., & Tronick, E. Z. (1998). Non-interpretive mechanisms in psychoanalytic therapy. The "something more" than interpretation. The Process of Change Study Group. *International Journal of Psycho-Analysis, 79,* 903–921.

Stern, H. (1978). *The couch: Its use and meaning in psychotherapy.* New York: Human Press.

Suzuki, S. (1970). *Zen mind, beginner's mind.* New York: Weatherhill.

Swartz, C., Wright, C., Shin, L., Kagan, J., & Rauch, S. (2003). Inhibited and

Uninhibited infants 'grown up': Adult Amygdalar Responses to novelty. *Science,* 300(5627), 1952–1953.

Swimme, B., & Berry, T. (1992). *The universe story.* San Francisco: HarperSanFrancisco.

Taylor, K., Cousino-Klein, L., Lewis, B., Gruenewald, T., Gurung, R., & Updegraff, J. (2000). Biobehavioral responses to stress: Tend and befriend, not fight or flight. *Psychological Review, 107*(3), 411–429.

Trevarthen, C. (1990). *Brain circuits and functions of the mind.* Cambridge, UK: Cambridge University Press.

Tucker, D. M. (2001, April). Embodied meaning: An evolutionary–developmental analysis of adaptive semantics. University of Oregon, Institute of Cognitive and Decision Sciences: Technical Report No. 01–04. Eugene: University of Oregon.

Trunpa, Chogyam (1985). Acknowledging death as the common ground of healing. *Naropa Institute Journal of Psychology, 3,* 3–10.

Van der Kolk, B., McFarlane, A., & Weisath, L. (Eds.) (1996). *Traumatic stress: The effects of overwhelming experience on mind, body, and society.* New York: Guilford Press.

Webster's New Universal Unabridged Dictionary, 2nd Ed. (1983). NY: Simon & Schuster.

Whitehouse, M. (1963). *Physical movement and personality.* Paper presented at the Analytical Psychology Club of Los Angeles.

Winnicott, D. W. (1965). *The family and individual development.* London: Tavistock.

Wolf, J. M. (1968). *Temple Faye, M.D.: Progenitor of the Doman-Delacato treatment procedures. Springfield, IL: Charles C. Thomas.*

Wright, R. (1994). The moral animal: Why we are the way we are. New York: Vintage Books.

Yalom, I. (1989). *Love's executioner.* NY: Harper Collins.

Yehuda, R., Teicher, M., Levengood, R., Trestman, R., & Siever, L. (1996). Cortisol regulation is posttraumatic stress disorder and major depression: A chronobiological analysis. *Biological Psychiatry, 40,* 79–88.

Young, C. (Ed.) (2002). *EABP bibliography of body-psychotherapy.* Amsterdam, the Netherlands: European Association of Body Psychotherapy.

Zajonc, R. (1982). *Animal social psychology: A reader of experimental studies.* New York: Wiley.

Index